Child Protection

Child Protection
An Introduction

Second Edition

Chris Beckett

SAGE Publications
Los Angeles · London · New Delhi · Singapore

© Chris Beckett 2003, 2007

First published 2003
Reprinted 2004, 2005, 2006
This second edition published 2007

SAGE Publications Ltd
1 Oliver's Yard
55 City Road
London EC1Y 1SP

SAGE Publications Inc.
2455 Teller Road
Thousand Oaks, California 91320

SAGE Publications India Pvt Ltd
B 1/I 1 Mohan Cooperative Industrial Area
Mathura Road, New Delhi 110 044
India

SAGE Publications Asia-Pacific Pte Ltd
33 Pekin Street #02-01
Far East Square
Singapore 048763

British Library Cataloguing in Publication data

A catalogue record for this book is available from the
British Library

ISBN 978-1-4129-2091-9
ISBN 978-1-4129-2092-6 (pbk)

Library of Congress Control Number: 2006933391

Typeset by C&M Digitals (P) Ltd., Chennai, India
Printed on paper from sustainable resources
Printed in Great Britain by The Alden Press, Witney

Contents

Introduction   1

PART I   CHILD PROTECTION WORK   3

 1   Different Perspectives   5

 2   The Multi-agency System   16

 3   Making Things Different   32

 4   Personal and Professional   46

PART II   CHILD MALTREATMENT AND ITS CONSEQUENCES   61

 5   Recognizing Child Abuse and Neglect   63

 6   Disabled Children   78

 7   Harm   91

PART III   CAUSES AND CONTEXTS   107

 8   Origins of Abuse and Neglect   109

 9   Parents with Substance Use and Other Mental
      Health Problems   123

10   Parents with Learning Difficulties   141

11   Violent Homes   155

12   Poverty and Social Exclusion   169

PART IV   PROBLEMS AND DILEMMAS   185

13   Abusive Systems   187

14   Facing Reality   201

References   214
Index   225

Introduction

This book is intended for students and practitioners in all the disciplines involved in child protection work, by which I mean the work of trying to meet the needs of children who may have been abused or neglected, and/or who are thought to be seriously at risk of abuse. It draws both on the research literature and on my own experience.

For this second edition two new chapters have been added, one on approaches to intervention (Chapter 3) and one on families where there is domestic violence (Chapter 11). Chapter 2 has also been completely rewritten to take account of new guidelines for multi-professional work and the rest of the book has been revised, and in many places also completely rewritten, to bring in new material and reflect the development of my own thinking about this complex topic. Having spent 18 years in the child protection field as a social worker and a manager of social workers, I have now been an academic for seven years. As time passes, my perspective changes, and I think this is reflected in some of the changes in this book.

The legislative and procedural framework described by this book is that which operates in England and Wales. This means that Chapter 2, and some passages elsewhere in the book, will not be of direct relevance to readers from outside of this jurisdiction. However, this book draws extensively on material from the US, Australia and elsewhere and I hope that most of its contents will be relevant and interesting to readers beyond this island.

Using this book

Part I of the book is about what is entailed in child protection work and the demands it makes of the professionals engaged in it. Part II looks at the different ways in which children can be abused and neglected and considers the indicators and warning signs in each case, as well as the long-term consequences. It includes a chapter on the abuse of children with disabilities. Part III considers the causes of abuse and neglect. What leads adults to mistreat their children or fail to provide the care and protection they need? Finally, in Part IV, I look at some of the difficulties and dilemmas involved in child protection social work.

Each chapter is interspersed with what I have called (for want of a better word) 'exercises'. These invite the reader to reflect on what is being discussed and to relate the discussion to specific situations such as might be encountered in practice. If you prefer not to break the flow of your reading by pausing to work on exercises of this kind, then of course you do not need to do so. However, you should read through them rather than skip over them, because I sometimes refer to them in the subsequent text.

Since many of these exercises are based around case examples, I should emphasize that these are *fictional*. Real-life elements have been included but they have been combined together, modified and mixed with imaginary elements, and names chosen at random. The cases are intended to be realistic, but *none* of them is a portrait of a real-life human beings.

In the text, for the sake of simplicity, I tend to refer to 'parents' when talking about the adult carers of children. Of course in many families children are cared for by step-parents, grandparents, foster-parents and others, and the word 'parent' can generally be taken as including any adult acting as a carer of a child. I also tend to refer to child protection professionals as 'she' because in Britain the majority of professionals involved in child protection work *are* women. No disrespect is intended to my fellow-members of the male minority. I just find it cumbersome to be continuously writing 'he or she'.

Acknowledgements

My thanks are due to Anglia Ruskin University and to my colleagues there for providing me with an environment in which it has been possible to reflect and write about my experience of child protection practice, to my students for all the many valuable insights and awkward questions that come from seeing child protection practice with fresh eyes, and to my former colleagues and clients.

I am also very grateful to my parents, Philip and Elspeth, my three children, Poppy, Dominic and Nancy, my three sisters, Vicky, Kate and Pippa, and my wife Maggie for all the many things they have taught me about childhood, parenthood and family life.

Part I

CHILD PROTECTION WORK

1 Different Perspectives

- The modern child protection system
- The historical context in Britain
- International comparisons
- Cross-cultural complexities
- Different disciplines
- Safeguarding children

Children – and especially small children – rely on the adults who care for them to meet both their physical needs and their needs for security, safety, love and a sense of belonging. But children are often harmed by those who they rely upon for protection. Occasionally they are killed. More often they are injured, or used for sexual gratification, or treated in ways that may not do any obvious physical harm, but which have long-term emotional and psychological consequences. More often still they are just poorly cared for to the point that their basic needs go unmet, whether this is because their carers are indifferent to these needs, unable to recognize them, or simply too preoccupied with their own. I suspect that every society, at every stage in history, has recognized that this is a problem about which 'something should be done'.

What is comparatively new though is a professional child protection system of the type which now exists in Britain, the USA and many other countries, set up and regulated by the state and expected not only to respond to specific incidents of child abuse and neglect, but also to anticipate and prevent serious harm being done to children. It is a system which provides work to thousands of social workers, doctors, nurses, judges, lawyers, police officers, civil servants, academics and many others, and a system upon which high expectations are placed by the community at large. It is this system that is the subject of Part I of this book. This chapter will give a broad overview of the subject. Chapter 2 looks in more detail at the multi-professional system as it is defined – and has recently been redefined – in the particular context of England and Wales. Chapter 3 looks more closely at what the professionals who operate the system can do to bring about change on behalf of children. Chapter 4 looks at what is entailed for, and required of, the individual worker.

The modern child protection system

In the next chapter I will describe the child protection system that operates in England and Wales. Many of the essential elements of that system are similar to those that exist in other jurisdictions in the industrialized world. Briefly, the system and its social context include the following:

1   All agencies involved in working with children or parents are expected to share information about children who may be at risk. This obligation generally overrides each agency's duty of confidentiality towards its service users.
2   Central government provides detailed guidelines as to the duties of the various agencies and the arrangements for them to co-operate.
3   At the local level agencies are required to establish collaborative structures within which to co-ordinate and develop local child protection strategies and procedures.
4   Social work agencies and the police have a joint responsibility to investigate incidents of abuse.
5   Social work agencies have legal duties to investigate families causing concern and, if necessary, to seek powers from the courts allowing them to intervene and impose solutions, which can include temporarily or permanently removing a child from her carers.
6   Although the day-to-day running of the child protection system is not of huge interest to the general public, its perceived failures cause widespread concern. These perceived failures include both incidents where the system has failed to prevent children from dying, or suffer serious mis-treatment at the hands of carers, and incidents where the system is seen to have behaved overzealously and interfered needlessly in families.

As I have said, I will leave more detailed discussion of the system to the next chapter. For the present I simply want to draw your attention to the fact that in England and Wales at present there is a particular system, and a particular way of looking at child protection. It has not always been so, and it is not so in other places. We should bear in mind that the system as it now operates is only one of many possible approaches. Reminding ourselves of this enables us to remain open to the possibility of changes and improvements.

The following, for instance, are objections that might legitimately be raised to the system I have described:

•   Historically it would have been the extended family and the community that dealt with abusive parenting. Some might argue that the more the state intervenes in family life, the less the extended family and the community become involved, so that, in the long run, society's informal protective networks are weakened. If concerned neighbours can pick up their telephones and report their concerns about a child, they may well feel they have discharged their responsibili-ties to that child just by doing this. If the option of reporting it to a professional agency was not available, they might feel that they needed to take more action themselves. Though not writing specifically about child protection, David Schwartz expresses this general anxiety about the professionalization of care as follows:

> Each year more of the world passes out of the sphere of the vernacular and into the sphere of systems. Mom-and-Pop stores fall to chain convenience stores, the neighborhood doctor and midwife become employees of health maintenance organizations, and small-scale personal efforts to help people become human service corporations. (Schwartz, 1997: 36)

- The child protection system is too much about monitoring and policing and not enough about helping and supporting. The preoccupation with information gathering erodes privacy and alienates families (see Munro, 2004, who also questions whether the information sharing that would be made possible through a national database would actually increase the effectiveness of children's services).
- Most of the abuse and neglect that is detected occurs in poor families. One of the main factors in abuse and neglect is poverty and social exclusion (as will be discussed in Chapter 12). It is possible to argue that social workers and other welfare professionals provide a fig leaf for structural injustice by making people into 'cases' and their problems look like individual failings, and that the inter-agency child protection system, constitutes a form of state surveillance to which the poor are subjected, but which more powerful members of society generally avoid.
- The child protection system in Britain has largely been shaped by a series of public inquiries about child deaths – and by newspapers and public opinion demanding that child deaths should not happen again. Trying to predict child deaths, though, is like trying to find a needle in a haystack. Arguably the whole system has been shaped by a goal which will never be reached. (For further discussion on this, see Chapter 14.)
- The system is geared towards detecting abuse, but much less thought has been given to how best to help abused children or their families once their abuse has been detected, or to whether the services now offered are actually always helping. For example, in recent years increasing numbers of children have been taken into public care. But the care system is not always successful, often failing to provide children with the security and stability that they need. (For more on this see Chapter 13.)

All these arguments, I would suggest, have some validity. The difficulty of course is trying to construct an alternative system that retains the benefits of the present system without suffering from any of the disadvantages. The system will probably always be an uneasy compromise between equally important but mutually contradictory objectives.

To make things more complicated, the system is very much a *political* creation which means that it is not just a compromise between mutually contradictory objectives in terms of the needs of children and families, but a compromise which also has to take into account the needs of politicians and the demands of various interest groups; for example, all governments feel under pressure to improve public services, including the child protection system, but all governments are also under pressure to limit public expenditure. This can result in a kind of tokenism in which public services, such as the child protection system, are periodically required to go through the motions of implementing changes which are trumpeted as revolutionary, though in actual fact they are not provided with the resources that would be needed for these changes to be anything other than cosmetic ones. Thus Eileen Munro and Martin Calder criticize the political agenda set out in the Green Paper *Every Child Matters* (DfES, 2003), as follows:

> [The government] want to shift practitioners' focus *towards* preventative services; this has the logical implication of shifting the focus *away from* its current emphasis on child protection. The consequences of this have not been explicitly addressed, leaving it to agencies and individual practitioners to grapple with the inconsistency of being told to focus on family support without taking attention away from child protection. (Munro and Calder, 2005: 444, their emphasis)

The historical context in Britain

Ideas about how children should be treated by adults, and about the community's responsibilities towards children, have changed over the centuries, although this is not to say that in the past adults were not concerned to protect children from harm. The fact that it was a serious matter to harm children in Biblical times, 2000 years ago, seems to me to be illustrated, for example, by the following famous verse:

> And whosoever shall offend one of these little ones that believe in me, it is better for him that a millstone were hanged about his neck, and he were cast into the sea. (Mark 9: 42)

It would be impossible to establish the prevalence of child abuse in historic times with any degree of certainty, since even today much abuse is never discovered. Attitudes as to what *constitute* abuse and what constitute appropriate chastisement have also changed, as illustrated by another Biblical quote: 'He that spareth his rod hateth his son' (Proverbs 13: 24. By contrast in several countries today *any* kind of physical punishment is now illegal while, in England and Wales, section 58 of the 2004 Children Act spells out that 'battery of a child cannot be justified on the ground that it constituted reasonable punishment'.)

Child protection as a distinct state-sponsored professional activity is a relatively recent phenomenon. During the nineteenth century the industrial revolution in Britain led to the growth of big cities and new state institutions began to appear. It was in 1856, for instance, that it became mandatory for the first time for local authorities to set up police forces. Attitudes to child welfare also changed over the course of the century. Some indication of the distance we have travelled in Britain is given by the fact that the 1833 Factory Act prohibited children under nine years old from working in factories, but the employers of nine-year-olds could still quite legally require them to work a *48-hour week*.

State regulation of childcare began with efforts to regulate the practice of 'baby-farming' (essentially private fostering), common in the nineteenth century. A series of pieces of legislation, beginning in 1872 with the Infant Life Protection Act, laid down requirements for baby-farmers to register with local authorities and to meet certain minimum standards. In 1889, the Prevention of Cruelty to Children Act empowered police to search premises for children thought to be in danger and to remove them if necessary to a place of safety (a power which continues to exist under section 46 of the 1989 Children Act). Meanwhile, in the 1880s, the precursor organizations to the modern NSPCC – the National Society for the Prevention of Cruelty to Children, the first child protection agency in England – had begun to take shape.

However, although what we now call the 'welfare state' had been developing over the previous century, the so-called 'post-war settlement', the period after 1945, is generally seen as representing a sea change in welfare provision in Britain. The establishment of the National Health Service is probably the best-known achievement of that period, but another change was the requirement of local authorities under the 1948 Children Act to set up Children's Departments employing welfare officers. These Child Welfare Officers – children and family social workers – were subsequently incorporated, along with welfare officers for the elderly and others, into the new generic Social Services departments in the 1970s. At time of writing, in 2006, Social Services departments are once again being broken up across England and Wales, following the *Every Child Matters* Green Paper and section 17 of the 2004 Children Act, and social work services (referred to as Local Authority children's social care) are being placed, along with Education, within the remit of new Children's Services Directors.

During the 1960s, there was a growing awareness of the prevalence of physical abuse of children ('the battered baby syndrome' as it was originally described). The death of Maria Colwell in 1973 was the first of many cases which brought child protection into the spotlight and the first of many to be presented in the media as failures by gullible or incompetent professionals. Following the public inquiry into this case, much of the framework was put in place that we would still recognize as the modern multi-agency child protection system. Public inquiries from then on emphasized again and again the importance of detecting indicators of abuse, improving communications between agencies and acting decisively to protect children from harm. But in 1987, there was a different kind of outcry about the activities of child protection professionals:

> If previous inquiries demonstrated that welfare professionals, particularly social workers, failed to protect the lives and interests of children and intervened too little too late into the private family, the concerns focussed around Cleveland seemed to demonstrate that professionals ... paediatricians as well as social workers, failed to recognise the rights of parents and intervened too soon and in too heavy-handed a way into the family. (Parton, 1991: 79)

The 1989 Children Act (which actually came into effect in 1991) was supposed to strike a new balance between support and compulsory intervention in families. 'The most important and far-reaching reform this century of the law on children', said *The Times* newspaper at the time, 'a fundamental shift from the adversarial legal system. The new emphasis is away from courts imposing solutions or orders and towards parents, relatives and local authorities working in partnership ...' (*The Times*, 8 October 1991). But in fact, the expected fundamental shift did not take place (McKeigue and Beckett, 2004) and, after an initial drop, the number of children annually made subject to Care Orders rapidly increased, tripling over the period 1992–2004, in spite of various efforts to shift the emphasis of child protection work in the direction of family support. It remains to see whether the changes associated with the 2004 Children Act will have more success.

International comparisons

We have seen how the growth of the formal child protection system in Britain did not emerge until the country industrialized in the nineteenth century. Very similar developments were occurring at the same time in other industrialized countries, and similar dilemmas were being encountered, dilemmas which we still struggle with. Neil Guterman observes, for example, that in nineteenth-century America,

> a schism arose between the investigative, protective and 'child rescue' approach taken by the New York SPCC and an approach that emphasized family strengthening and abuse prevention, as represented by the Massachusetts SPCC. (Guterman, 2001: 79)

But of course there are still many countries in the world which have not yet industrialized or are still in the process of industrializing. And in many of these countries, as in pre-industrial Britain, the regulation of family life is left much more to informal systems, with much less of a role for the state.

Even in the industrialized world, there are differences between different countries as to how the problem of child abuse is seen and responded to. Cooper et al. (1995), for instance, offer a comparison between the British and French child protection systems, and suggest that there are quite significant differences in approach at either end of the Channel Tunnel. 'They don't seem to have to panic', commented one British social worker enviously about French child protection social workers (1995: 11), while a French social worker was struck by 'a semi-obsession with getting evidence' that seemed to preoccupy the British child protection worker, who seemed to have become 'a bit like a detective' (1995: 10).

Cross-cultural complexities

For child protection workers in modern Britain – and indeed in most other countries – there are more immediate reasons for being aware of the different attitudes of different cultures to children, families and child protection. Child protection professionals themselves come from a wide variety of cultural backgrounds and are involved in work with children and families from a similarly diverse range of cultures. The child protection worker may find herself dealing, for example, with a Sudanese family for whom clitoridectomy of little girls is normal, or a Bangladeshi family where the mother married the father at the age of 12, or Romany families who choose to keep their children out of school because they are opposed to sex education. British child protection professionals – like those in most Western countries – work with families from diverse traditions with profoundly different attitudes to discipline and parental authority, physical punishment, sex, the role of men and women, and the nature of the obligations that exist between parents, children and the extended family. Even attitudes to matters like educational achievement may be very different, with some migrants from poor countries placing an emphasis on their children's educational achievement that may look like undue pressure, and even cruelty, to European, Australian or North American eyes, though they may see themselves as ensuring that their children can provide for themselves and avoid destitution.

Exercise 1.1

The following behaviours are regarded as normal in various cultures, or are methods of punishment used by families in this society. How should we respond to them when they occur in this society?

- Circumcision of boys (the cutting-off of the foreskin either in infancy, in the case of Jewish or Muslim culture, or in adolescence, in the case of some African cultures).
- Arranged marriages of 12-year-old girls (normal in many Asian and African societies).
- Beating with a stick (accepted as a normal method of punishment in many cultures and recommended, as we have seen, by the Bible).
- Clitoridectomy (removal of the clitoris, or 'female circumcision', common in Middle Eastern and African cultures).

Comments on Exercise 1.1

It is difficult to take an entirely consistent view of these things. It seems reasonable on the one hand that a society should have a consensus view of minimum standards which apply to everyone in it, regardless of their culture of origin, and in fact at least two items on this list are quite simply illegal under English law. On the other hand, it is important to be aware that every culture has its own system of values and meanings.

It is also important to be aware that the abusiveness of any act cannot be understood except in context. Being beaten with a stick may be undesirable in any context, but its meaning will be very different for a child who knows that all his friends are punished in the same way, and that his parents love him and genuinely believe it is for his own good, than for a child who knows that none of his friends are beaten, and that his parents seem to do it as an expression of feelings of rage and hatred. Similarly, for a Muslim child circumcision is a normal part of being a boy. If a circumcision were to be performed for no reason at all, 'out of the blue', by a parent with no cultural reason for doing so, it would be a bizarre and very abusive act.

It is important to bear in mind too that differences in parenting practices, and views about what is appropriate, exist not only between different ethnic groups but also within the same ethnic group, between different neighbourhoods and social classes. An Israeli author (Shor, 2000: 165) finds significant differences in attitudes towards things like parental authority and the use of corporal punishment between low-income and middle-income groups, with the former being more supportive of more authoritarian methods. He suggests that some parenting behaviour considered excessively punitive or authoritarian by middle-class parents may, in fact, be appropriate in the context of preparing children for life in a 'deprived' neighbourhood. Certainly middle-class professionals need to be wary of challenging parental practices which are regarded as entirely normal in the communities where they occur.

Different disciplines

As well as different approaches to child abuse and child protection in different places, different times and different cultures, different perspectives and approaches are also taken by different professional disciplines within a single culture. Each discipline has its own particular approaches, its own characteristic ways of understanding the world.

The medical approach

Naturally enough a medical approach to child protection – that is, an approach led or inspired by the medical profession – will tend to place emphasis on those aspects of the problem that are clearly in the province of medicine: the interpretation of physical symptoms. Even when talking about those aspects of the problem that are not specifically physical, it will tend to use the language of illness and treatment. Consider the term 'battered baby syndrome', for example, introduced by C. Henry Kempe and his colleagues in 1962. These doctors did a great service to the cause of child protection by drawing attention to the fact that many supposedly accidental injuries to young children were, in fact, the result of being hit by adults. But 'battered baby syndrome' is, when you think about it, a curious use of the word 'syndrome'. (Would we speak of the 'playground punch-up syndrome', or 'pub brawl syndrome'?) Words like *treatment, therapy, pathology, prognosis,* all borrowed from medicine, are often used by medical and non-medical workers alike in case discussions that have nothing to do with any kind of organic illness. But if we use medical analogies, we need to be aware that the analogy with illness is not the only one that can be used, and may not always be the most useful.

There are many areas in which doctors do indeed possess special expertise, but we should not assume that this expertise extends to all aspects of the problem. There is no reason to assume that a doctor should be seen as having special expertise into *why* a parent injured a child, for example, even if the doctor is better qualified than others to tell us *how* the parent did so. Non-medical professionals should also be careful not to assume that medicine is more of an exact science than it is, even within its own particular area of expertise. Many physical symptoms are hard to interpret, and two doctors will often disagree as to how they were caused. Accepted medical opinion also changes with time, as is the case for example with Münchhausen's Syndrome by Proxy (MSBP) and Shaken Baby Syndrome, which I will mention later in this book.

In the Cleveland report, social workers were criticized for accepting too readily the diagnosis of sexual abuse made by two paediatricians. More recently, uncritical acceptance of medical opinion by other professionals has been criticized in the cases of Victoria Climbié and Lauren Wright, whose deaths at the hands of their carers in London and Norfolk respectively were well publicized in the British media.

The report made a series of recommendations – the main one being that professionals in any child care agency should challenge decisions that do not accord with their professional judgement. *(Guardian* Society, 1 October 2001, summarizing a report prepared on the Lauren Wright case for Norfolk Area Child Protection Committee)

Early suspicions of non-accidental injury were overruled by consultant paediatrician Dr Ruby Schwartz, who diagnosed scabies … Another doctor wrote on the notes that there were 'no child protection issues', a phrase repeated in the referral letter to social services … Inquiry counsel criticised both Hines [senior social worker] and Dewar [police officer] for accepting Schwartz's diagnosis without question. (*Community Care,* 2002: 18–19, on the Victoria Climbié inquiry)

Psychological perspectives

It is difficult to draw a hard-and-fast line between medical and psychological approaches, because psychological theories are often influenced by the medical model. For example, classical Freudian theory draws extensively on medical language, using words such as *pathology, neurosis* and *trauma* that were used originally in physical medicine, and adopts a model in which the sick patient comes to the trained expert for diagnosis and treatment (a model which British social care services, with their heavy emphasis on *assessment* have arguably also adopted).

But psychological theory provides a range of ideas that can be used to try and make sense both of why child abuse happens and what its effects are. Indeed it would be impossible for anyone to work with abusive and neglectful families – or abused and neglected children – without having *some* sort of psychological theories in her mind about abuse, even if those theories were only derived from her own life experience. If you had no ideas about what makes people abuse children, or about how abuse harms children, how could you decide what action to take?

I will be drawing on various psychological approaches to abuse in this book, particularly in Chapter 7, where I consider the long-term consequences of abuse for children, and in Part III, where I discuss the origins of abusive and neglectful behaviour by adults.

Sociological and political perspectives

The big limitation of purely psychological theories is that they locate the origins of the problem at the level of the individual or the family, and therefore are in danger of ignoring the wider social and structural factors. Exactly the same criticism can be made of traditional casework with individuals and with families.

In reality, child maltreatment takes place within a social context. To fully understand child abuse we need to look beyond the particular individuals involved, or the particular family, and think about the workings of a society in which individuals and families are only parts. We need to think of things like the way that relationships between adults and children are constructed in this society, for example, and about power differences between men and women. Why is it that more abusers are men than women, for example? (I will discuss gender and abuse a little more in Chapter 11.)

One hugely important issue that is left out of the equation by a purely psychological approach is that of class, poverty and structural inequality. As I will discuss more fully in Chapter 12, abuse and neglect are linked to poverty and social exclusion. This has major and difficult implications, for if one looks at abuse and neglect as phenomena linked to poverty and social deprivation, it is possible to argue that the kind of intervention that is typically carried out in the USA and Britain in child protection cases is not only inappropriate, but may actually make the problem *worse*. Intervention may simply add to the feelings of powerlessness and alienation that lead parents to physically abuse or neglect their children in the first place.

A sociological perspective helps to remind us too that the concept of 'child abuse' itself is a socially constructed phenomenon, unique to particular types of society at a particular point in time, as is the idea of 'child protection' in the sense that we now understand it.

The police and the legal profession

Two other professional groups closely involved with the child protection process are the police and the legal profession.

The police approach in child protection, as it is in other areas of police work, tends to place more emphasis on establishing whether an offence has taken place and, if so, prosecuting the offender, than does the approach of other professionals. Such an approach has an important place in a society that wants to give a clear signal that mistreatment of children is a crime. But in individual cases, it can cut across the interests of a child. An abused child, for example, may want the abuse to stop, but she may not want her abuser to go to jail.

Lawyers play an important role in our child protection system, helping to ensure that all parties, including parents and children, have articulate advocates who are conversant with the law. On the negative side, the adversarial British legal system can result in polarizing views, turning the process into a protracted battle.

Safeguarding children

This book will focus on the 'acute' end of the spectrum of services to children, that is on protecting children who have already been subjected to serious maltreatment, or who are imminently at risk of being seriously maltreated. Of course it would be much better if we could find ways of avoiding getting to this point in the first place, by providing services to vulnerable children and families at an earlier stage that would prevent maltreatment from ever occurring. At the time of writing, the UK government is attempting to strengthen these types of early intervention, and is using the phrase 'safeguarding children' to suggest a somewhat broader approach than is implied by the words 'child protection'.

The provision of universal services for children and families, and more specialized services for children and families with particular problems and needs, is of course all part of protecting children in the broadest sense. And in fact *all* the work done by professional agencies is itself really only a small part of the work that is done in every society to protect children by parents, relatives, friends and neighbours. However, the focus of this book will be the 'acute' end of the spectrum, or what the UK government calls 'responsive work to protect children who are suffering, or at risk of suffering, harm' (DfES, 2006: 49).

Chapter summary

In this chapter I have tried to sketch out the basic characteristics of child protection work as an organized professional activity in the modern world, and a variety of perspectives that can be applied to it. I have discussed:

- the development of the child protection system as we know it in the UK over the past century and a half
- the differences between child protection systems operating in different countries

(Continued)

- the particular issues raised by different cultural attitudes to children and families
- the existence of different professional and conceptual perspectives on child abuse and child protection
- a wider aspect to safeguarding children which involves providing services to vulnerable children and families which might help prevent them from ever coming to need 'child protection' in the narrower sense which is the focus of this book.

In the next chapter I will focus on the specific legal and procedural framework that exists in England and Wales at the present time.

2 The Multi-agency System

- The Children Act 1989
- The Children Act 2004 and its wider context
- *Working Together to Safeguard Children*
- The social work role
- Challenges of multi-agency and inter-disciplinary work
- Groupthink

In the previous chapter I discussed the modern concept of child protection as an organized professional activity. In this chapter I will look at a particular way of organizing it – the multi-agency system that (as of 2006) operates in England and Wales.

I will begin by briefly discussing the 1989 Children Act. I will then mention the 2004 Children Act and the wider *Every Child Matters* policy context of which this piece of legislation is part (DfES, 2003). I will then look at the government guidelines *Working Together to Safeguard Children* (DfES, 2006). *Working Together* sets out the system which child protection social workers and other professionals are now expected to implement in England and Wales. I will consider the central role within the system that is given to social workers employed by Local Authority children's social care agencies, before concluding this chapter with some reflections on the challenges of multi-agency and inter-disciplinary work.

The Children Act 1989

The 1989 Children Act brought together most of the law relating to child protection in England and Wales in a single piece of legislation. The following are a few key points:

General principles of the Children Act

Section 1 of the Act makes clear that the child's welfare should be the paramount consideration in all court proceedings. It provides a checklist for the courts to use in determining what is in the child's best interests and, for the first time in English law, it specifically states that delays in court proceedings are harmful to a child and should be avoided. In spite of this, however, court proceedings have grown steadily longer since the Act came into effect (see McKeigue and Beckett, 2004), a reminder that the aspirations expressed in laws, regulations and guidelines do not necessarily always work out.

Section 1(5) states that the court must not make an order 'unless it considers doing so would be better for the child than making no order at all'. This means that when a local authority takes a case to court it needs to prove not only that a child is being harmed in her family, but that the local authority *will be able to do better if an order is made.* (Of course there is only ever any point in doing anything if it is likely to make things better rather than worse.)

The duty to investigate

Sections 37 and 47 set out a local authority's duties to investigate cases of alleged harm to children. Section 37 relates to situations where a court decides that an investigation is needed in relation to a case which is before the court for other reasons (for example, a divorce case). Section 47 relates to the more common scenario where a local authority receives information about a child within its area who may be suffering, or likely to suffer, 'significant harm', and sets out the action the local authority should take:

- It should make sufficient enquiries to allow it to determine what action needs to be taken to protect the child.
- It should arrange for the child to be seen, unless sufficient information can be obtained without doing so.
- If denied access to a child, or refused information about the child's whereabouts, it should apply for a court order (an emergency protection order, a child assessment order, a care order or a supervision order).
- More generally it should decide whether it is in the interests of the child to initiate court proceedings.

The NSPCC (National Society for the Prevention of Cruelty to Children) can also undertake investigations, and is the only body, other than local authorities, specifically authorized under the Act to initiate care proceedings.

Immediate protection

If immediate action is needed to protect a child – for example, a child needs to be removed from a parent's care, or a parent needs to be prevented from taking a child out of a hospital or foster-home – then a social worker can apply to a court for an Emergency Protection Order (EPO), under section 44. To grant the order the court must be satisfied that there is good cause to believe that the child will suffer significant harm if the order is not made.

NSPCC officers can also apply for an EPO, as can other professionals, though the latter is rare. The EPO *is* only a provision for use in emergencies. If a child is at risk of significant harm and needs to be removed from home but the danger to the child is not immediate, then an Interim Care Order rather than an EPO should be used.

Police officers have another method of protecting a child in an emergency, which is to take a child into 'police protection', under section 46 of the Act. This they can do without going to court. Police protection lasts a maximum of 72 hours, during which time the child can be placed in local authority care. The police can also obtain a warrant allowing them to force entry and search for a child.

Neither an EPO nor police protection confer powers to insist on a medical examination of a child. If permission is refused for a medical by the parents *or* child, then it is necessary to seek specific directions from the court.

Children in need

The Act also places a duty on local authorities to assess and meet needs. These are set out in Part III of the Act, with the general principles being set out in section 17. There is a large grey area between 'children in need' (section 17) and 'children in need of protection' (section 47). The former is preferable if at all possible because it can be a very traumatic experience for both parents and children to be on the receiving end of a child protection investigation, however sensitively it is handled:

> The adversarial and stigmatizing nature of protective services intervention, although aimed at promoting children's safety, can rather jeopardise parents' feelings of support and confidence during a highly vulnerable time. To the extent that such intervention thus engenders in parents deeper feelings of powerlessness and adds additional ecological challenges, it may even heighten the risk of child maltreatment – precisely the opposite of the stated purpose of the intervention. (Guterman, 2001: 49)

The Children Act 2004 and its wider context

The Children Act 2004 is not a comparable piece of legislation to the 1989 Act and does not supersede the earlier Act in respect of any of the provisions discussed above. However, it introduces a miscellany of reforms to the system, many of which have their origins in the recommendations of the Victoria Climbié inquiry (Laming, 2003) and the Green Paper *Every Child Matters* (DfES, 2003). These include:

- The establishment of a Children's Commissioner for England (sections 1–9)
- Provision to allow the government to establish a database of children in England (section 12) and for the devolved Welsh Assembly to make similar arrangements in Wales
- The requirement on local authorities to appoint 'Directors of Children's Services' (section 18). These bring together all a local authority's services for children and families – both social care and education – under one overall umbrella.
- The establishment of 'Local Safeguarding Children's Boards' (sections 13–16) in each Local Authority area.

Local Safeguarding Children's Boards

LSCBs are responsible for co-ordinating efforts across local agencies to safeguard and promote the welfare of children in that area. They must include representatives of statutory agencies and relevant voluntary agencies such as the NSPCC. Their remit is wider than that of their predecessors, the Area Child Protection Committees. They are expected to co-ordinate activity at three levels:

- 'Activity that affects all children' (DfES, 2006: 76)
- 'Proactive work that aims to target particular groups' such as children identified as 'in need' or groups of children known to be more vulnerable than the general population (DfES, 2006: 76)
- 'Responsive work to protect children who are suffering, or at risk of suffering, harm' (DfES, 2006: 77).

The last of these three areas of work is the one covered by this book. In this area, LSCBs are required to draw up local policies and procedures, covering thresholds for intervention, training, recruitment of staff who work with children and investigation of allegations about staff working with children. They also have responsibility for looking into issues arising from child deaths.

The wider context

The 2004 Children Act is part of a widespread reform of the way services to children and families are delivered in the UK. I have already mentioned the establishment of new Children's Services Directors and LSCBs. Another development is the concept of local *Children's Trusts,* intended to bring together all the agencies with responsibilities for children and families in a locality in order to co-ordinate and commission new services in a particular geographical area. The hope is that these trusts will promote the well-being of children and young people in a more creative way that is less hamstrung by agency demarcation lines than has been the case with more traditional modes of service delivery. In particular the hope is to improve services for vulnerable children and their families prior to the point where they become 'child protection cases' and thereby prevent them ever having to enter the child protection arena. (It would certainly be a wonderful thing if more families could be helped at an earlier stage, particularly if we could somehow stop resorting so often to legal compulsion to break up families. However I am a little sceptical about the extent to which these hopes will actually be realized as a result of the current reforms because I think that *very* substantial additional resources would be required to (a) develop preventative services of sufficient depth and reach to make a really substantial impact of this kind, while simultaneously (b) bringing about the improvements to the child protection system which the government also claims to be making. I will return to this in the final chapter.)

For the present my focus will be on the current framework for responding to suspected abuse and neglect, as laid out in *Working Together*. Before discussing this, though, it may be useful to briefly reflect on what it would feel like to be on the 'receiving end' of the child protection system.

Exercise 2.1

- Have there ever been any situations in your own extended family that could possibly have resulted in child protection issues, but were in fact dealt with within the family? (A young mother suffering severe post-natal depression, for example, or parents at the end of their tether because of a marital crisis, or a crisis brought about by external factors such as redundancy.) If you can think of a situation of that kind, consider what kind of professional intervention might have been helpful, and what would have been unhelpful.
- If a teacher at your children's school was concerned about one of your children and decided to inform social services, how would you feel if they did so without consulting you?
- How would you feel if you were to discover, long after the event, that one of your children had been the subject of discussions between their school, social services and your family doctor without you being informed?
- What would your first feelings be if you received a telephone call from a social worker who wanted to interview your child at school without you present?
- What would your feelings have been, when you were a child of, say, 10, if a social worker you had never met before was to come to your school and ask you questions about the way that you were treated by your parents?

Comments on Exercise 2.1

If you work in the child protection field, it is easy to become preoccupied with procedures and routines at the expense of the human side of the job. It is therefore important to ask yourself from time to time how you would like yourself and your children to be treated, if your family became the subject of a child protection investigation and to consider whether your own practice is actually consistent with this.

It is also important to think about how you would react in that situation. It is easy to label people as 'awkward', 'unco-operative' or 'anti-authority' when they behave in an angry or difficult or aggressive way during an investigation, but I suggest that professionals would be more careful about applying such labels if they considered how they would react in the same situation. While it isn't always possible or desirable to avoid upsetting people, it is important to think about why people get upset, so that you are able to acknowledge and allow for it.

Working Together to Safeguard Children

Detailed arrangements for inter-agency working are drawn up for each area by LSCBs, which means that professionals need to be familiar with local procedures, but the overall framework within which professionals are required to operate is described in *Working Together to Safeguard Children* (DfES, 2006). This document refines rather than overturns the model provided by the previous version of *Working Together* (Department of Health, 1999), and most of the elements set out in the earlier document – the *strategy meeting*, the *key worker*, the *initial case conference*, the *core group*, the *core assessment* – remain in place.

In the discussion below, when I refer to *Working Together* or give paragraph numbers, I will always be referring to DfES (2006).

Initial responses

Local Authority children's social care is required to carry out an 'initial assessment' (Department of Health, 2000) on each child referred to them. This has to be completed in seven days but may be much quicker than this if it becomes apparent that the criteria are met for initiating enquiries under section 47 of the 1989 Children Act, namely that the child is suspected to be suffering, or is likely to suffer, significant harm (para 5.37).

At this point, if there is a risk to the life of a child, or a risk of immediate serious harm, it may be necessary to take immediate action to protect a child, though in most cases this will follow a strategy discussion. In the rare event that the situation is so urgent that a single agency has to go ahead and act on its own, a strategy meeting should be set up as soon as possible afterwards (paras 5.49–5.53).

Strategy discussion

Paragraph 5.54 of *Working Together* states that 'Whenever there is a reasonable cause to suspect that a child is suffering, or is likely to suffer significant harm, there should be a strategy discussion involving LA [local authority] children's social care and the police, and other bodies as appropriate (for example, children's centre/school and health).' LA children's social care is responsible for convening these meetings, and participants needs to be senior enough to be able to make decisions on their agency's behalf. Hospital staff must be involved if the child is an in- or out-patient and, where a medical examination is needed or has taken place, a senior doctor from the relevant health agency should be involved.

The purpose of the strategy discussion, which can if necessary take place over the telephone, is to share information, decide whether section 47 enquiries should be initiated or continued, plan how the enquiries will be carried out and by whom, agree what action is needed immediately to protect the child, and determine what information about the meeting will be shared with the family. It should also decide whether any legal action is needed.

Various matters to be considered in the meeting are itemized in para 5.56, including 'the race and ethnicity of the child and family ... how this should be taken into account, and ... whether an interpreter will be needed' (from para 5.56).

Exercise 2.2

I suggested earlier that you consider how you would like to be treated – and how you would like your children to be treated – if you were on the receiving end of a child protection investigation. What I would like you to do now is consider that question again, but this time imagining that you are a parent in a country where:

(Continued)

(Continued)

- The language spoken by the majority, and by public officials, is different from your own, and you are not able to speak it very well, if at all.
- The dominant culture is different from your own and you are well aware of the fact that this culture disapproves of many things that you regard as normal, and tolerates many things that you regard as wrong.
- You are aware that there is widespread prejudice against your ethnic group, and you have been treated rudely by public officials in the past.
- You are visibly different from the majority population, so you can be immediately identified as not belonging to the majority before you have opened your mouth.

What would your fears be about the way the system would treat you and your child, if you heard that you had been reported to the authorities for suspected child abuse, and that the authorities were following it up? What would you hope for, or want from the investigating authorities?

Comments on Exercise 2.2

I don't know, of course, what your fears would be, but I would be fearful that I would not understand what was going on, and that my child would not understand either and would be frightened. I would also fear that the authorities would not understand me, or listen to me properly, or that they would believe the worst of me. I would be concerned that they would be prejudiced against me. I would fear that the situation would be completely out of my control and that I would be prevented from providing reassurance to my child at a time when she really needed it. I would perhaps be frightened of ending up in jail or of having my child removed from me.
The sorts of things that I imagine would help would be:

- *If a good interpreter was provided, who could not only translate words for me, but also explain the cultural differences.*
- *If the public officials carrying out the investigation acknowledged to me and my child that they could see this was difficult for us, and assured me that they would do their best to take the cultural differences into account.*

The purpose of this exercise, obviously, was to look at what a child protection investigation would feel like if you were a member of an ethnic minority. Professionals operating in areas where there is only a very small ethnic minority population may be tempted to think that it is not relevant to them. Actually this is very mistaken, since it may well be *precisely* in situations where members of ethnic minorities feel themselves to be in a very small minority, that they are most likely to feel vulnerable. And it may be precisely in such situations that, if a professional is a member of the ethnic majority, she will be *most* in danger of getting out of her depth.

The reverse situation also often occurs, in which you as a *professional* come from an ethnic minority or from another country, while the family comes from the majority culture. (This is an increasingly common scenario in the UK, where employers of social workers, nurses, doctors and teachers actively recruit abroad.) Here too, I think, the onus is on the professional, who is in a powerful position relative to the child and family, to be sensitive to cultural differences and to the possibility of communication problems.

Core assessments

The term 'core assessment' (from Department of Health, 2000) describes a more thorough assessment following on from the brief initial assessment, and is the framework within which a section 47 enquiry should be carried out (para 5.60). The core assessment should start with the issues identified during the initial assessment but should go on to build a rounded picture of the entire context, using the various 'dimensions' set out in the *Assessment Framework* guidelines (Department of Health, 2000). The responsibility for this rests with Local Authority children's social care agencies, but other agencies have a legal obligation to assist (para 5.61).

When a parent or child is disabled, they may need to have help with communication in order to allow them to participate fully, and interpreters may be needed for people whose first language is not English. In the case of children whose age or understanding precludes them from taking part in an interview, their wishes and feelings need to be judged as far as possible by observation (para 5.63).

The importance of talking to children themselves is emphasized in para 5.64, which points out that 'children are a key, and sometimes the only, source of information about what has happened to them, especially in sexual abuse cases'. The need for sensitivity in interviewing children is emphasized and the point is made that 'children may need time, and more than one opportunity, in order to develop sufficient trust to communicate any concerns they may have' (para 5.64).

The guidance notes that in certain exceptional circumstances it may be necessary to interview children without the knowledge of the parent or caregiver (para 5.65), discusses the need for interviewers to have specialist training and experience (para 5.66) and notes that courts are obliged to make special arrangements for child witnesses, including the use of pre-recorded videos and the use of live video links.

Core assessments are supposed to be completed within 35 working days, though some specialist assessments such as psychiatric assessments may not be completed within this time frame (para 5.144).

Initial child protection conferences

The initial case conference (*Working Together,* paras 5.80–5.106) is supposed to take place within 15 working days of the strategy discussion. It brings together all the relevant agencies and members of the family concerned and is chaired by 'a professional who is independent of operational or line management responsibilities for the case'. Its purpose, as described in the guidance, is to:

- bring together and analyse in an inter-agency setting the information that has been obtained about the child's developmental needs, and the parents' or carers' capacity to respond to these needs to ensure the child's safety and promote the child's health and development within the context of their wider family and environment

- consider the evidence presented to the conference, make judgements about the likelihood of a child suffering significant harm in future, and decide whether the child is at continuing risk of significant harm; and
- decide what future action is required to safeguard and promote the welfare of the child, how that action will be taken forward, and with what intended outcomes (para 5.80).

Paragraphs 5.93–5.100 of *Working Together* set out what the conference should make decisions about. The central question is 'Is the child at continuing risk of significant harm?' in which case, the guidance says, safeguarding the child requires 'interagency help and intervention, delivered through a formal child protection plan' (para 5.95) and the conference should work out, in as much detail as is feasible, the outline of that plan. The chair of the conference determines what category of abuse or neglect the child has suffered or is likely to suffer. (There will be more on the various categories and their definitions in Chapter 5 of this book.)

If there *is* to be a formal child protection plan, the conference needs to settle whether the 'lead statutory body' will be the NSPCC or Local Authority children's social care, and to appoint a 'key worker' from that body. It also needs to identify the membership of a 'core group', agree timescales for the meetings of that group and for the completion of the child protection plan, and set a date for a review case conference.

In some cases an initial child protection conference may be held before the actual birth of a child (see para 5.140).

Recording that a child is the subject of a child protection plan

Under previous guidelines, children subject to a child protection plan were placed on a 'child protection register'. The word 'register' is no longer used in the current guidance but LA children's social care are required to record in a child's case record that a child is subject to a child protection plan and must be capable of producing a list of all such children in the area (paras 5.141–5.148).

The old register was accessible to the relevant agencies not only in working hours but out of them, so that, for example, when a child was admitted with an injury at eight o'clock at night to an accident and emergency department in a hospital, the staff could check the register in the event that there was any possibility that the injury might not be accidental. The new guidance greatly extends this principle because it states that other agencies and professionals should be able to access information not only about children 'judged to be at continuing risk of significant harm and who are the subject of a child protection plan' but also about 'other children who are known or have been known to the LA'. It goes on:

> Consequently, agencies and professionals who have concerns about a child should be able to obtain information about a child that is recorded on the LAs ICS IT system ... It is essential that legitimate enquirers such as police and health professionals are able to obtain this information both in and outside office hours. (*Working Together*, para 5.142)

This is one aspect of the new *Working Together* framework which *does* constitute a very substantial shift from the earlier guidance, a shift which is entirely consistent with the emphasis on information sharing that is evident in *Every Child Matters* (DfES, 2003) and in the 2004 Act. Some have reservations about its wisdom. Discussing the proposals for data sharing in the then Children Bill, which was to become the 2004 Act, Eileen Munro commented that they removed 'all right to confidentiality for all children and young people under the age of eighteen'. She raised several concerns about this, including the following:

> A perceived lack of control over what happens to personal information is already having a detrimental effect. Research among adult survivors of parental abuse found that two thirds of the victims had never reported the abuse because of concerns that professionals would react inappropriately and leave them powerless. The Bill proposes removing an advocate's right to offer confidentiality to a child and this is likely to increase the number of children who will conceal their problems. (Munro, 2004: 4–5)

In my experience children can indeed feel very powerless when information about them is shared in ways over which they have no control. I give a fictionalized example of this in Exercise 7.4 on page 104.

The key worker role

The person who is appointed key worker may come from either the NSPCC or from a local authority, but must be an experienced social worker. She is responsible for making sure that the outline child protection plan is developed into a fully realized plan. She is required to complete the 'core assessment' of the child and family, drawing on the assistance of other agencies. She is also the 'lead professional' for the inter-agency work and must run the core group meetings and 'co-ordinate the contribution of family members and agencies' to working out the details of the plan. She must also make sure that the plan is carried out and that its progress and effectiveness are properly reviewed (paras 5.115–5.118).

The core group

This group must be established at the initial conference and should hold its first meeting within ten days, meeting regularly thereafter to co-ordinate efforts and share information. The members should include the key worker, who leads the group, the child where appropriate, family members and those professionals (including foster-parents) who will have direct contact with the family. The first task of the core group is to 'flesh out' the plan agreed at the child protection conference and decide how to complete the 'core assessment' on time (paras 5.110–5.115).

Child protection plan

The guidance sets out in detail (paras 5.116–5.118) what the child protection plan should include. It should indicate what developmental needs of the child have been identified, and include specific outcomes which the plan aims to achieve, as well as strategies and specific actions to achieve them. It should include contingency plans in the event of changes of circumstances and set out the roles and responsibilities both of professionals and family members, including the 'nature and frequency of contact by professionals with children and family members'. It should set dates for progress to be reviewed and the criteria by which progress will be judged.

The plan should 'take into consideration the wishes and feelings of the child, and the views of the parents, insofar as they are consistent with the child's welfare' (para 5.118) and one of the key worker's tasks is to try to ensure that family members understand the outcomes, accept the plan itself and 'are willing to work to it'. If the preferences of family members are not followed, the reasons for this needs to be explained to them. They need to know about how to make complaints and representations if they want to do so. Parents and children should have the plan explained to them in appropriate language and at an appropriate level, both orally and in writing.

Intervention

The guidance offers some comments on intervention in paras 5.121–5.127, pointing out that intervention may include several different components:

- action to make a child safe;
- action to promote a child's health and development – i.e. welfare;
- action to help a parent(s)/caregiver(s) in safeguarding a child and promoting his or her welfare;
- therapy for an abused child; and
- support or therapy for a perpetrator of abuse (para 5.123).

It makes the point that when working to bring about change one important question is 'whether the child's developmental needs can be responded to within his or her family context, and **within timescales that are appropriate for the child**' (para 5.125, original emphasis). If a parent needs to be able to make major changes in order to be able to provide an adequate level of care and safety for that child, the question is not just 'can this parent change?' but 'can this parent change within the time that the child can reasonably be kept waiting before other plans need to be made?' In practice children are sometimes kept waiting, effectively in limbo, for periods of time that seem out of kilter with a child's developmental needs. For example, Bridget McKeigue and I cited a case of a child we called Michael:

> Michael was just short of his second birthday when he was removed from home on an emergency protection order. A full care order was not made on him for another two years and five months. He was then four years and four months old. However it was another year and a half before he was placed with an adoptive family, by which time he was nearly six. (Beckett and McKeigue, 2003: 33)

In this case the length of time that passed before final placement, during which two separate unsuccessful attempts were made to rehabilitate 'Michael' with his father, resulted in it being much harder to find another home for him, and in a considerably increased likelihood that his eventual adoptive placement would break down. It also resulted in this child spending four years, at a crucial time in his development, without a secure family base.

Child protection review conferences

The Child Protection Review Conference is discussed in paras 5.128–5.135. With the same membership as the initial conference, a review case conference should be convened within three months of the initial conference, and thereafter at a minimum of every six months while the child's name remains on the register. The meeting's purpose is to:

- review the safety, health and development of the child against planned outcomes set out in the child protection plan;
- ensure that the child continues to be safeguarded from harm; and
- consider whether the child protection plan should continue in place or should be changed. (*Working Together*, para 5.129)

The guidance gives a collective responsibility to the core group for producing conference reports. It also sets grounds (para 5.133) under which a child should no longer be subject to a child protection plan. These are that the child is no longer at risk of significant harm, or that he or she has moved permanently to another local authority area (in which case the new authority should convene a conference within 15 working days of being notified), or that the child has reached 18 years of age or died, or left the UK. The ending of a child protection plan does not necessarily mean that the local authority should withdraw its help.

The social work role

Every professional group within the multi-agency system has a distinctive role to play, and no single professional group has either the expertise or the authority to operate the system single-handedly. Thus, for example, while it is Local Authority social care (or the NSPCC) and the police who carry out initial investigations of suspected cases of abuse, these agencies are almost entirely reliant on others, such as teachers, to pick up the signs of abuse in the first place.

However, social work agencies do have a central co-ordinating role in the system as it stands, undertaking not only direct work with children and parents alongside other professionals, but also work in social work's characteristic 'executive' capacity (see Beckett, 2006: 10ff) in which the social worker is involved in recruiting and supervising input from others, and, where necessary, acting as the agent of state power to impose aspects of a plan.

Social workers' tasks include the following:

- Taking child protection referrals from the public and other agencies. ('If somebody believes that a child may be suffering, or be at risk of suffering, significant harm, then s/he should always refer his or her concerns to LA children's social care' (*Working Together*, para 5.16).
- Carrying out initial investigations, usually jointly with the police. This includes a responsibility for setting up and participating in strategy discussions.
- In the event of an investigation coming to the conclusion that no further action needs to be taken under child protection procedures, following this through with the family and checking whether there is any other help that they need.

- Taking any immediate action necessary to protect the child, which in some circumstances could include going to court for an EPO.
- Requesting an initial child protection conference and providing the conference co-ordinator with preliminary information and details of those to be invited. ('Where the agencies most involved judge that a child may continue to suffer, or to be at risk of suffering, significant harm, LA children's social care should convene a child protection conference' (*Working Together*, para 5.79).)
- Undertaking an initial assessment and providing a report to the initial child protection conference.
- Informing the family and child about the case conference and the child protection process. Preparing the family and child for the child protection conference.
- In the event of a conference deciding that it is not necessary for a child to be subject to a child protection plan, following this up with the family and discussing whether they need other help.
- In the event of a child being made subject to a child protection plan, taking on a key worker role, and carrying out the following tasks:

  (a) carrying out a core assessment within the prescribed timescale
  (b) leading the core group in the development of a child protection plan
  (c) ensuring that there is good communication between the family and the agencies involved – and ensuring in particular that the child is consulted and informed about what is going on in a way that is consistent with her age and understanding
  (d) taking a lead role in the implementation of the protection plan
  (e) preparing reports for review case conferences.

- If any court proceedings are required, initiating them, working with lawyers in the preparation of statements and giving evidence in court, while simultaneously offering support to the family and child.
- If a child is to be removed from the family home (whether as a result of a court order, or by being accommodated in foster- or residential care on a voluntary basis), managing this, which includes the following tasks:

  (a) locating appropriate placements and managing the logistics of placement
  (b) supporting the carers
  (c) supporting the child and the family, ensuring that all parties are kept informed and are able to express their wishes and feelings
  (d) managing contact between parents and child
  (e) ensuring that the necessary visits, reviews and paperwork are completed, that the child's needs are met as far as possible, that the child is kept informed about what is happening, and that the child's views and wishes are sought and taken into account.

Challenges of multi-agency and inter-disciplinary work

One would like to think that the multi-agency system was entirely rational, guided purely by the need to secure the best possible outcome for the child. But we are human beings, not robots. All kinds of factors intrude, at the individual level, at the inter-personal level, and at the level of group dynamics which may distort decision-making and communication. Too much or too little weight may be given to one piece of information. Too much or too little influence over the outcome may be allowed to one participant. Sometimes the process can even become a battle between different agencies in which the child's needs get lost.

Every individual participant in the child protection process, and every profession or agency, necessarily sees things from his, her or its own particular standpoint and has his, her or its own particular 'axes to grind'. It is important to bear in mind that no one participant possesses the pure and unadulterated 'truth': not even you!

Some common areas of difficulty in inter-agency/inter-professional communication are the following:

- Status differences and different areas of expertise. It can be hard to challenge people who we perceive as being of higher status, and/or to challenge people in their own area of expertise (or, if we are high-status experts ourselves, or see ourselves as such, it can be hard to accept challenges from others). But exaggerated deference to any one participant is likely to be counterproductive and is potentially dangerous.
- Negative stereotypes of other agencies or other professionals. Agencies can develop negative stereotypes of each other which can get in the way of good working relationships. One source of friction comes about because different agencies have different jobs to do and limited resources to do these jobs, which may mean that when one agency asks another for help, help is not always forthcoming.

   Schoolteachers, for instance, often express frustration about the fact that social care don't follow up enough on their referrals about children who are causing them concern. Often it simply isn't physically possible for social workers to follow up every concern referred to them, but teachers cannot see all the other cases that social work agencies have to deal with, so that social care's failure to follow up their concerns may just look negligent or uncaring. But in the same way, social workers sometimes get frustrated with schools who exclude children from the classroom. This too can seem uncaring to social workers who know the traumas that lie behind a child's difficult behaviour, but don't have to think about the other children in a class whose learning may be completely disrupted by one difficult pupil.

   Agencies' negative perceptions of one another can lead to distrust, antipathy and even outright hostility. It is necessary to make a conscious effort to see things from the point of view of other professionals and to understand the particular pressures that they face.
- Focussing on different aspects of the problem. Different professional groups have different jobs to do with the result that they may also have different ideas about the correct order of priorities for dealing with a given situation. Police officers, for example, may be more inclined to prioritize securing a conviction than, say, doctors or social workers, and their views on an appropriate protection plan may be different as a result.

   These kinds of differences can be positive: they can result in a 'creative tension' in which each professional group is forced to examine its own assumptions. But they can also result in conflict and stalemate.
- Differences as to primary client. In a case where the parents have learning disabilities, the learning disability agencies will see the parents as their primary clients, but health visitors, teachers and children's social care workers will see the children as theirs. The same situation can arise when parents have mental health or drug and alcohol problems. Since each member of the family has different needs, it can be very useful for each to have their own advocate within the professional system, but it can also lead to conflict if there is not a constructive dialogue between the professionals involved – and this in the end can work against the interest of all family members.

Conflict can occur around information sharing. Agencies whose primary concern is child protection may feel that all the information about a given family should be on the table, but agencies whose primary clients are the parents may feel that they have a duty of confidentiality to their service users which can only be waived in respect of information which has a *direct* bearing on child protection issues.

Groupthink

A case conference or core group, like any other group, has its own dynamics. While there are certainly many advantages in group decision-making, there can also be dangerous distortions caused by the way that groups work. Eileen Munro (2002) refers to the phenomenon of 'groupthink' described by Irving Janis (1982). This occurs when group members' desire to achieve a consensus and avoid conflict has the effect of inhibiting their ability to realistically weigh up the situation under discussion:

> The tendency of groups to reach consensus does not lead to middle-of-the-road decisions, but to 'extreme' ones; that is, the group will shift to one extreme or the other of being very cautious or very risky. (Munro, 2002: 155–6)

The major features of groupthink, as summarized by Munro, are given in the following list in italics. I have added my own comments.

- *An illusion of invulnerability, shared by most or all group members, that leads to overoptimism and excessive risk taking.* Most of us experience a reduction of anxiety when we are sharing decision-making with a group of other people – the weight is no longer on our shoulders alone – but our sense of reassurance may allow us to jump to conclusions that are not supported by the evidence.
- *An unquestioned belief in the group's inherent morality.* We may become complacent, assuming that the group will necessarily 'do the right thing', and cease to be sensitive to the possibility that the group will act in a way that will make things worse for children rather than better.
- *Collective efforts to rationalize or discount warnings.* Having 'made up its mind' groups may collectively act to discount and discredit information that might suggest that the consensus is wrong.
- *Stereotyped views of adversaries as too evil to make negotiating worthwhile, or too weak and stupid to pose a serious threat.* As I discussed earlier, 'professional groups involved in child protection often develop negative stereotypes of each other' (Munro, 2002: 156) and this provides a means by which one professional group can simply discount and reject the input of another group.
- *Pressure directed at any group member who dissents from the majority view.* Sometimes in case conferences, it can be hard to express a minority view without being placed under pressure by other participants to retract or modify it.
- *Self-censorship of deviations from the apparent group consensus.* We may keep our own dissenting views to ourselves if we feel that we would otherwise invite censure from the rest of the group. It can be difficult, for example, to express the view that parental behaviour is not as abnormal or abusive as other conference members seem to think, if you fear that you will be perceived as unprofessional or collusive.
- *A shared illusion of unanimity.* If dissenters are discouraged from expressing their views, or censor themselves, the rest of the group may not realize that there *is* disagreement. It could even happen that the *majority* of the group privately disagreed with the apparent consensus view, yet each dissenting individual assumed him/herself to be in a minority of one.

- *Self-appointed 'mindguards' who protect the group from information that might challenge the group's complacency.* Individuals may take on the role of 'policing' the input of other participants, finding ways to discredit dissenting views or discourage their expression. Participants may take upon themselves the mantle of 'expert' and then challenge or undermine the contributions of others who dissent from their 'expert' view.

The dangers of poor decision-making resulting from groupthink can be reduced if all agency participants in a group decision-making process – and especially those seen by others as leaders – cultivate an atmosphere of openness within which the expression of dissenting views is actively encouraged. It is very important to avoid a sense of there being only one permissible orthodox view from which no one dare dissent for fear of, as it were, being branded a heretic. This can result in disastrous decisions being taken on very inadequate evidence. There have been tragic occasions when groups of child protection professionals, a little bit like participants in a medieval witch-hunt, have allowed groupthink to bring them to conclusions which rational consideration of the evidence really doesn't support. Several high-profile UK examples occurred in the late 1980s and early 1990s when, as a result of widespread fears about so-called ritual abuse, children were needlessly removed from their families; for example, in Rochdale and in the Orkney Islands (Clyde, 1992).

Chapter summary

In this chapter I have looked at the framework within which child protection professionals are required to operate, at the beginning of the twenty-first century, in England and Wales. Topics covered included:

- the legal framework provided in England and Wales by the 1989 Children Act
- the multi-disciplinary system in England and Wales, as prescribed by the *Working Together* guidance
- the diverse tasks undertaken by social workers within this system
- the challenges of working with people from other agencies and other professional disciplines
- the dangers posed by 'groupthink' for the child protection system

I have described a framework. In the next chapter I will consider what child protection professionals can actually do, within that framework, to make things better for children.

3 | Making Things Different

- Some constraints and principles
- Protecting the child from immediate danger
- Child-directed work
- Parent-directed work
- Work directed at the wider environment
- Permanent substitute care

> When procedures become the primary focus of concern, a dangerous and false sense of security can develop. Professionals then have a tendency to invest faith in the formal processes, as if these structures, and not the work done with and by families and communities, actually decrease risk. (Burton, 1997: 6)

It is easy to fall into the trap of thinking that, simply by discussing a child, or agreeing that she should be the subject of a child protection plan, we have somehow helped or protected her, but this is an illusion, related to the phenomenon of 'groupthink' that I discussed in the previous chapter. What protects children and helps them to recover from harm is not a meeting taking place in a faraway office, or a completed assessment form on a file, or data in a computer, but *actual positive changes in the child's own environment*. Assessments, meetings and records are of value only in so far as they help to bring such changes about.

I say *positive* changes, because actually it is quite easy to bring about change of some sort, but considerably harder to bring about changes that will result in lasting benefits. When a child has entered the child protection arena, all kinds of services and arrangements are sometimes 'put in' – a student of mine recently described to me a case in which *12* different services were all simultaneously involved in working with one family – and there can be little doubt that any substantial intervention will make a difference of *some* kind. But change can be for the worse as well as for the better. Families and children can be bewildered, overwhelmed and undermined by being compelled to accept 'help' which really isn't helpful at all.

The art of successful child protection work – the real challenge of it – lies in finding ways of intervening that are genuinely helpful to children. Many commentators have observed that the child protection system in the English-speaking world has become overly focussed on surveillance, information gathering and risk assessment, at the expense of actually doing things to make a difference. Neil Guterman in the US, for example, worries that a preoccupation with 'screening, decision making and monitoring activities' will drive out 'any remaining capacity to provide direct services to families' (2001: 44). Given the detailed official guidance that exists in Britain on information gathering and information sharing, it is surprising how little guidance exists about what actually to do to make things better, yet it seems to me that it is actually often easier to see what the problem *is* than to find the lever that will move things on.

This chapter will look at the levers that are available.

Some constraints and principles

Before looking at what can be done, it is worth considering what the constraints and limitations are that child protection professions have to take into account. The principles of good professional practice must be consistent with those constraints, because a course of action is only useful if it can actually be put into effect.

Legal constraints

Child protection agencies cannot simply impose whatever intervention they want on a family. Under the law of England and Wales, if a family declines to co-operate with a proposed protection plan, then there are two alternatives. The plan can be changed to a form which family members *would* be willing to work with, or the local authority can request a court to make an order which would allow the agencies to insist on a plan.

It is far better to proceed by negotiation than by resorting to the courts, if this is possible without compromising the welfare of the child. And it is important in any case that professionals do not simply impose their will on the assumption that they must know better than the family what sort of intervention is needed. Of course child protection workers cannot simply accept the parents' view of the world – their primary duty is to the child – but they would be extremely foolish to ignore it.

Working with involuntary clients

Most child protection cases don't end up in court. Even so, parents normally feel they have to work with the child protection system at least to some extent, whether or not they want to. The term 'involuntary client' is used in social work texts to describe both service users who are compelled by law to deal with social workers and those who, while not legally compelled, nevertheless feel obliged to do so. (Ronald Rooney [1992: 4] calls the first group 'mandated' and the second group 'nonvoluntary'.) In the case of child protection work, parents are often involuntary clients not only of social workers but of all the other professionals involved in delivering the protection plan.

But people cannot be forced to change the way they think or feel or to share their inner selves. The child protection system – backed by legal force – certainly has a great deal of power (power which, as I'll discuss in Chapter 13, can be abused) but it is nevertheless limited power and if we want to help people to change in any deep way, we still have to secure their co-operation.

Chris Trotter (1999, 2004) suggests four groups of skills that are associated with positive outcomes when working with involuntary clients:

- Accurate role clarification. We need to be clear about our role and our expectations. What is the purpose of our contact with the family? What are our expectations of them? What are the basic ground rules in respect of matters like confidentiality? What aspects of the child protection plan are negotiable and what are not?
- Collaborative problem-solving. In work with involuntary clients, better outcomes are associated with approaches based on 'modest, achievable goals which are the client's rather than the worker's (or at least collaboratively developed), and identifying strategies with the client to achieve the goals' (Trotter, 1999: 21). Of course, in the child protection context, it is often not possible to allow the clients to set all the goals. Nevertheless, although some goals will be non-negotiable from the professional worker's point of view, there is almost always scope for other goals to be placed on the agenda by family members.

  Collaborative working must include being open to the possibility that you are wrong. Involuntary clients are often labelled as 'anti-authority', 'uncommitted' or 'resistant to change' if they question the arrangements that professional agencies seek to impose on them. And some parents *are* all of these things. But professional agencies do often get things wrong, and parents should be entitled to object to arrangements that seem to them unhelpful without being negatively labelled for it, particularly when one considers that parents have to accept very personal criticism in very public arenas, and are expected to acknowledge and take responsibility for their own short-comings. Being open to constructive criticism is something that we ought to be modelling.

- Pro-social modelling and reinforcement. Collaborative problem-solving can however slide into collusion, if you end up uncritically accepting the parent's point of view. In child protection work you need to be clear about the behaviours you are trying to promote and you need to consistently and firmly reinforce and model them. Some professionals feel uneasy about imposing a particular set of values on service users. Social work training courses, for instance, quite rightly emphasize the importance of being non-judgemental, but sometimes with the result that:

  > we sometimes find practitioners tolerating harmful circumstances for some family members in their efforts to avoid appearing judgemental of other family members – usually the older ones. (Milner and O'Byrne, 2002: 169–70)

  If you are going to work in the child protection field you really *have* to be able to sign up to the position that certain parenting practices are unacceptable, which is actually an entirely different thing from being 'judgemental' in the sense of making moral judgements about people's worth as human beings. You have to be able to give a consistent message, being careful not to fall into the trap of giving one message but then undermining it, perhaps by seeming to apologize for it, or by contradicting it with your actions or body language. Inadvertently undermining your own message is quite easy to do if you are uncomfortable with the authority that you hold in a context of this kind.

- Worker/client relationship. The quality of the working relationship itself is linked to positive outcomes:

> When child protection workers understand their clients' point of view, when they make appropriate use of self-disclosure, when they make appropriate use of humour and when they are optimistic about the potential of the client to change, they tend to have good relationships with their clients. In turn the good relationships may lead to improved outcomes. (Trotter, 2004: 23)

No confidentiality

In the multi-agency context of child protection work, professionals are expected to share information freely. This means that confidentiality in the sense that it is normally understood, really cannot be offered. In fact I sometimes feel that all child protection professionals should, like the police when making an arrest, caution their clients that 'everything they say will be taken down and may be used in evidence'. I think it is interesting and significant that the word 'confidentiality', like 'confidence' and 'confide', has its origins in a Latin word meaning 'trust' and I have already alluded in the previous chapter to concerns that by eroding the principle of confidentiality, the modern child protection system reduces the likelihood that parents or children would want to confide in it.

But we can limit the damage to trust to some extent by being very clear about the ground rules in this area. If you are a counsellor, for example, working with a parent or child as a component of a child protection plan, you need to be clear both with the family and with the professional group about what you will share with others and what will stay in your consulting room. This may involve some negotiation with your professional colleagues.

Resources

A major constraint that child protection professionals face is to do with the resources that are available to do the job. Bringing about large-scale changes in the way that families operate is an enormously ambitious task. It is the social equivalent, one might say, of open-heart surgery. Yet, given the scale of the task, the resources available to carry it out are often extremely modest. Professionals may have only a very limited amount of time that they can devote to any one family, and an even smaller proportion of that time to spend in actual face-to-face contact.

Perhaps because it is politically uncomfortable this is seldom discussed but any useful plan will have to take into account what the participants are actually able to put into it in terms of time and money, and goals have to be set at a realistic level accordingly. It is not heroic of child protection workers to set themselves unrealistic goals, any more than it would be heroic for a surgeon to operate without adequate equipment or support. (It is even *less* heroic, incidentally, of policy makers to set unrealistic goals for others, but this is something I will come back to in the final chapter.)

No such thing as 'playing it safe'

Almost any intervention into family life carries its risks as well as its benefits. In theory the law recognizes this and the 1989 Children Act was supposed to protect children 'both from the harm which can arise from failures or abuse within the family and from the harm which can be caused by unwarranted intervention in their family life' (Department of

Health, 1989: 5). Any decision about intervention has to try to strike a balance at the point where the benefits intervention will bring are likely to exceed the harm it might do, rather in the way that a surgeon needs to strike a balance between the medical benefits of surgery and the not inconsiderable risks that surgery poses.

Recognizing strengths

While intervention is necessarily aimed at changing things, it should not just focus on the negatives. No one responds well to purely negative criticism and most of us are much more likely to learn and to change and to keep *at* things if we are given encouragement. Therefore, just as we should be aware of the possible negative effects of intervention when deciding a course of action, we should also take sufficient account of the positive aspects of what a child's family has to offer.

A corollary of this is that it is important not to make excessive demands on parents. The aim of child protection work is not to get to a point where the parents never get anything wrong. The aim is to get to a point where the standard of parenting is such that it would normally be considered acceptable. We should not demand of families that they achieve a level of parenting that is *higher* than the standard that would be regarded as acceptable in others. It is quite unrealistic to expect the child protection system to turn every family that comes its way into a model happy family.

Avoiding overload and fragmentation

A fragmented tick-box approach is rather common in which those drawing up a protection plan (a) list all the problems a family has, and then (b) try to match each identified problem with its own separate specialist service. Apart from overwhelming people with multiple services and confusing them with multiple messages, this approach also runs the risk of unnecessarily professionalizing some of the problems being experienced. The fact that there is an agency out there that deals with Albanian migrants, does not necessarily mean that every Albanian migrant will find this agency useful. The fact that a child has had a traumatic experience does not necessarily mean she needs psychotherapy. (She *may* do, but she may get over it herself in a safe environment with supportive carers.) Chris Trotter comments that:

> there are advantages in having one worker who understands her or his clients in a broad context and who helps those clients work through a range of issues which are of concern to them. When a client sees several professionals in relation to multiple problems the client may be required to repeat his or her story over and over. Not only would this be tiresome but it might also lead to poorer outcomes given the time it takes to develop an effective client/worker relationship. (Trotter, 2004: 11)

I do not think it is necessarily appropriate to confine family contact to *one* worker – the professionals involved in a child protection plan typically include several, like GPs and teachers, who would expect to be involved with a family anyway in the normal way of things – but I do suggest that the tendency to involve large numbers of workers and agencies in simultaneous direct work with families and children is more about managing our own anxieties than about really meeting children's needs.

Micro and macro planning

A good plan involves what I call micro and macro elements. The macro plan refers to the broad services that are going to be provided. The micro plan relates to the precise practical details of how this is going to work. The micro plan therefore includes things like transport arrangements, babysitting arrangements (if the parents need to attend sessions away from home) and the precise means by which the child and family members are going to be communicated with, consulted and kept informed. I suggest that getting the micro elements right is very important to the overall success of a plan. A good child protection plan creates an environment in which the child not only is safe but *feels* safe, and in which parents also feel safe enough to address problems and make changes. Poor logistics – numerous different people involved in transporting children, poor timekeeping, multiple changes of venue, frequent breakdowns in communication – create an atmosphere of muddle and confusion which does not feel safe at all. Good, respectful, regular communication with child and parents about what is going on can make a huge difference to the success of the overall plan.

Protecting the child from immediate danger

Where a child is at an immediate risk of acute harm, the first step to be taken is to reduce that risk. This sometimes involves physical removal of the child from the family, or removal from the family of the person thought to be the source of the danger. Sometimes it may be possible to secure an agreement from family members to alter their behaviour in a way that will reduce the risk, though in these circumstances you obviously need to have a solid basis for believing that the agreement will stick.

Exercise 3.1
What immediate steps might be taken in each of the following three situations in order to protect the child from danger?

1 John is ten. His Uncle Ralph is a paedophile and John is at risk of sexual abuse if he has any contact with him.
2 Helen is 18 months old. Her father, Dave, has assaulted her so severely as to cause serious injury, not just once but on several occasions. It is likely to happen again if she is ever left in his care.
3 Judy has been left on her own by her mother Lisa for long periods on a number of occasions. She is only five and on one occasion nearly started a fire by playing with matches.

(Continued)

(Continued)

Comments on Exercise 3.1

1   In John's case, preventing his Uncle Ralph from having unsupervised contact with him will reduce the risk of his being sexually abused. It may be that simply making John's parents aware of the risk posed by Ralph will be sufficient to achieve this. But if there is reason to believe that John's parents cannot stand up to Ralph and/or do not take the risk he poses seriously, then additional steps might need to be taken. Perhaps the supportive network for John's parents could be strengthened so they would be better able to stand up to Ralph? Or perhaps steps could be taken to deter Ralph from attempting to have contact with John? If you had reason to believe that his parents were actively colluding in making John available to Ralph then you would want to consider removing John from their care.

2   A child of Helen's age is at real risk of fatal injury if she is not protected from Dave's violence but perhaps Helen's mother, or another carer, would be able to ensure that Helen never does have unsupervised contact with her father? If there is reason to believe that Dave is capable of intimidating Helen's carer, then additional support might be needed. In some circumstances, it might even be necessary for Helen to be removed into care if no member of her family is able to protect her from Dave.

3   The immediate danger to be avoided here is that Judy will once again be left on her own. This might be achieved by securing an undertaking from Lisa that she will not do so, but there would have to be some means of checking up on this, and you would need to have confidence that Lisa would take this sufficiently seriously for it to deter her from leaving Judy alone again. Checks might involve a system of spot checks, including checks out of office hours, by one or more of the agencies implementing the child protection plan. It could be that the extended family might also play a role.

Child-directed work

I am moving on now to look at interventions whose aim is to bring about longer-term change, beginning with those focussed directly on the child.

Developing strategies for self-protection

Of course we could not expect 18-month-old Helen in Exercise 3.1 to be able to do anything at all to protect herself against her father Dave, but in the case of John there may be quite a lot that could be done to help him keep *himself* safe. I do not mean by this that John can or should be expected to take sole responsibility for protecting himself because it is up to adults to keep him safe. But one of the ways that adults can help him is by giving him guidance about avoiding putting himself in risky situations and what to do should he find himself in one. He could be given the names and numbers of people he would contact if he felt uncomfortable or at risk. He could even be given strategies for what to do should he find himself unexpectedly in contact with his uncle.

Supporting recovery

The child protection system cannot prevent all abuse and neglect before it has had time to do any harm. Therefore an important component of child protection work is aimed at helping children to deal with abuse or neglect *already* suffered and, as far as possible, to help them come to terms with it and get on with their lives. This might include counselling or therapy, or just talking and listening, at a level appropriate to a child's age, aimed at helping the child to make sense of what has happened and move on from it, addressing in particular the destructive and mistaken ideas about themselves and others (internal working models) that children who have been mistreated tend to develop: 'I deserved it', 'I provoked it', 'I'm not worth anything better', 'you can't trust anyone'…

Psychiatrists, psychologists and play therapists might be involved in this. But formal counselling or therapy is only ever part of this work of promoting recovery, and not necessarily the main part. There is a danger that, by setting 'therapy' too much on a pedestal, we forget how much can be achieved by family members, foster-parents, teachers and others simply being available to a child, respectful of the child's point of view, sensitive to a child's needs at any given moment and careful both to explain and to listen. And supporting recovery involves thinking about practical needs as well as emotional ones. For example, it is common for children who are experiencing abuse or neglect to have problems with schoolwork and they may need additional help in that area to catch up and to fit in again with other children.

Addressing special needs

Sometimes children themselves can make enormous demands on parents which may have contributed to pushing a parent 'over the edge'. This is the case with some children with behaviour problems or other special needs. Some interventions might be aimed at helping change a child's behaviour or a parent's response to it. Sometimes practical help is needed. For example, some day care or respite care might be necessary.

Communicating with children

Whatever the overall 'macro' plan, it is important that the child's own view of things is heard and that the child is kept informed of what is going on in a way that is appropriate to her age. This does not mean that every professional involved in the child protection plan should feel that she must constantly be talking to the child. A social worker's task, for example, is to make sure that the work gets done, not to do all of it, and there may be others with an easier, closer relationship with the child who are better placed than the social worker – a teacher, perhaps, or a school nurse – to do most of the work with the child.

Effective work with children and young people is certainly a skilled activity, but we should beware of over-professionalizing it or making too much of a mystique out of it because this can make some professionals unnecessarily fearful that they do not possess those skills. But work with children does need to take into account the child's stage of development and recognize the power difference between children and adults.

Adults are often very inconsistent, sometimes acting as if children think and understand just like they do, sometimes behaving as if children do not think at all about the world around them at all. The fact is that children think *just as much* as adults do but not in *the same way.* Small children in particular think in more concrete terms than adults and have more difficulty with abstract concepts, so it often useful to use concrete things such as toys, drawings, books and puppets as communication tools.

Recognizing the difference in power between adults and children is always important for any effective work with children. Children in abusive situations are particularly aware of the potential for adults to misuse their power. They may have learnt – or been explicitly taught – not to speak their own minds but rather to try and guess what adults want them to say. Children in neglectful situations, on the other hand, may also have a lot of experience of adults *failing* to use their power appropriately. An example of this might be a four-year-old who is allowed to wander round the streets on her own and to cross busy roads. Such children may see any exercise of authority by adults as threatening or intrusive.

Children who have been abused in an extreme, systematic way by adults may need specific help in recognizing that one particular adult – the abuser – is not in fact all-powerful and that other adults, be they other family members or professionals, are powerful enough to protect them. But it is important too to remember that most children, even children in families where there is some abuse, do look to their parents for protection, and therefore *need* to see their parents as powerful. Professional interventions should not humiliate and undermine the parents unnecessarily in the eyes of their children and should not put children in a position where they are made to feel they are betraying someone whom they care about.

Parent-directed work

If a child is being mistreated or neglected in some way by his or her parents then an effective plan of action needs to focus not only on the child but on the parents, and on the relationship between child and parents. In the case of Judy in Exercise 3.1, for instance, there may be various short-term measures which would remove the immediate dangers posed, but in the long-run what one would really want is for Judy's mother Lisa to be able to take responsibility *herself* for meeting Judy's need for safety and security. This in turn would involve looking at Lisa's needs and her feelings about her relationship with Judy.

Exercise 3.2

Judy, in Exercise 3.1, had been left on her own by her mother Lisa for long periods at the age of only five. Let us suppose that a case conference has been held which has determined that Judy needs a child protection plan (on grounds of neglect). What kind of work might help to ensure that Judy's needs were more adequately met in the future?

Comments on Exercise 3.2

You will probably agree with me that my question is impossible to answer unless you know a bit more about why Lisa was leaving her daughter on her own. You need to understand the context in order to know how to respond, something I will discuss in more detail in Chapter 8 and subsequent chapters. But here are a few possibilities:

(Continued)

- *Lisa is a heroin addict whose subjective experience of needing the drug sometimes gets so extreme that she loses sight of Judy's needs entirely. If this is the issue, then obviously any plan for long-term change will have to look at Lisa's drug problem.*
- *Lisa's own understanding of the needs of children is so limited that she simply does not understand that it is inappropriate to leave a child alone at that age. If this is really the issue then it may be that the plan should include education for Lisa on parenting skills.*
- *Lisa is driven to distraction by Judy and the demands she makes, to the point where she feels she must go out and leave Judy alone for fear that she will otherwise end up hurting her. The situation is more complicated here and raises further questions which you'd need to explore before knowing what kind of work was needed: Is Judy exceptionally demanding? Has Lisa had very distressing childhood experiences which are constantly being triggered by Judy?*
- *Lisa does not have any feeling of loving or caring for Judy, and has very little interest in her welfare other than a rather minimal sense of guilt and obligation. This might be a temporary feeling, resulting from stresses or distresses of one kind or another. If she has always felt that way, though, and sees no prospect of this changing, you might wonder whether Judy should really be in her care.*

Parent-centred work involves trying to bring about change in a parent's behaviour. This might mean change in the way that they function *as parents*. For example, it might mean trying to get a parent not to hit a child. Alternatively it might mean change in another area of a parent's life which was impacting on their parenting, which could for instance mean addressing the parent's heroin use, as discussed in the case of Judy and Lisa above.

Boundary setting

The typical way in which the child protection system works with parents is to set boundaries ('you must ensure your child is never left without adult supervision', 'you must ensure that your child is not left alone with his Uncle Ralph') within which the parents must demonstrate they can work if the child is to cease to be subject to a child protection plan (or, in some cases, if the child is to remain in their care). The professional group then (a) monitors compliance with the boundary that has thus been set, and (b) tries to offer support and encouragement to the parent in doing so.

Whether this is successful or not will depend on a number of factors: the nature of the problems that the parents are required to address, the reasons for them having the problem, the quality of the support and encouragement that is on offer, the extent to which the parents are able to acknowledge that their behaviour has been a problem and the degree to which parents feel involved in discussing and agreeing the tasks to be worked on. Based on his own Australian research, Chris Trotter concludes that the best outcomes in child protection work are associated with workers who are able to convey to their clients that they are operating in both a 'helping' and an 'investigatory' role, while the worst outcomes are associated with those who are only able to convey to their clients that they are there in an investigatory role (Trotter, 2004: 54). Occasionally perhaps, it may be sufficient to simply draw a boundary, perhaps in situations where the incident does not seem to be part of a pattern and where a parent seems very clear that it will not be repeated. But normally parents need help with change. If parents are prone to fly into a rage and lash out at their children, for instance, they might need some help with recognizing the sources of their anger, the things that trigger it, and alternative strategies for coping in those moments.

Intensive or specialist therapeutic work

Many problems are simply too entrenched and complex for the simple 'boundary setting' approach to work without intensive additional input. For example, in a case where a child has been sexually abused by a family member, intensive work is needed by professionals with extensive knowledge of this field to establish whether there is even a realistic possibility of that family member being able to change and, if so, to provide a therapeutic experience of sufficient intensity to achieve it. Likewise it would be naïve to expect a heroin user to simply stop using the drug. These are both areas involving behaviour patterns which are known to be very hard indeed to stop – drug addicts and paedophiles are adept at fooling not only others but themselves about their habit – and also areas in which ordinary 'common sense' simply does not apply. They are therefore both areas in which input from professionals with specialist knowledge and experience is needed, as is the case also when parents have serious mental health problems.

Complex and long-term problems in family functioning cannot be expected to change as a result of a few boundaries being set. The specific abusive incident that triggers the involvement of the child protection system is in many cases simply a symptom of much more general problems, and some families have had patterns of abusive or neglectful behaviour not just for years, but for generations. Various therapeutic approaches to working in more intensive therapeutic ways with abusive or neglectful families are discussed in the literature. Arnon Bentovim (2002), for instance, gives an overview of approaches involving systemic family therapy. But child protection professionals should not be under the illusion that these specialist services represent some kind of infallible scientific fix for family problems. Geraldine MacDonald, discussing outcome studies carried out on a range of different interventions, concludes that cognitive-behavioural approaches, particularly when integrated with other services, seem to score most highly, while 'the effectiveness of other forms of family therapy, such as systemic family therapy, is not yet clear but merits further investigation' (MacDonald, 2001: 192).

Parenting skills training

Sometimes a factor in neglect is a lack of understanding about what children need. Some parents, for instance, have quite unrealistic expectations of what a child is capable of at a given age. This lack of understanding may be the result of childhood experiences which failed to provide role models. It may also sometimes be the result of parents having learning difficulties which make it harder for them to absorb information.

Parenting skills training, like any other sort of training, needs to be accurately pitched if it is to be of help. Some parents lack very basic practical skills, like correctly mixing baby milk, others struggle with more complex skills such as responding appropriately to a child's challenging behaviour. A one-size-fits-all approach to skills training is unlikely to meet the needs of both these groups of parents and may result in one group feeling patronized and infantilized. It's also important to remember that when people are not doing something properly it doesn't necessarily mean they don't know *how* to do it. (If I break the speed limit in my car, it doesn't necessarily mean that I don't know how to use the accelerator or brake.) I illustrated this in the commentary on Exercise 3.2. If Lisa does not know that it is inappropriate to leave a five-year-old on her own, that is a skills problem. If she knows this but sometimes sets it aside due to the urgency of her need for heroin, then this is another problem entirely and referring her for parenting skills training might be entirely irrelevant.

Work directed at the wider environment

Interventions aimed at 'addressing issues that impact on parenting capacity' shade into, and overlap with, interventions aimed at, so to speak, the bigger picture. Abuse and neglect is more likely to occur when a family is under stress, or lacks a network of support.

Tackling stress factors

Not all child abuse or neglect is linked to stress. Some abuse is deliberate and calculated. Some is the result of deep-seated relationship problems. Some is the result of ignorance. But in many cases, addressing stress factors is a crucial component of any intervention. This is particularly so when we bear in mind that (unfortunately) being the subject of child protection investigations is, for most parents, itself very stressful.

Sometimes it is possible for the professional agencies to alleviate stress in practical ways, for example by helping sort out money problems or, if a family is living in unsuitable accommodation, by helping them to move. Often it is *not* possible to remove all the problems that are causing stress to the parent but it may be possible to help people develop better strategies for coping. (The 'task-centred' casework method in social work is precisely intended as a method of helping families deal with multiple stressors. See Marsh and Doel, 2005.)

Building protective networks

Looking back at the case of John in Exercise 3.1, it is obvious that the immediate risk comes from his Uncle Ralph who is a known paedophile. If John's parents were made aware of this risk and were entirely willing and able to ensure that John was never alone with Ralph, then this might be adequate protection for him (perhaps coupled with some work with John on self-protection strategies, as discussed above) and John might not even need to be the subject of a child protection plan. But if there was some doubt about his parents' ability to do this, then a protection plan might be needed. (Perhaps they are scared of Ralph, or are easily manipulated by him, or just don't seem to be able to see the seriousness of the risk he poses.) Under these circumstances it may be necessary to try and recruit a wider protective network that would look out for John, monitor Ralph, and check up on the protection offered by John's parents. This network would include professionals such as health visitors, teachers and GPs, but in the long run the most effective strategy might be to encourage the child's own extended family to provide a protective network. This is one of the main ideas behind Family Group Conferences, in which the extended family of a child are brought together and encouraged to negotiate their own solutions. For more on this concept, originally developed in New Zealand but now incorporated into child protection practice in many countries, see, for example, Marsh and Crow (1998).

Permanent substitute care

Some children are removed into public care as a result of intervention by child protection agencies and, of these, a proportion end up being placed permanently in substitute families. This occurs in situations where the professionals involved conclude, and are able to convince the courts, that parents are unable or unwilling to change their behaviour sufficiently to be able to provide their children with a home that will protect them from significant harm, or at any rate not in a timeframe that the child can afford to wait. There are also some relatively rare situations where the abuse is so extreme, deliberate or malicious and/or the child's relationship with the carer so negative that even to attempt to return the child is inappropriate. Permanent substitute care can of course transform a child's emotional environment, in some cases from one of rejection and fear to one of love and security, though it is important to remember that abuse can occur in substitute families too, that unhappy placements and placement breakdowns are quite common and that some children who have suffered abuse and neglect can be extremely hard for substitute carers to successfully reach.

The difficulty faced by child protection professionals and the courts lies in striking the correct balance, so that children are not removed from parents unnecessarily, but are also not left to suffer real, long-term harm in deeply unhappy or frightening situations where there is no realistic prospect of things getting better. This is made even more difficult by the fact that the older a child is, the worse is the prognosis for the child being able to make a good adjustment to a new family. (See, for example, PIU, 2000, for a summary of data on the increasing likelihood of permanent family placements breaking down, the older a child is at time of placement. Older children are also harder to find placements for in the first place.) Waiting and seeing is not an alternative to making a decision, in other words, but itself a decision which creates new risks for the child.

Chapter summary

This chapter has balanced the more procedural emphasis of the previous chapter by looking at what can actually be done, in practical terms, to help bring about change for children who have been maltreated or are at risk of maltreatment. I have discussed the following:

- The practical constraints and basic principles which need to be considered when coming up with a protection plan for a child

(Continued)

- Steps that can be taken to protect children from immediate danger
- Work directed at children themselves, including work on self-protection and work on supporting recovery from maltreatment
- Work directed at changing the behaviour of parents, including what I have called 'boundary-setting', therapeutic work and skills training
- Work directed at the wider environment surrounding a family, including dealing with stress factors and developing protective networks
- Permanent substitute care as a way of meeting a child's needs in the event that parents cannot do so

In the next chapter I will look at the difficulties faced by the individual involved in child protection work at a personal level, and the way that personal feelings relate to professional judgement.

4 | **Personal and Professional**

- Personal feelings and professional practice
- Acknowledging fear
- Child rescue versus family support
- Focussing on the child
- Respecting family relationships
- Bureaucracy
- Your own needs

Child protection work is difficult because it involves dealing with human pain, and because it involves operating at a point where two of society's most strongly held beliefs meet and clash: the belief that children should be protected against harm, and the belief that out-siders and strangers should not intrude into personal, intimate relationships. Children being hurt and families being violated: these are disturbing things to contemplate, let alone be part of, but child protection professionals are often in a position where to avoid one they may have no choice but to be implicated in the other.

Whatever we do, we will be condemned, is how child protection workers sometimes feel. They can be condemned for failing to intervene to protect a helpless child from cruelty but they can just as easily be vilified as 'child-snatchers' and 'interfering do-gooders' who break up loving families.

But, to make things harder, the conflicting values I have just described do not just exist *out there*. They exist also within each of us as an individual. Child protection work can violate deep taboos and touch deep emotions which go down to our very roots. It felt like going 'against the laws of nature', said one social worker who had been involved in remov-ing a baby from his mother at birth (Corner, 1997: 25).

This chapter is about the interaction between child protection workers with the children and parents with whom they work, but it is impossible to consider this without thinking also about another kind of interaction that goes on between a worker's professional duties and her identity as a human being.

Personal feelings and professional practice

Every professional involved in child protection work brings different personal experiences to the job. Some will themselves have experienced abuse at the hands of parents or other adults. Almost all will have had at least some childhood experiences of being let down by adults. All who *are* parents will have had at least some experience of having been less good a parent than they would like to be. Some will have experience of poverty, or single parenthood, some of drug abuse, or alcoholism, or mental illness. Men will have had different experiences to women, black people different experiences to white people.

In child protection work it is important to reflect on your personal style, your approach, your priorities, and to consider how these are linked to your own experience. You need to be aware, for instance, of which kinds of poor parenting you find most unforgivable and which kinds you find easiest to understand. You need to know what kinds of situations arouse in you the desire to 'rescue' and what kinds of people make you feel punitive. You need to have some sense of how your own needs may get in the way of your judgement of the needs of others. Do you have a strong need to be liked? Do you get particularly anxious about conflict and confrontation? Are there certain things parents do that make you so angry you find it hard to even look them in the eye? We cannot necessarily change our feelings, but professional priorities should not automatically be based on them, and this means we need to know what those feelings are.

Exercise 4.1

Have a look at the statements below. They represent various stances in relation to child protection work.

For each statement consider (a), what might be a *strength* of a child protection professional taking the stance which it represents, and (b), what might be a weakness. (For example, in the case of the first statement you might think that a strength of a social worker taking this stance would be that she would work hard to make parents feel listened to and involved. A weakness might be that she might be reluctant to take any step which might result in an angry and hostile response, even if this was necessary for the safety of the child.)

Notice also which statements seem closest to your own viewpoint.

(a) I do not like to be seen as the 'bad guy' and I want to work *with* people not against them.
(b) I am repulsed and appalled by the idea of adults abusing children.
(c) I was abused myself as a child; I know how awful it is and I just want to stop any other child going through what I went through.
(d) I am a parent and can very easily understand why some people lose their temper with their children and go over the top.

(Continued)

(Continued)

(e)   I think most children engage in sexual play. I know I did. It doesn't mean they have been abused.

(f)   I want to help and empower people, not to take away their children.

(g)   I was sometimes beaten as a child, but I don't think it did me any harm.

(h)   I identify very strongly with the powerless position of a child in an abusive family.

(i)   I don't feel it is my job to order people around or to tell other people how they should live their lives.

(j)   I think that heavy-handed intervention can often increase the risk of abuse.

(k)   I feel strongly that middle-class values should not be imposed on poor working-class families.

(l)   I think child abuse, like many other 'social problems', is often the result of social injustice: the abusing parents are often as much victims as children.

(m) I can understand why a parent might hit a child, but sexual abuse I will never understand.

(n)   I think different cultures have different ways of disciplining children, and we should be very wary about defining abuse in white European terms when dealing with black or Asian families.

(o)   I am there to protect children, not to help parents.

Comments on Exercise 4.1

Good child protection work does involve striking a balance. Any of these stances has its strengths, but can be dangerous if not balanced by other considerations. I suggest you take particular note of those statements with which you identified personally, and give some thought to what that tells you about possible strengths and weaknesses in your own practice. Awareness of possible strengths and weaknesses allows you to avoid pitfalls, and to seek help when you are entering an area of work that will be difficult for you.

The following are a few thoughts on some of the statements above. If you can identify with abused children and their powerless position, this may help you to be clear about your priorities and help you to avoid being deflected by the needs of carers and others. But, even though protecting children is the first priority in child protection, there are dangers in over-identifying yourself with the child. The child is not you and has her own needs and loyalties (including perhaps to the abuser), which you will not necessarily understand from your own experience. If you try to form an alliance with the child against the carers, this can have effects within the family which may make things worse for the child rather than better.

If you can identify with the feelings that lead parents to abuse children, then this may help you to establish a rapport with the parents and to work constructively with them to improve things for the child. But you need to be careful not to enter into a 'cosy' or collusive relationship with the parents that makes you overlook or minimize the harm they are doing to the child.

'I can understand this but I will never understand that' is a statement often made with the implication that what we understand is forgivable but what we can't understand is not. Actually there is something quite arrogant about the idea that our own personal experience should be the criterion by which we forgive or condemn others. Child protection work really isn't about making judgements of this kind. It is about trying to prevent suffering. Our own personal experience is an invaluable source of information for this work, but it is not everything and it can mislead as well as assist us.

Acknowledging fear

It is natural for us to try and avoid things that we find painful or frightening but this very natural impulse can be very dangerous in child protection work because it can make you avoid seeing things that are important, or avoid doing things that need doing. Many social workers in my experience will admit to having once or twice knocked very quickly on the door of a house and then hurried back to their office to record 'Visited. No answer.' Many social workers can probably also think of instances when their anxiety or distress resulted in their missing out on important pieces of information. In the case of Jasmine Beckford, who was to die as a result of physical abuse, a social worker visited Jasmine's family several times when Jasmine was present and still managed to avoid noticing that Jasmine had several broken bones (London Borough of Brent, 1985). Perhaps she just could not bear to let herself see it.

Fear of various kinds is a major feature of child protection work: fear of causing upset, fear of making a mistake and being blamed, fear of the anger and hostility of others, and sometimes, when dealing with violent, threatening people, fear for your actual physical safety. Fear can be hard to own up to, even to yourself, but you need to be aware both of what your fears may be telling you and the way they affect your behaviour and judgements. Martin Smith (2005: 11) likens 'the need to be aware of fear and its potentially helpful and unhelpful manifestations' with the need to be aware of fire procedures in buildings. It is dangerous to ignore a fire alarm or to pretend to yourself that you cannot hear it, but it is also dangerous to be panicked by it into hasty, ill-considered action.

Fear of blame

Professionals in the child protection field operate in a 'blame culture'. When something goes wrong there tends to be a search for someone to blame and occasionally the identified culprits are disgraced and vilified in very public ways. Most British social workers are very conscious of members of their own profession whose names ended up emblazoned on the front pages of the newspapers under shaming headlines condemning them as bungling incompetents.

A natural result of this is that professionals can end up being as much preoccupied with protecting *themselves* as with protecting the child. This can result in defensive practice in which actions are taken simply to avoid the potential accusation of not having done enough and in panicky knee-jerk responses that may have seriously harmful consequences for children.

Other professional participants in the child protection process can be intimidating, and particularly so in an atmosphere where people are anxious to shift blame and responsibility onto others. Sometimes professionals at case conferences may be afraid to speak their minds for fear of the reaction that they will get from others. We are hier-archical creatures and we may be particularly afraid to contradict people we perceive to have high status. We may also be fearful of speaking out against what seems to be a group consensus and this can lead to irrational and dangerous decision-making, some-thing which I have already mentioned in Chapter 2 when I discussed the phenomenon of 'groupthink'.

Fear of hostile family members

People tend to come into the helping professions, naturally enough, because they like the idea of helping other people and the idea of partnership sits very naturally and comfortably with this. But, although child protection work *is* of course intended to help other people – namely children – it is not always *experienced* as helpful by parents and carers who are suspected of neglect or abuse, or even necessarily by children themselves. If you are a parent you will probably not find it hard to imagine just how frightening it would be to be visited by a social worker or a police officer and accused of mistreating your children, and how angry it might make you feel.

Child protection work often involves confrontation and it often involves dealing with anger and hostility, sometimes overt, sometimes hidden. In some cases, the people involved are known to be violent, are very intimidating and make explicit threats. All of this is uncomfortable and there are various unhelpful strategies that child protection workers sometimes adopt in order to manage their anxieties. One is to become distant, cold and punitive, dealing with parents as if they had forfeited the right to actually be treated as parents. Another is to hide behind procedures and your official role. Another again is to collude and placate, trying to fend off anger and hostility by undermining your own authority ('Of course, if it was down to me I wouldn't make you go through this'), avoiding asking difficult questions, forgetting the child and forming a kind of alliance with the parents.

Janet Stanley and Chris Goddard (2002) suggest a link between the experience of child protection workers working with intimidating clients and so-called 'hostage theory'. This is a body of psychological theory which tries to explain the phenomenon known as the 'Stockholm syndrome' following an incident in Stockholm in 1973. Hostages captured by terrorists or criminals sometimes display behaviour that is quite different from what one would expect. Instead of condemning those who threatened their lives and put them through a terrifying ordeal, they end up 'negotiating on behalf of their captors, trying to protect their captors from the police and ... refusing to testify against the terrorists' (Stanley and Goddard, 2002: 108–9). Stanley and Goddard suggest that something like this may sometimes occur in child protection work:

> When a worker is explicitly, or implicitly, threatened with violence, he or she may unconsciously act as a hostage. Previously learned behaviour may be lost because of a sense of isolation and powerlessness in a hostile environment. The victim or worker may develop characteristics of the Stockholm Syndrome, and adopt defences in response to the need for self-preservation and relief from severe stress. These defences may include:

- denial of the threat;
- rationalisation;
- intellectualisation of the situation;
- identification with the aggressor or adopting the aggressor's viewpoint;
- reaction formation, or adopting a viewpoint opposite to what the person truly believes;
- creative elaboration; and
- black humour. (Stanley and Goddard, 2002: 119)

So anxiety about dealing with a parent who is hostile and menacing can paradoxically result in social workers *underestimating* the threat posed by the parent to his or her children. Stanley and Goddard asked a number of child protection workers to describe the extent to which one of nine different categories of family violence was present in families they were working with. They found that – in the case of eight of their nine categories of violence – workers consistently underestimated the level of violence that was actually on record in the current case files. 'On average, violence was recorded in the case file twice as often as that reported by the workers' (Stanley and Goddard, 2002: 130).

If you are aware of this phenomenon, though, you can look out for it, noticing in yourself those times when you seem to want to minimize the violence of parents, and noticing the same phenomenon in others. It also provides an insight into the psychology of the children and partners of violent and menacing adults, and why they sometimes seem to protect and side with those who treat them so badly. If professional workers who only *visit* a house can start to act like hostages and experience distortions in their thinking as a result, what kind of effect does the atmosphere in that house have on those who actually have to live there and who may, to all intents and purposes, really *be* hostages?

Celia Doyle (2006) draws just these parallels between the experience of abused children and the experience of hostages, making the important point that the Stockholm syndrome occurs in situations where the captors show at least some signs of kindness towards their captives, rather than situations where the hostility is unremitting. (It is not so hard to imagine how, in such a situation, you might be desperate to hold onto this kind side of your captor and desperate to avoid provoking the return of his violent side.)

Fear of causing or facing distress

But, uncomfortable though it is to admit it, there are probably often times when the Stockholm syndrome works the other way around: it is the parents who feel like hostages and the child protection system that feels like the captor they need to placate. Many parents in child protection cases are not in the *least* bit threatening and intimidating. There are many situations in which children are neglected because their parents are so consumed by their own problems and unmet needs that they are simply unable, whether in the short or the long term, to attend to their children's needs, and many of these parents are not violent or threatening at all.

However, the fear of upsetting people is also a factor that can result in distortions in practice. Child protection workers may so dread giving a parent a painful but necessary message that they put it off, or water it down, so that the parent never receives the information that they actually need to have. Professionals often feel so uncomfortable about making critical comments that parents will hear or read, that they dilute their actual views and paint a picture that is less bad than the reality which they have actually observed. Some professionals are reluctant to speak their minds at case conferences where parents are present for fear of hurting the parents' feelings, with the result that the conference is deprived of information that it needs to make an accurate judgement about the level of risk. Some professionals (like many members of the public) also seek to pass on information to other child protection agencies in a way that releases them from having to face the parents themselves.

Exercise 4.2

A primary school teacher telephones a children's social care agency to pass on her concerns about Yasmine, an eight-year-old girl, who she feels may be being abused or neglected at home. After passing on various details about how withdrawn and unhappy Yasmine has become, and how reluctant she seems to go home, she asks the agency to try and look into it, 'but please don't tell the family that it was me that contacted you, because we have a good working relationship with these parents and we don't want to lose their trust.'

What are your thoughts about this request?

Comments on Exercise 4.2

Although it is easy to see why such requests are made and to see why agencies such as schools, which rely on parental co-operation, might wish to distance themselves from child protection investigations, it is actually very difficult to see what the social care agency could usefully do with this information if it is not able to reveal its source. A social worker is not likely to get very far by visiting Yasmine's family on the basis that 'we have reason to be concerned about Yasmine, but we can't tell you why we are concerned.'

In the British system, social care agencies do have a lead role in child protection, and it is perfectly appropriate for the teacher to refer her worries to them, but in a multi-agency system, it simply isn't possible for one agency to be the sole bearer of difficult messages for all the other agencies. In a child protection case, sooner or later, the parents are going to need to know about the views and concerns of all the relevant agencies. The damage to working relationships will often be greater if the parents only find out some time after the event about the involvement of a professional with whom they thought they had a working relationship of trust. Most people do appreciate openness even if they don't like the message they hear. (After all, to criticize someone is actually not a betrayal of trust, but to deceive them certainly is.)

Another point about this scenario is that, while social care does have a lead role, it is not always the agency best placed to make initial enquiries in situations of this kind where there is no definite child protection issue. In this situation it might well be that the teacher, or one of her colleagues, is best placed to make initial enquiries with Yasmine and/or her parents and to introduce the idea of involving the social care agency. The social care agency might find that the most helpful contribution it could make at this initial stage would be to help the school think through how to go about this in the most constructive way possible.

As well as the fear of distressing people, there is also a normal human reluctance to be in the presence of another person's distress. We know, for example, that people who have experienced a bereavement sometimes find that their friends avoid them or avoid talking about their loss, because it makes them uncomfortable. In the child protection context, this fear may mean that workers only engage with desperate and unhappy parents in a superficial way. And it is surely one of a number of reasons why child protection workers often neglect to ensure that children are properly listened to. The distress of a seriously abused child can be very hard to bear.

Child rescue versus family support

In a paper on the workings of teams managing child protection cases, Alan Carr used the psychoanalytic term 'counter-transference reaction' (CTR) to describe a process in which a worker experiences 'an intense emotional reaction' to the characteristics of a particular case, as a result of these characteristics triggering off something from that worker's own 'significant prior experiences', without the worker being consciously aware of it. We need to understand these strong emotional reactions, which could otherwise 'interfere with the capacity for collective balanced decision-making about child protection' (Carr, 1989: 87).

Carr identified five characteristic CTRs:

1 rescuing the child
2 rescuing the parents
3 rescuing the mother and child while persecuting the father
4 rescuing the father
5 persecuting the family

The first two seem to me to be particularly common and so I will discuss them further below. In my experience, while different situations can pull us in all kinds of different directions, most child protection professionals incline towards one of these two characteristic responses.

Rescuing the child

This is characterized by an 'intense emotional desire to protect the child' which may be

accompanied by an additional desire to persecute the parents. The child is experienced as someone who would gladly be forever separated from the parents. The parents are experienced as 'sick' or 'bad' and therefore undeserving of the child. Evidence which points to parental competence and the child's desire to be with the parents is minimized, denied or discounted … Workers with this CTR become involved in angry disagreements with team members who point to factors which suggest that family rehabilitation is possible. (Carr, 1989: 89)

Carr suggests that this CTR is 'likely to occur in workers who have, in the past, erroneously assessed a family as safe', in which case the family currently being assessed is being identified by the worker with the family where the failure occurred. It is also likely to occur with 'young workers who are struggling to achieve a personal sense of autonomy from their families of origin', in which case the worker is identifying with the child and identifying the family with her own family of origin (Carr, 1989: 89–90).

Rescuing the parents

In this CTR the professional

construes the parents as victims of a hostile social environment and a punitive child protection system … The worker experiences a strong desire to support the parents and ensure that they retain custody of the abused child ... Anger towards extended family members and help-giving agencies who are unsympathetic to the parents' plight is also experienced. Evidence which points to parental incompetence, and factors which suggest that the child is at risk ... is mimimized, denied or discounted. (Carr, 1989: 90)

Carr suggests that 'workers who have insecurities about their adequacy as parents and their capacity to meet their own children's need for nurturance and safety' might be particularly prone to this CTR, which arises as a result of the worker identifying with the parents of the abused child (Carr, 1989: 91).

Effects of CTRs on decision-making
Carr observes that

within child abuse teams, when one member experiences a CTR, another typically experiences a complementary CTR. For example if one worker begins to rescue a child, another will try to rescue the parents. If CTR's remain outside awareness, such polarization will continue until inter-worker or inter-agency co-operation becomes impossible. (Carr, 1989: 95)

What is dangerous, though, is not the fact that these phenomena *occur*. They are inevitable, part of being human, and, what is more, by noticing what feelings are triggered off in ourselves by a family, we can often learn something about what is going on in that family (just as, to refer back to the discussion earlier, we can learn something about a family if we find that one member is making us behave like a 'hostage'). Noticing their own reactions to the different facets of a family situation, can help the members of a team or multi-agency group to build up an understanding of how that family works. What is dangerous is if we are unable to recognize the *personal component* in these reactions, the part that comes from our own lives and our own circumstances rather than from the family in question, and insist that our professional judgement is simply *the truth*, entirely balanced and uninfluenced by personal factors of any kind.

Exercise 4.3
In my experience, some professionals tend to incline towards being *child rescuers*, while others have instincts that incline them towards being *family supporters* (or *parent rescuers* in Alan Carr's terminology). Where do you think you yourself would stand on this spectrum? If you are not sure, I suggest that you refer back to Exercise 4.1. If you identified more with statements (a), (d), (f), (i), (j) and (l) then you may be inclined towards being a *family supporter* (and are therefore more prone to the *parent rescuer* CTR). If you identified with (b), (c), (h) and (o) then you may be inclined to the *child rescuer* side.

Comments on Exercise 4.3

I do not wish to force you into a pigeon hole. I also think we should be careful not to assume that the way we respond to statements on paper necessarily corresponds to our response when faced

(Continued)

with a real situation. However, I do suggest that it is useful for child protection workers to think about where they stand on this continuum.

If you are inclined to be a child rescuer then you will need to work hard to remind yourself that removing children from their families is not necessarily the solution. You will also need to keep a close eye on your working style to ensure that you do not undermine parents unnecessarily. If you are inclined to be a family supporter, then you will need to work on ensuring that you don't enter into excessively cosy or collusive relationships with parents and that you don't 'turn a blind eye' to or excuse parental behaviour which really is seriously harmful to children.

To do effective child protection work you need somehow to be able to maintain a focus on the child and to be able to respect and support family relationships wherever possible, but it is a hard balance to strike and most people are better at one side of it than they are at the other. Sometimes it can be very useful to co-work cases with people whose instinctive approach is the opposite to your own.

Focussing on the child

It is very easy for a professional worker to become engrossed in the complexities of her working relationship with parents to the point where the child's needs end up being a secondary concern. It may happen for a number of reasons. A professional worker is an adult, after all, and may well find it easier to identify with adults and their needs than with children, particularly if she finds the problems of the adults interesting or touching in some way. If adults are intimidating, then the worker may put all her energies into coping with this and this may leave little mental space for thinking about the child. Or, if parents are grateful for help, they may be extremely rewarding to work with, perhaps more so than their children. It is also possible to become so preoccupied with the logistics of the case, or with the working relationships with other professionals that it entails, or with the interesting issues that it raises, that you forget that the child is not just a 'case' but an actual human being. As was observed in the Cleveland report:

> There is a danger that in looking to the welfare of the children believed to be the victims of sexual abuse the children themselves may be overlooked. The child is a person and not an object of concern. (Butler-Sloss, 1987: 245)

In many cases it is perfectly appropriate for a child protection plan to focus mainly on work with the parents or carers, rather than work directly with a child. Indeed it is possible to do *too much* direct work with a child if this work has the effect of undermining the parents. But if it is the case that the plan does not involve much contact with the child, then the professionals implementing it need to keep checking that what they are doing really is still focussed on the child's needs and has not become deflected by their own needs or the needs of the parents, and they really do need to be sure that they have some direct means of knowing what is actually going on for the child.

Something that often gets in the way of professionals consulting children, though, is that many adults are actually quite shy of children, or feel foolish trying to get down to a child's level. Such feelings may be difficult for a childcare professional to own up to, but I suggest that they are quite commonplace, even in professions which are entirely centred on children, such as teaching and paediatrics. Fear of children, which I imagine is related to our own childhood experiences, should really be added to my earlier list of fears that get in the way of effective work. Like the other fears I discussed it is one that needs to be recognized, otherwise workers who are afraid of children end up finding rationalizations for not communicating with children at all, and this can have disastrous consequences.

I mentioned earlier the fear of facing the distress of others. I think this is particularly acute when it comes to facing the distress of children, because it triggers feelings of distress, terror and helplessness from our own childhoods. It is significant, I think, that physical abuse, including fatal abuse, is quite commonly inflicted by an adult with very unhappy childhood experiences *who simply cannot bear to hear a child crying.*

'Family supporters' need to keep checking that they are not turning their backs on the distress of the child.

Respecting family relationships

Being respectful of the position of parents is not incompatible with making the child's needs paramount. In fact, to fail to respect the importance of parents and family to a child would, in the great majority of cases, be to ignore one of a child's most basic needs.

What can be forgotten by child protection professionals is that most parents, including those who are sometimes neglectful or abusive, see themselves as the primary protectors of their children against external threats. So parents who are resistant to intervention by child protection agencies are often in fact trying to protect their children. If, for instance, parents are resistant to a social worker or police officer interviewing their child, this does not necessarily indicate that they have something to hide, or that they are reluctant to let the child have her say. Most parents would be hesitant about letting their children be interviewed about personal matters by a complete stranger and there are perfectly good reasons for this, such as concern about the worry it will cause the child, or doubts that the stranger will handle it properly, or distrust of the stranger's motives.

There are some very cold and rejecting families, and some parents who are sadistic and cruel, and certainly many families where the children's attachments are very insecure, but in most cases the love that parents – even quite abusive parents – feel for their children is something of an altogether different order than the professional concern felt by child protection workers, however committed and caring, and child protection workers need to be very careful not to trample on this.

Of course there *are* circumstances in which it is right to 'rescue' a child from his family, but even in these situations, the child's family of origin is important to him, a part of his identity, whether positive, negative or (as is the case for most of us) a mixture of the two. It is not something that can simply be erased or swept aside. In the majority of cases children are not removed from their families, and in these circumstances, for a worker to try to form an alliance with a child against the rest of the family is likely to isolate that child and create more problems for him, because the whole family needs to be engaged if the child is to be helped.

'Child rescuers' do need to hold such impulses in check.

Bureaucracy

Child protection work takes place within a tight procedural framework and under much scrutiny. The advantage of this is that it provides checks and balances on individual practice, and, at least some of the time, helps to set some minimum standards.

One disadvantage is that meeting the needs of the system – completing records, filling in the prescribed forms, compiling the prescribed reports – takes up a very large proportion of a worker's time. Another disadvantage is that the system places many limits to the individual professional's autonomy. This means that workers may at times have to work in ways that they do not necessarily agree with. Sometimes it can feel as if a child protection agency's priorities are as much about protecting the agency itself as about protecting children, and there are times when the relative inflexibility of the bureaucratic system can seem oppressive, even abusive, in itself. Sometimes the need to do things 'by the book' may have the effect of inhibiting professionals from using their own judgement, even their own common sense. So part of the challenge for a child protection professional is to find her own way of operating as part of this system, without sacrificing her ability to apply her own intelligence and experience and think for herself.

There are times when it is just not practicable to adhere to an agency's procedures. There may, for instance, simply not be enough hours in the day. In such cases it is important to be clear with agency managers and co-workers that this is the case, and why. If this is not done not only do workers make themselves vulnerable to disciplinary action, but the system as a whole begins to function in a dangerous way because no one knows what is really going on. There will also be times when rigidly following procedures as laid down may be counterproductive. But again, it is important that a decision to set them aside is collectively taken. Safe, balanced practice requires that child protection workers do not attempt to work in isolation. And this applies not only to individuals but to agencies, which also need to avoid trying to work in isolation from one another, or assuming that their particular perspective is the 'right' one. The failure of agencies to communicate properly with each other has been a frequent factor when serious abuse has failed to be picked up.

Procedures and bureaucratic systems do undoubtedly have an important place. But, while child protection systems collapse into dangerous chaos if their individual participants simply disregard agreed procedures and act in isolation, they do not work either if their participants behave like cogs in a machine, without using their own judgement or standing up for their own views. In this chapter I have been discussing various ways in which professionals unconsciously defend themselves against the fear and distress that is entailed in this kind of work and how these defences, while entirely natural, can result in dangerous practice if not properly understood. Retreat into bureaucratic systems can also be a defence mechanism, a way of avoiding reality, because it has the effect of depersonalizing the child and parents and distancing the worker from their distress. Isabel Menzies Lyth discussed this phenomenon in a famous study on hospital nurses, first published in 1959:

> The protection afforded by the task-list system is reinforced by a number of other devices that inhibit the development of a full person-to-person relationship between nurse and patient, with its consequent anxiety. The implicit aim of such devices, which operate both structurally and culturally, may be described as a kind of depersonalisation or elimination of individual distinctiveness in both nurse and patient. For example, nurses often talk about patients not by name, but by bed numbers or by their disease or a diseased organ: 'the liver in bed 10' or 'the pneumonia in bed 15'. Nurses themselves deprecate this practice, but it persists. (Menzies Lyth, 1988: 52)

Child protection professionals certainly use language that has the effect of depersonalizing what they do. Impersonal expressions like 'core group', 'strategy meeting', 'child protection plan', 'non-accidental injury' all place a certain distance between workers and the human suffering that is the actual subject of their work. Some distancing and depersonalization is unavoidable, a necessary survival mechanism which allows people to keep on doing their jobs without being overwhelmed, but too much can result in a system which no longer serves its original purpose of alleviating and preventing suffering and becomes a sort of end in itself. And it can result in the kind of dangerous magical thinking, discussed at the beginning of the previous chapter, in which merely following procedures becomes confused in people's minds with the actual work of protecting children. When I discuss case examples with groups of social workers and ask what action they would take to protect the child, I sometimes get the response 'we would hold a meeting', 'we would involve such-and-such a team', 'we would carry out an assessment'. These might be useful steps, but they will not *in themselves* protect the child.

Your own needs

Child protection is a difficult and distressing area to work in. Confronted with abuse, neglect and misery, it is quite easy for a professional in this field to feel that her own needs are trivial compared with those of the children with whom she works. But I hope I have shown in this chapter that a child protection professional who does not take her own fears and needs seriously and does not recognize her own limitations as a human being, is actually dangerous.

No one would want to be operated on by a surgeon who was so tired she could barely keep her eyes open. By the same token, a child protection worker who is not thinking straight because of stress or fear, or because she is no longer able to disentangle her own personal history from the history of the family in front of her, is not likely to be of much help to children, and may well make things worse rather than better.

Child protection workers who actually want to be helpful to children need to be assertive in demanding a reasonable workload. Those closely involved in day-to-day work with the parents and children also need proper professional supervision and support if they are to unravel personal feelings from professional judgement. Any worker in this area, however experienced, who does not regularly check out her own thinking with others is likely to make serious mistakes.

Chapter summary

In this chapter, I have looked at some of the ways in which child protection work is especially challenging at a personal level, and at the ways that personal and professional issues can interact. I have looked at:

- the ways in which personal experience affects how social workers approach their job, the things that they notice and the things they fail to notice
- fear, in various forms, as a major factor in child protection work
- the tendency of workers to fall into one or other pattern of response, linked to their own life experiences: in particular 'child rescue' or 'family support'
- the difficulties involved in staying focussed on the child
- the importance of family relationships, and of taking family relationships seriously
- working as part of a bureaucratic system
- the fact that professionals have their own needs which must be met if they are to offer the best service.

In the next chapter I will move on to the second part of this book, which considers the nature of child abuse.

Part II

CHILD MALTREATMENT AND ITS CONSEQUENCES

5 Recognizing Child Abuse and Neglect

- Physical abuse
- Sexual abuse
- Emotional abuse and neglect
- Other categories

This is the first of three chapters that will look at the nature of abuse and neglect in terms of its implications for children. In this chapter I will discuss definitions of the different forms of child abuse and neglect, and at the signs which suggest that abuse is happening. Chapter 6 will consider particularly the case of disabled children. Chapter 7 will look at the consequences for children of abuse and neglect – the harm that it does.

Most of the content of this chapter will be organized under the headings of 'physical abuse', 'sexual abuse' and 'emotional abuse and neglect', though in practice abuse and neglect do not necessarily fall neatly into one or other of these categories. Different kinds of maltreatment typically co-exist, and the boundaries between one and another – and indeed between maltreatment and other kinds of problems with parenting – are often blurred.

Physical abuse

Physical abuse is defined in *Working Together* as:

> hitting, shaking, throwing, poisoning, burning or scalding, drowning, suffocating, or otherwise causing physical harm to a child. (DfES, 2006: 37)

This definition does not, however, clarify what degree of physical harm is to be considered abusive. Smacking, for example, is not treated as abuse in England and is regarded by much of the population as an acceptable form of punishment. (In Sweden, Germany and several other countries *any* kind of corporal punishment is an offence, but this is not the case in England and Wales, though Section 58(3) of the 2004 Children Act states that 'Battery of a child causing actual bodily harm to the child cannot be justified in any civil proceedings on the ground that it constituted reasonable punishment.')

Physical abuse is defined by the fact that it results in physical injury. Looking at it as something that people *do*, however, we can see that it covers a very wide range of behaviours. It includes both impulsive acts of anger and frustration, ranging from excessively hard smacks to fatal assaults, and deliberate, premeditated acts.

Recognizing physical abuse

Examining injuries and determining what caused them is, of course, a job for a doctor, but children sustain many injuries, most of which are accidental and most of which do not require medical attention. This means that other professionals do have to exercise some judgement as to which injuries should be regarded as suspicious, and which injuries merit asking for a medical opinion.

Non-medical professionals also need to remember that the precise cause of many injuries cannot be necessarily determined by examining the physical symptoms. For example, a bruise caused by a child accidentally banging her head on the corner of a table is not necessarily physically distinguishable from a bruise caused by the child being hit on the head with an object. Often we can get some sense as to whether an injury is accidental or not, only by looking at the social context and the history.

Certain injuries are pretty clearly indicative of abuse, including hand-shaped bruises, bite marks, multiple cigarette burns and the long bruises and/or lacerations caused by blows from sticks or other implements. This is not to say, however, that there may not sometimes be innocent explanations for most of these injuries.

Cuts, fractures or bruising on babies who are too small to move about are obviously also very suspicious. Bruising and lacerations on soft parts of the body and parts which are unlikely to be injured as the result of falling over or walking into something, may also be indicators of physical abuse: bruises on the face, buttocks or back of the thighs, for example.

Patterns of injury can also be suspicious. It is worrying when a child may have far more bruises than average, even if none of the individual injuries clearly points to abuse. Some children do, however, suffer from medical conditions which result in their bruising very easily.

Often concern that an injury is not accidental arises not so much from the nature of the injury itself, but because of circumstances. The following are some examples:

- There is a previous history of abuse.
- The child is evasive about how the injury occurred, or gives an account of it that he seems to have been taught to say.
- The child tells contradictory stories about the injury, or gives a different story to the one given by a carer.
- A child returns to school after time off and there are signs of a fading injury.
- The child is frightened when questioned about the injury.
- The injury occurs in a context where there are already concerns about a child's relationship with her carer(s). For example, the child may seem frightened or uncomfortable with a carer, or the

carer may speak of the child in an angry, rejecting or punitive way. Or angry altercations may have been seen or heard between the child and a carer.

- A carer has a previous history of violence. A person who is violent towards adults, or indeed towards animals, is also likely to be violent towards children.
- There is a history of marital violence.
- The family is known to be under exceptional stress.
- The carers are known to have difficulties managing the child's behaviour.
- Injuries seem to coincide with other events in a child's life: the arrival of a new adult in the family home, for example, or weekends spent staying with a non-custodial parent.
- The injury occurs in a context where there have been causes for concern about a child's emotional well-being. Children who are being physically abused may show low self-esteem or seem to avoid social contact. They may be excessively anxious to please, or show excessive anxiety about being told off. In extreme cases, physically abused children may also show 'frozen watchfulness': they have learnt not to do anything or to show any feelings, but simply to watch those around them and try and anticipate further mistreatment. Alternatively, children who are being abused may show an extremely short concentration span, and be very restless or hyperactive.

Exercise 5.1

Robert, who is nine, turns up at school with a large, unusually shaped bruise on his back. A teacher notices this when Robert is getting changed for gym. It strikes her as an unusual injury for which she can think of no obvious explanation.

If you were the teacher, what sorts of additional information might reassure you that this was an accidental injury?

What sorts of additional information might make you feel that this could be a non-accidental injury and an indicator of possible abuse?

Comments on Exercise 5.1

I would be much less concerned about this injury if Robert was able to give a plausible explanation of it without any sign of discomfort or embarrassment. ('Oh yes, I was climbing in a tree and I slipped and this branch stuck into my back. It really hurt.') I would also be reassured if I heard him give the same explanation to his friends, or if I heard the same explanation from whichever of his parents came to collect him at the end of the day.

I would also not be very worried about this injury if Robert was a confident sociable boy, who was popular with his peers, seemed to have a good relationship with his parents, and did not have a history of other injuries outside of the normal range of childhood bumps and bruises.

I would be much more concerned about the injury if Robert avoided looking me in the eye when I asked about it, gave an explanation reluctantly and tried to get away from me as quickly as possible. I would also be concerned if he seemed to have given different explanations to different people and (of course) if the explanation he gave did not seem to fit the injury.

I would be even more concerned if Robert had a history of injuries for which there had not been clear explanations, or if I observed Robert to be (or to have recently become) an unhappy or anxious child. I would also be more concerned if I was aware of particular relationship difficulties between him and his parents or carers, or if I had other reasons to be concerned about the level of care he was getting at home (for example, if he habitually came to school without having eaten, or in dirty clothes), or if I had noticed him being uneasy in the company of a carer.

Fabricated or induced illness

In addition to what I have already quoted, the *Working Together* definition of physical abuse goes on to say that:

> Physical harm may also be caused when a parent or carer feigns the symptoms of, or deliberately causes ill-health to a child. (DfES, 2006: 8)

Fabricated or induced illness is sometimes called 'Münchhausen's syndrome by proxy' (MSBP), by analogy with Münchhausen's syndrome *per se,* where a person deliberately harms *herself* to feign illness and obtain sympathy and attention. 'The commonest methods for inducing illness seem to be poisoning, including the misuse of prescribed medication, and suffocation' (Foreman, 2006: 978). Disturbed and unhappy people do sometimes do extraordinary things to get attention or to make themselves feel in control, and this very occasionally includes harming their own children.

Recently in Britain there has rightly been much publicity given to cases where doctors have misdiagnosed MSBP in cases of sudden infant death syndrome (cot death), with the appalling result that bereaved mothers have been unfairly accused of killing their own children, had their other children removed from them and been sent to prison, a particularly devastating example of the way in which the child protection system can get things wrong. Some commentators have been inclined to dismiss the whole notion of MSBP, as a result. Virginia Sherr (2005), for instance, likens accusing women of MSBP to the blaming and persecution of women that occurred in medieval witch-hunts. And yet some parents do intentionally make their children ill, or pretend their children are ill when they are not. (For a personal account see Julie Gregory, 2004.) The difficulty for the child protection system now is that of the little boy in the story who cried wolf. How are we going to protect children in the rare cases where parents really *do* harm or try to kill their children in this way, while avoiding the errors of the past?

Sexual abuse

The definition of sexual abuse in *Working Together* is:

> forcing or enticing a child or young person to take part in sexual activities, including prostitution, whether or not the child is aware of what is happening. The activities may involve physical contact, including penetrative (e.g. rape, buggery or oral sex) or non-penetrative acts. They may include non-contact activities, such as involving children in looking at, or in the production of, sexual online images or watching sexual activities, or encouraging children to behave in sexually inappropriate ways. (DfES, 2006: 38)

One issue that is not covered by this definition is age. Two seven-year-olds examining each others' genitals is not 'abuse', although an excessive preoccupation with sexual play on the part of children *can* be symptomatic of their having been abused by others. But what if one of the children was seven and one was nine? Or one was seven and one was seventeen?

What is not spelled out in the DfES definition is the fact that *unequal power* is central to sexual abuse (as it is to other kinds of abuse). Non-consenting sex is always abusive. Consenting sexual activity between two little children is not abusive (even though it may be a cause for concern), and consenting sex between two adults is likewise not abusive. But sex between an adult and a child *is* abusive, *whether 'consenting' or not*, because of the huge differences in power and understanding between the two parties.

Recognizing sexual abuse

In the case of sexual abuse, physical symptoms are not likely to be the signs that first draw the attention of an outside observer. Many forms of sexual abuse do not result in any physical evidence. Where there *is* physical evidence, which is mainly when abuse has involved penetrative sex, then this is usually something that is identified after the possibility of abuse has come to professional attention in another way. The interpretation of medical evidence is also sometimes controversial, as in the case of the 'anal dilation' test whose use in the 'Cleveland crisis' (see Parton, 1991: 79–115), resulted in a rather similar controversy to that now surrounding MSBP.

The signs and symptoms I will now look at, therefore, are mainly the behavioural and circumstantial ones that can alert us to the possibility that sexual abuse is taking place. The other way in which it sometimes comes to our attention is, of course, when the child herself – or someone who knows the child – makes a specific allegation of abuse.

Among the observable effects of sexual abuse on children are the following:

- Depression and social withdrawal.
- Anxiety.
- Self-harm.
- Inappropriate sexual behaviour towards adults. For example, touching adults in the genital area or on breasts, inserting the tongue when kissing, striking 'seductive' poses.
- Age-inappropriate sexual behaviour with other children. Although some sexual play is normal for children, it is suspicious when small children lie on top of one another and simulate sexual intercourse, or attempt to penetrate themselves or others with objects. (See Calder et al., 1997: 10, for an overview of studies looking at the spectrum of sexual behaviour by children.)
- Age-inappropriate sexual knowledge or preoccupation with sex.
- Sexually abusive behaviour towards other children.
- Behaviour problems or learning problems in school.
- Aggressive or anti-social behaviour.
- Frequent urinary tract infections (UTIs).

None of these symptoms *necessarily* indicates that sexual abuse is going on (urinary tract infections, for example, are quite common among small girls generally), but a combination of several of these together should certainly alert professionals to the possibility of sexual abuse.

For example, the profiles in the following exercise would suggest to me a child who may well be the victim of sexual abuse.

Exercise 5.2

Dana, aged seven, is difficult in school, unpopular with other children and socially isolated. When her teacher tries to get her to sit and read with her, Dana is restless and several times has touched her teacher's breasts, asking 'Do you like that?' She also tells her teacher, 'I fancy you, I want to give you a kiss.'

Helen, aged 13, is very thin, pale and withdrawn. Reports from primary school suggest that she has not always been so. But now she is dreamy and pays little attention in class. She has lost weight. She is frequently absent from school with headaches and similar minor complaints. She has deep scratches on her arms where she has cut herself. 'Because I was bored,' she says when asked by her class teacher. When the class teacher suggested meeting and talking with her mother and step-father she is tearfully adamant that she did not want this to happen, but will not say why. Her step-father joined the family about two years ago.

Suppose that in both these cases, the respective schools had contacted the Local Authority's children's social care service for advice as to how to proceed. What approach might be agreed?

Comments on Exercise 5.2

Both these children are clearly unhappy and it is obvious that something is not right with their lives. The pattern of behaviour of both of them certainly suggests that they may be being – or have been – sexually abused, though it is impossible to say categorically that this is the case.

Neither of them has, however, made an allegation of sexual abuse and there is no single piece of evidence that points unambiguously to it. In the absence of other information it is not clear that a formal abuse investigation is warranted, or would be productive, but you will want to try and find out more.

The task of trying to look into this further is a delicate one, since in both cases it seems likely that, if abuse is going on, then it will be going on in the family home.

I would suggest that this would require close co-operation between the social care agency and the respective schools. The next step might be for someone who each girl knows, to try and find ways of talking to them and giving them opportunities to talk about what is happening to them. The person best placed to do this might well be a teacher, though the teacher would need to be clear about her role and her boundaries.

Emotional abuse and neglect

Emotional abuse and neglect are in some ways easier to identify than other kinds of mal-treatment and in some ways harder. You are unlikely to actually witness a child being beaten or sexually abused but emotional abuse and neglect may well take place right in front of you. On the other hand, emotional abuse and neglect do not necessarily involve specific incidents comparable to sexual or physical assaults. This means that we need to look at the quality of the parent–child relationship as a whole in order to determine whether emotional abuse or neglect is taking place, and to decide how severe it is. This can be quite difficult to do and often takes child protection workers into grey areas where there is a good deal of scope for disagreement.

In the DfES's *Working Together* guide, emotional abuse is defined as:

the persistent emotional maltreatment of a child such as to cause severe and persistent adverse effects on the child's emotional development. It may involve conveying to children that they are worthless or unloved, inadequate, or valued only insofar as they meet the needs of another person. It may feature age or developmentally inappropriate expectations being imposed on children. These may include interactions that are beyond the child's developmental capability, as well as overprotection and limitation of exploration and learning, or preventing the child participating in normal social interaction. It may involve seeing or hearing the ill-treatment of another. It may involve serious bullying causing children frequently to feel frightened or in danger, or the exploitation or corruption of children. Some level of emotional abuse is involved in all types of maltreatment of a child, though it may occur alone. (DfES, 2006: 38)

The definition of neglect in *Working Together* is:

persistent failure to meet a child's basic physical and/or psychological needs, likely to result in the serious impairment of the child's health or development. Neglect may occur during pregnancy as a result of maternal substance abuse. Once a child is born, neglect may involve a parent or carer failing to:

- provide adequate food, clothing and shelter (including exclusion from home and abandonment)
- protect a child from physical and emotional harm or danger
- ensure access to appropriate medical care or treatment.

It may also include neglect of, or unresponsiveness to, a child's basic emotional needs. (DfES, 2006: 38)

You can see that the definition of neglect shades into the definition of emotional abuse. What is more, while both these definitions make sense, they are somewhat blurred round the edges. What constitutes 'serious impairment'? How bad is 'severe'? (Presumably so bad as to constitute 'significant harm' in the language of the 1989 Children Act, but this still leaves the vexed question as to what constitutes 'significant'!) Such questions can make it difficult to decide whether, and at what level, to intervene. An additional difficulty is that it is much more challenging to find ways of bringing about a qualitative change in family relationships than it is to find ways of protecting a child against specific threats.

Recognizing emotional abuse

I've said that neglect and emotional abuse shade into each other. The following exercise illustrates this:

Exercise 5.3

Francesca (aged ten) suffers with cystic fibrosis. One of the features of this degenerative illness is that unusually thick and viscous mucus is secreted in the lungs. In order to prevent this from building up too much, it is necessary for a child's carers to carry out a

(Continued)

(Continued)

physiotherapy procedure several times a day, involving rigorous pummelling on the back. Failure to do this means the mucus builds up, resulting in a persistent cough and serious chest infections – and, ultimately, a shorter life expectancy. It is also necessary for sufferers to take special enzymes before every meal.

However, Francesca's parents are very preoccupied with their own highly turbulent personal lives, and consistently fail to provide the necessary physio or to give the correct dosage of enzymes. Although they express affection for Francesca when they see her, they refuse to make her medical needs a priority, though this has a demonstrable effect on her health and on her life expectancy. When she was admitted to hospital recently, it was four days before either parent visited her.

Would you describe the behaviour of the parents as emotionally abusive or neglectful?

Comments on Exercise 5.3

The failure of the parents to provide the necessary physiotherapy is a form of neglect – a form sometimes categorized as 'medical neglect'. In this case it is potentially fatal. But it is surely also a form of emotional abuse, as is the failure to visit Francesca in hospital, since emotional abuse includes conveying to children that they are 'worthless or unloved, inadequate, or valued only insofar as they meet the needs of another person'.

Such messages can be conveyed in words, but they can also – and probably much more powerfully – be conveyed in deeds. Few of us would accept that someone loved us just because they said so, if in fact they behaved as if we were very low on their list of priorities.

The fact that Francesca's parents do not make the effort to visit her in hospital is giving her a message that she is not important to them, and that her needs are much less important to them than their own. The fact that they are not prepared to provide her with the help she needs at home not only places her health at risk, it also gives her a rather clear message as to her own value to her parents.

In fact any kind of neglect, physical abuse or sexual abuse conveys to a child a negative message about her worth to her parents – and this is why emotional abuse is present in all forms of child abuse and neglect, and is therefore, in a sense, the primary form of abuse.

Emotional abuse is about *messages*, verbal or non-verbal, given by a carer to a child. The fact that long-term psychological and physical harm can result from emotional abuse decisively refutes the old saying that 'sticks and stones may break my bones but words can never hurt me'. Words can do as much harm as sticks and stones, as can non-verbal messages such as those given to Francesca in the above example.

One difficulty with emotional abuse is that unlike sexual or physical abuse, almost all children are subjected to it to some degree. Even the most caring of parents does at times give children quite negative messages. When we are preoccupied, or tired, or busy, our children may find that it is hard to interest us in their issues, and may get the message that they are a nuisance and that we would rather they were not there. Probably most parents have at some time also said or done hurtful things to their children in anger, which they later regret.

A key word in the definition therefore is *persistent*. All children have some resilience, and are capable of understanding that even loving adults lose their temper, get tired and have bad moods. It is when the negative message becomes the predominant one that the situation becomes seriously abusive. In practice it is really when (a) the negative message can be seen to be persistent and (b) when the child's behaviour is such as to suggest that the negative messages are doing real psychological harm, that professional intervention under a child protection remit starts to be indicated.

The following are some parental behaviours that would generally be considered emotionally abusive. It is not an exhaustive list.

- Deliberately humiliating a child.
- Making a child feel ashamed for not being able to do or understand something which she is, in fact, developmentally incapable of.
- Expecting a child to put the needs of other family members before her own, and dismissing the expression of her own needs or wishes as selfish. This might involve consistently singling one child out, like Cinderella in the story, for inferior treatment as against her siblings.
- Shutting a child into a small space.
- Persistently verbally abusing a child.
- Persistently threatening to leave a child on her own as a punishment. This is abusive whether or not the threat is actually carried out, but obviously more so if a child is actually left alone.
- Making threats of other cruel and excessive punishments and/or carrying them out. A very extreme example of this that I am aware of is a case where a father killed family pets in front of his children, with the implication that the same might be done to them too.
- Telling a child that he was not wanted, was a mistake, or was the wrong gender. ('I never wanted a boy.')
- Exposing a child to age-inappropriate activity. For example, exposing a small child to horror videos (exposure to pornographic videos is generally regarded as sexual abuse).
- Isolating a child, preventing him from socializing with his peers.
- Persistently putting a child under unfair moral/emotional pressure.

The sort of evidence that might suggest that the abuse was doing significant harm to the child would be:

- The child is depressed, or withdrawn, or very passive, or has very low self-esteem.
- She is excessively anxious to please others and very frightened of criticism.
- The child is socially isolated.
- The child has behaviour problems.
- The child is underachieving.
- The child seems reluctant to go home, or shows signs of fear in the presence of a carer.
- Some children who behave in ways that seem indicative of sexual abuse (for example, compulsive masturbation) may in fact be *emotionally* abused rather than sexually, and may be seeking some way of providing the comfort to themselves that their carers are not providing.

As with sexual abuse, there will be times when children choose to disclose emotional abuse that is happening at home. The following exercise provides an example of this.

Exercise 5.4

At school Harriet (11) is an exceptionally hard-working and well-behaved child in the classroom, though quiet, serious and hard to get to know. She and her older sister (Dawn, aged 14) live with their mother, Ruth. Ruth is divorced from their father, who lives in another part of the country. Ruth is seen by the school staff as a 'difficult' parent, who is prone to come in and 'make a scene' when something happens at school which she disagrees with. She is also known to suffer with depression.

One day at school, Harriet spills some ink over her dress. To her teacher's surprise Harriet's reaction is one of utter terror. The teacher finds an opportunity to take her aside and ask her what the matter is, and eventually Harriet tells the teacher that her mother hates dirt of any kind and is furious when Harriet gets any kind of mark or stain on her clothes. Last time something like this happened (a glue stain on a tee-shirt), her mother screamed and shouted at her that she was a thoughtless, selfish little slut. She made Harriet scrub the tee-shirt at the sink for more than an hour, and then threw it out and said that she would not be giving Harriet a birthday present this year because the money would go on a new tee-shirt.

Harriet also tells the teacher that her mother makes her get up at 6 a.m. every day and hoover the house from top to bottom, and that her pocket money is stopped if her mother does not regard the house as cleaned to an acceptable standard.

She also says that she longs to see her father, whom she has not seen for several years, but that her mother flies into a rage if she or her sister Dawn so much as mention him.

Harriet agrees to the teacher talking about this with children's social care, but she begs for a reassurance that her mother will not be told that she has complained about her.

As the teacher, or a social worker responding to a call from the teacher, what would your thoughts be about the next step?

Comments on Exercise 5.4

Ruth will doubtless have a different story and we should not assume that Harriet's story is the only legitimate version of events. But her distress at spilling the ink does not seem likely to have been premeditated or staged. Indeed, even if she turned out to have made up the entire story, this would suggest that there was some quite serious problem with her relationship with her mother.

It would certainly appear that unrealistic demands and expectations are being placed upon Harriet, cruel and disproportionate punishments are being meted out, and that she is being given negative messages about herself.

The difficulty, of course, is that, as Harriet fears, any intervention will have to be carefully planned if it is not to result in making Harriet's situation even more difficult. This is a case that one would not wish to rush into. On the other hand, Harriet is frightened about what is going to happen tonight.

As much information as possible needs to be gathered (for example, from Dawn and her school, from the family doctor and Harriet herself) before any intervention in the family. (How is it going to be presented to Ruth? How, as far as possible, is Harriet not going to be put in the position of the one whose fault it is?)

Recognizing neglect

To recap on the *Working Together* definition given earlier, neglect is 'persistent failure to meet a child's basic physical and/or psychological needs'. It can include:

- Failure to feed a child adequately; for example, some children are not provided with regular meals, or are left to fend for themselves, or are fed on a diet of crisps and sweets.
- Failure to provide appropriate clothes or bedding; for example, a girl is sent to school in mid-winter in a thin summer dress and sandals; a boy wears the same clothes to school the next day, even though he wet himself in them and makes him stink of urine; a girl goes to school in crumpled clothes, some of which she has put on backwards; three children sleep on a dirty mattress without sheets and with only a single blanket.
- Failure to provide basic physical care; for example, a girl of four has never been helped to wipe herself after using the toilet or brush her teeth, and has never been taught how to do so; a six-month-old baby is left in dirty nappies for many hours, resulting in very severe nappy rash.
- Failure to provide a routine; for example, children aged five and six are allowed to stay up until the early hours of the morning; a child of eight is habitually late for school, and often also has to wait for up to an hour to be collected from school.
- Failure to provide boundaries or consistency; for example, a mother finds it amusing that her seven-year-old son smokes and watches his parents' collection of adult movies; a family of children are described by neighbours as completely wild and 'like little wild animals', whose parents do not seem to enforce any kinds of rules of behaviour; a baby is passed around to numerous different carers.
- Failure to provide safety; for example, a small child is in the habit of climbing outside his upstairs bedroom window, and nothing is done to prevent him; children aged seven and nine are left alone all evening while their parents go out.
- Failure to attend to medical needs; for example, a child of seven is fed a diet of sweets all day and all her front teeth are visibly rotten, but her parents do not take her to the dentist.
- Failure to meet or recognize a child's emotional needs; for example, a mother seems indifferent to her child's crying, or not to notice his repeated attempts to ask a question; a little girl is expected to call her mother's new boyfriend 'daddy' on the second time of meeting him, even though her real father was a member of the household only two weeks previously.

Under- versus over-protection

There is a balance to be struck between the harm caused by failing to protect children from danger, which is an aspect of neglect, and the harm that is caused by 'overprotection and limitation of exploration and learning' (DfES, 2006: 38), which is a form of emotional abuse.

The difficulty is that we do not all choose the same point in between these two extremes. Middle-class professionals, for example, may sometimes regard as neglectful a practice that is seen as normal in poor working-class communities: letting children play on their own in the street, for instance.

Exercise 5.5

Looking through the following list, pick out the practices that you would see as neglectful, as against those that you would see as acceptable:

(Continued)

(Continued)

- Leaving a ten-year-old alone in a house for an hour.
- Leaving a three-year-old alone in the house for an hour.
- Leaving a ten-year-old alone in a house for an evening.
- Sending a seven-year-old to school on her own, which involves crossing a main road.
- Letting a six-year-old play with other children in a street which is used as a through-route by traffic.
- Letting 13-year-olds smoke.
- Letting a ten-, eight- and seven-year-old (all swimmers) spend a whole day on their own in a meadow next to a river, providing them with a picnic and swimming things.
- Letting a seven-year-old boil a kettle and make a cup of tea.
- Leaving a baby in the charge of a 12-year-old babysitter for two hours.
- Leaving an eight-year-old in hospital for three days without visiting him.
- Leaving an eight-year-old in a private boarding school for four weeks without visiting him.
- Letting children play in a park where there are dog faeces.
- Letting children get involved in (a) rugby football or (b) boxing.
- Letting a 16-year-old or 17-year-old girl bring her boyfriend home to sleep with her.

Comments on Exercise 5.5

All of these are practices which place children at a degree of risk. The difficult question is what constitutes an acceptable level of risk. This is something that different people have different views on. It is also noticeable that attitudes have changed over the generations. Nowadays a parent who would let small children spend a day by themselves swimming and picnicking by a river would be considered irresponsible both on health and on safety grounds, but a generation or two ago this was much more normal – my sisters and I used to do it regularly as children – and it could be argued that modern parents are exposing their children to new risks by restricting them more to the home.

My point here is not to argue that neglect is impossible to define, but to demonstrate that neglect cannot necessarily be defined in absolute terms. Like other forms of child mistreatment, neglect needs to be interpreted in context. The following are some questions that may help you to think about this in relation to specific instances of alleged neglect:

- *Is the behaviour normal in the community where it is taking place?* If an entire neighbourhood regards a certain practice as normal and acceptable, it would very definitely be inappropriate to try and deal with individual instances of this practice as child protection cases, though it *might* be appropriate for public health services to attempt to bring about changes in attitudes.
- *Is the behaviour (a) pretty certain to be harmful, or (b) risky, in that it may cause no harm at all but carries some risk of a very serious negative outcome?* An example of the former would be sending children to school in urine-soaked clothes, which is fairly certain to result in the children being stigmatized and isolated. An example of the latter would be letting children play in the street,

which can be fatal, though only in a minority of cases. The former seems to me to be neglectful, though a formal child protection response is not necessarily warranted; the latter is more of a 'judgement call' and is dependent on questions like the age of the children.

- *In the case of behaviour which is certain to be harmful, what is the extent of the harm that is likely to be caused and the evidence for it? Is it such as to warrant intervention,* bearing in mind that intervention itself can have negative effects?
- In the case of risk-taking behaviour, you could ask the following: *Is the risk proportionate to the benefit? Have the risks been properly thought through or is the risk-taking being allowed only as a result of parental indifference or resignation?*
- Most fundamentally, *Is the parents' overall relationship with the child neglectful? Do the particular instances of apparently neglectful behaviour reflect a more pervasive parental indifference?*

Other categories

The four categories *physical abuse, sexual abuse, emotional abuse* and *neglect* are the four most commonly used in the child protection literature to describe child maltreatment and are the ones used in British government guidance. However, there are some other terms in use, and some areas of parental behaviour which do cause harm to children but which perhaps do not fit neatly into one of the four categories:

Ritual abuse

This is physical, sexual or emotional abuse carried out as part of some kind of magic, satanic or religious ritual practice. There was a lot of concern about this in the UK in the 1980s and 1990s, though the idea was very much discredited by several incidents in which children were removed from their parents when professionals managed to persuade themselves, on the basis of very little evidence, that ritual abuse was going on (La Fontaine, 1998). These episodes should remind us that, fuelled by 'groupthink', child protection processes can indeed sometimes take on the character of the witch-hunts of the past in which,

> fascinated and horrified by its sexual content, many of those who heard evidence of witchcraft suspended their critical judgement. They unsceptically accepted accounts of crimes which were unlikely or impossible and came to believe unreservedly in the reality of an evil conspiracy which did not exist. (Webster, 1998: 36)

Having said this it does seem to be the case that the horrific abuse suffered by Victoria Climbié was motivated in part by a belief, endorsed by pastors of African churches, that Victoria was possessed by evil spirits (Laming, 2003). There is evidence that this was not an isolated incident, and that a form of ritual abuse of children is sanctioned by the belief systems of some African churches. A BBC investigation in Angola provided the following report of a child being quite openly tormented in a way that is disturbingly reminiscent of the treatment meted out to Victoria Climbié, although she came not from Angola but from Côte d'Ivoire:

On the dusty streets of the Palanca Township, we stumbled upon a small Pentecostal church. Entering a small concrete out-house, we found a shocking sight. Sitting on the floor was a terrified, near naked girl of eight, her head shaven. She cowered as her mother and a pastor shouted at her. This was an exorcism, the pastor told us. The mother's marriage had broken down, it was the child's fault as she was possessed with Kindoki. Something had been rubbed into the girl's eyes as part of this ritual. Her ordeal had already lasted three days, and there was another 24 hours to go. The pastor dismissed the risk the child could die from such treatment. He said: 'Why should the child die? If the child dies, it means the child is evil.'
(BBC News, 2005)

System abuse

This refers to the ways in which children can be emotionally abused or neglected, usually unintentionally, by the system intended to protect them. I discuss it in detail in Chapter 13.

Psychological abuse

Some writers make a distinction between 'emotional' and 'psychological' abuse (for example, Kieran O'Hagan, 1993). Geraldine MacDonald (2001), on the other hand, uses the term 'psychological maltreatment' in a way that encompasses what I am calling emotional abuse.

Exposure to adult violence

Children in homes where there is violence, typically violence by a father-figure against their mother, are now generally recognized to themselves be indirect victims of that violence, even if it is not actually directed at them. This is why the *Working Together* definition of emotional abuse, quoted earlier, included 'seeing or hearing the ill-treatment of another'. I will discuss this separately in Chapter 11.

Other parenting problems

Children can be harmed by parenting practices that would not normally be categorized as abusive. For instance some children suffer as the result of their parents being unable to set consistent boundaries for them, or to stand up to their challenging behaviour. Maggie Mamen (2006) suggests that pampering or over-indulging children may result in behaviour resembling ADHD (Attention Deficit Hyperactivity Disorder), as well as depression and learning problems. In other words, as folk wisdom suggests, it is possible to *spoil* a child. I do not suggest that these sorts of problems should be brought under the umbrella of the child protection system, but I simply note that they too can result in long-term harm to a child's social development. In our desire to protect children against the abuse of adult power, we should not forget that adult authority is important to the healthy development of children, and should not be unnecessarily undermined.

Chapter summary

In this chapter I have looked at definitions of the various kinds of abuse and at ways of recognizing that they are going on, drawing attention to the overlapping nature of the different forms of child maltreatment, and to the need to look not just at incidents in isolation, but at the context in which they occur. I have discussed:

- physical abuse and its signs and symptoms, and considered the case of fabricated and induced illness
- sexual abuse, drawing attention to the need to consider the power relationship between the alleged abuser and victim, as well as to the actual acts
- emotional abuse and neglect, noting these overlap in many respects, and that emotional abuse underlies all forms of abuse, while also being on a continuum with some kinds of negative behaviour which occur in any family
- various other categories, 'ritual abuse', 'system abuse', 'psychological abuse' and exposure to adult violence, as well as forms of poor parenting, such as excessive indulgence, which would not normally be categorized as abuse or neglect but which are nevertheless harmful to children.

Having considered what is involved in defining and recognizing abuse and neglect, I will consider in the next chapter the particular case of children with disabilities, and the special difficulties and challenges that arise in their case.

6 | Disabled Children

- Vulnerability of disabled children
- Working with disabled children
- Assessing families

In the previous chapter I looked at how to define and recognize child abuse and neglect in general. In this chapter, I will look at the specific case of disabled children. They are sometimes neglected in the child protection literature, though for a variety of reasons they are more vulnerable to abuse than other children.

A lack of attention to this group of children in the literature may at times reflect a lack of attention in actual practice. Laura Middleton (1992: 99) refers to 'a common, compartmentalized view that child abuse is one thing, and disability another'. The way that services are typically organized can lead to a similar compartmentalization. On the one hand, child protection professionals may often not be very familiar with the needs of disabled children, while on the other, professionals specializing in work with disabled children may be reluctant to take on a child protection role, seeing their task as supporting families rather than policing them. Middleton (1999: 80) argues that this polarization is maintained by both groups 'seeking to preserve their own status as experts', and also by fear – a fear of disability on the part of child protection workers, and a fear of dealing with abuse on the part of disability workers – leaving disabled children unprotected 'in the middle'.

Vulnerability of disabled children

The evidence is that disabled children are more vulnerable to abuse and neglect than other children. In America, Patricia Sullivan and John Knutson (2000) found that children with disabilities were more than three times more likely to be the victims of maltreatment than non-disabled children. In the UK, Jenny Morris (1999) reported that disabled children only made up 2 per cent of the population aged 0–17 in one county, but accounted for 10 per cent of the children on the child protection register there. *Working Together* confirms that 'the available UK evidence on the extent of abuse among disabled children suggests that disabled children are at increased risk of abuse, and that the presence of multiple disabilities appears to increase the risk both of abuse and neglect' (DfES, 2006: 198). *Working Together* suggests that this is because some disabled children:

- have fewer outside contacts than other children
- receive intimate personal care, possibly from a number of carers, which may both increase the risk of exposure to abusive behaviour, and make it more difficult to set and maintain physical boundaries
- have an impaired capacity to resist or avoid abuse
- have communication difficulties which may make it more difficult to tell others what is happening
- be inhibited about complaining because of a fear of losing services
- be especially vulnerable to bullying and intimidation and/or
- be more vulnerable than other children to abuse by their peers. (DfES, 2006: 198)

The caveat 'some disabled children' is important, because, of course, disabled children are not a homogeneous group. The issues that arise for a highly intelligent mobile child with a hearing impairment are very different from those that arise for a child who has profound learning impairments and mobility problems as a result of brain damage, and these are different again for those that arise for a child with Down's Syndrome or one with autism. And of course, just as much as everyone else, disabled children will also differ in terms of their own individual characteristics and circumstances, ethnic background and so on. But subject to the same caveat, I would add to the list above the following family and social factors that may also make abuse more likely to happen, and less likely to be detected and/or defined as abuse.

Family factors

The birth of a child with an impairment is a difficult thing for most parents to come to terms with – and some do not succeed in doing so. Solnit and Stark (1961) suggested that it can involve a kind of bereavement in which the parents grieve the loss of the non-disabled child that they had envisaged. With grief, typically, comes anger and some of this anger may be directed at the child herself. If this is not resolved, there may be long-lasting ambivalence on the part of the parents towards the child, if not outright rejection. I am not implying that this is *necessarily* the case for all parents of disabled children, of course, and it is worth noting here that ambivalence and outright rejection can be experienced by non-disabled children too. (It can occur, for example, in some situations where a child is the result of an unplanned and unwanted pregnancy, or is the result of a failed relationship, or the product of a rape, or is not the gender that was wanted – and indeed for many other reasons.) But the birth of a child with a disability is another factor that can sometimes bring this about. And ambivalent feelings, angry feelings or a secret longing to be rid of a child, can precipitate abuse and neglect.

It is interesting that Morris (1999) found a 'different pattern of types of abuse' for disabled children: they were more likely to be placed on the child protection register under emotional abuse and neglect than non-disabled children.

Exercise 6.1

Harriet Davis is 13 and is learning disabled. Her language skills are limited, perhaps similar to those of a three-year-old non-disabled child. She attends a special school. One day she confides to a teacher there that she is upset with her brother, Greg, who is 16 (and is not learning disabled). He has been touching her in the genital area, and she does not like it. The teacher reports this to the social services and, after discussion with other agencies, a social worker follows it up by arranging to interview Harriet and talking to her parents.

When the social worker visits Mr and Mrs Davis, they tell her that they are convinced that Harriet has made the whole story up to get attention and sympathy, and to get Greg into trouble. Greg is an intelligent boy who could have a bright future ahead of him, they say. He puts up with a great deal from Harriet and it is grossly unfair that these allegations against him should now be taken seriously. When the social worker insists that the allegations made by Harriet do need to be taken seriously by the professional system, and that there will be a need for further follow-up, Mrs Davis becomes very angry. 'We are just fed up with all the things we have to do for that girl. All the problems she's caused for our family – meetings, special schools, doctors – and now *this!* She doesn't care or think about anyone except herself.'

What are your thoughts about Harriet's place in this family?

Comments on Exercise 6.1

As ever with these case examples, I would caution against drawing any firm conclusion on the basis of the limited information that I have presented. There could be other information, not yet come to light, that would completely alter your initial impression, and invalidate some or all of the points I am about to make.

However, initial impressions are important too, and you will probably agree that it is striking how Mr and Mrs Davis seem to view the meetings which they have had to attend on account of Harriet's disability as an imposition, by Harriet, on the rest of the family. The disability is seen as something that Harriet is inflicting on them (as opposed, say, to something which they and Harriet are dealing with together). Harriet's allegations about Greg seem to have been immediately placed in the same category: simply a further nuisance caused by Harriet.

It is worrying that the possibility that what Harriet alleges is true seems to be dismissed out of hand. What we know about sexual abuse suggests that the harm it does is likely to be compounded by the failure of others to believe in it. In fact the negative, dismissive attitude of Mr and Mrs Davis towards Harriet, if it is the normal pattern, could be seen as emotionally abusive in its own right. One might also speculate about the extent to which this family attitude might have allowed Greg to feel that it was somehow alright to abuse his sister.

I do not say that what Harriet says about Greg is necessarily true (though this would seem likely), but it is important that it is taken seriously. If it were not true, after all, there would still need to be serious thought given as to why Harriet would have made such a thing up.

(Continued)

Assuming that there has been sexual abuse of Harriet by Greg, the challenge in planning an intervention is the need to find a way to (a) support Harriet, in ensuring that abuse from Greg does not continue, (b) find ways of deflecting Greg from a pattern of abusive behaviour, while at the same time (c) not causing Harriet being cast even more as a sort of family 'scapegoat'.

Once again I am speculating, but this latter pattern may be linked to Mr and Mrs Davis' grief and disappointment at some much earlier stage on discovering that their daughter had a learning impairment: grief and disappointment which they have not been able to put behind them. It seems to me that this grief needs to be recognized, and their efforts and struggles acknowledged, if they are going to be able to hear the message that they need to take seriously what they are being told about the abuse of their daughter by their son. The primary goal of an intervention may be to protect Harriet, but this requires that the needs and viewpoints of other family members are properly addressed. Among the commonest mistakes that are made in child protection are attempts to 'rescue' children, which end up achieving nothing except to further isolate them.

In all this, it is equally important to bear in mind that Harriet has limited communication skills, and that time and effort need to be set aside to hear her point of view, if this is not to be swamped by the views of more articulate family members.

Even for the most unreservedly loving of families there can be no doubt that a child with disabilities can be a source of additional stress, since any disability will place at least some additional demands on the carers – and some disabled children need an enormous amount of extra time and attention compared to other children. And, while parents of non-disabled children can expect the initial heavy demands to reduce as time goes on – a small baby may wake her parents several times every night, but they can look forward to a day when this will no longer occur – parents of some disabled children cannot necessarily look forward to a reduction in the demands upon them in the same way.

The additional stresses that caring for disabled children places on families is illustrated, for example, by the higher incidence of divorce that has been found among parents of children with Down's Syndrome (Gath, 1977), and among parents of children with visual impairments. In the latter case, Hodapp and Krasner (1995) found the incidence of divorce to be 25 per cent, as against 15.3 per cent in a control sample whose children were not visually impaired. Since we know that stress is a factor in child maltreatment, it is therefore only to be expected that incidence of child abuse and neglect would also be higher for these groups of children.

Having said this, though, I do not wish to imply that child abuse or neglect – or indeed family breakdown – is in any sense an inevitable consequence of the presence of a child with a disability. Families may be strengthened too by the challenges and rewards of supporting a child with a disability. I am simply saying that the presence of a child's disability is a stressor, and hence an additional risk factor (as, for example, is poverty).

Exercise 6.2

Billy Thomas, aged eight, has been diagnosed as having an autistic spectrum disorder. Adults caring for him have always found his behaviour extremely challenging. It is difficult to get his attention, or to get him to retain information. He is restless all day and will not settle in his bed easily at night, coming downstairs again and again until midnight or later, and then waking very early the next morning. He is unsafe in the street, and, if not closely watched, is liable to run out across the road, or just wander off. In particular he is prone to getting into repetitive cycles of behaviour, which he may repeat over and over again, ignoring attempts to stop him or deflect him into other activities.

One day he becomes obsessed with pulling his little sister's hair. His father reprimands him and tells him to stop, but Billy then immediately goes and does the same thing again and again, without any apparent malice, but hard enough to hurt. When his sister leaves the room, he simply follows her and carries on. Billy's sister is distressed. Mr Thomas, Billy's father, is angry and upset. Mr Thomas cannot understand Billy's behaviour, which seems entirely pointless, and he cannot understand Billy's indifference to his sister's distress. Eventually Mr Thomas takes Billy by the arms, shaking him and shouting into his face to stop.

The next day, at school, Billy is found to have pronounced finger bruises, and some broken skin, on both his upper arms. In fact it is not the first time bruising has been noticed on his upper arms, and there have been several previous occasions when his teacher had wondered whether there might be some sort of physical abuse going on, but the school decided to take no action. On this occasion, though, it is very clear and the school makes a referral to the local social services child protection team.

The school does this with some reluctance, as Mr Thomas (a single parent as the result of his wife's death two years previously) is a strong supporter of the school, and is seen by teachers there as a good and caring man who has had a great deal to cope with, what with Billy's exasperating behaviour and Mrs Thomas' death. He never complains, is always cheerful and never asks for help – indeed he is always willing to help others. This is the general perception.

What do you notice about this case, and what thoughts do you have about how it should be taken up?

Comments on Exercise 6.2

You may well agree with the school that behaviour such as Billy's would be extremely wearing for most people, and that it is understandable that Mr Thomas should have lost his temper. It may well be true that Mr Thomas is indeed a 'good and caring man' who is doing his best.

However, it is dangerous to get too set in viewing any one situation in one way, without re-examining your assumptions. It seems that the school staff may have fallen into this trap, allowing their faith in and liking for Mr Thomas to prevent them from viewing repeated instances of suspicious bruising as physical abuse.

The fact that abuse 'is understandable', or that the person who inflicted it is basically well-meaning, does not alter the fact that it should not happen. Probably it is relatively easy for any adult to identify with Mr Thomas, because it is easy to see that Billy's stubbornly persistent behaviour must be maddening. The danger lies in the fact that it may be much harder to identify with Billy, whose behaviour and outlook are alien to most people's experience, and that therefore Billy's own needs may go unnoticed.

(Continued)

> *It would appear likely that this was not an isolated incident. It may also be a problem that is getting worse, seeing as the current bruising is the most serious to date. This is therefore a problem that needs to be addressed.*
>
> *This does not require that a punitive attitude is taken towards Mr Thomas, but it does require that his behaviour is challenged and explored. It may be that, following initial investigation, an appropriate intervention would simply be to provide more practical help and support to the family, and perhaps make arrangements that allow Mr Thomas and Billy some time away from each other, or allow Mr Thomas to spend time with his children separately. (Mr Thomas' self-reliance and resistance to outside help might need to be challenged.)*
>
> *These are things that need to be considered further down the line. It is possible that the relationship between Mr Thomas and Billy will, on further enquiry, turn out to be less benign than the school believes. Or it may turn out that there were other explanations for the other bruises, and that this may indeed have been an isolated incident.*
>
> *Obtaining information from Billy may prove difficult, because people with autistic spectrum disorders do not typically communicate like other people, and may not be able to carry on what would normally be understood as a conversation. It would therefore be essential to have advice from someone with some specialist knowledge of this area and who is comfortable working with children like Billy.*

Social factors

Families exist in a wider social context. The stress experienced by parents will be dependent in large part on the practical and emotional support that is available to them, and the messages they have received and internalized about the nature of disability. *All* of the factors cited by *Working Together*, which I listed above, are really just as much to do with social context as with the specific impairments that children may have. Indeed, disability itself is a matter of social context. Thus, for instance, the extent to which communication difficulties 'make it more difficult to tell others what is happening' may be dependent on the amount of skilled help with communication that is available. The fact that some disabled children 'have fewer outside contacts than other children' is not an inevitable consequence of having an impairment so much as a reflection of the opportunities that a particular society offers. Margaret Kennedy (2002: 149) argues that the dependent position which children who are disabled are placed in, and the messages and training they are given or not given, amounts to 'a situation in which children who are disabled have been taught to be good "victims" of sexual abuse'.

Widely held assumptions about disabled children may also increase the risk of abuse happening and/or failing to be detected. Several commentators even suggest that an unspoken view exists that disabled children are less important than other children, or that abusing them does less harm than to other children, or simply does not matter as much. Middleton (1992: 99) suggests that there has been an almost wilful failure of the child protection system to take seriously the problem of abuse of disabled children, given that research going back at least to the 1960s shows links between disability and abuse. 'Social work, it appears, does not WANT to know', she comments. Kennedy (2002: 148, 149) quotes the comment of a counsellor to the mother of a disabled child who had been abused: 'well it would have been worse if it had been one of your other [non-disabled] children', and the comment of a man with cerebral palsy about his childhood abuse: 'why bugger up a normal child when I am defective already?' Sympathy for parents of children with disabilities, who are seen to be trying to cope with enormously difficult challenges, may also (as can sympathy for parents in many other areas of child protection work) prevent professionals from paying attention to the perspective of the child – and encourage them to overlook or collude in behaviour that might be seen as neglectful or abusive in other circumstances.

In contrast to the view that abuse of disabled children is *less* serious than abuse of other children, though, a number of writers (Westcott and Cross, 1996, for example) have identified a widespread 'myth' that no one would abuse a disabled child: 'handicapped children are sacrosanct, not to be touched. Other children perhaps, but not the disabled' (Watson, 1989: 113). It is odd that this view should exist in parallel with its opposite, but both do seem to exist and both have the effect of reducing the likelihood that abuse will be detected and taken seriously. Burke and Cigno (2000: 99) observe that 'many people find it difficult to believe that disabled children may be the targets of abusers', and that this of course makes them 'ideal targets'. Failure of professionals to recognize the possibility of abuse will increase the likelihood that adults will attribute signs and symptoms of abuse to the child's impairment.

> It is important when we see bedwetting, fear of the dark or withdrawn behaviour also to consider the possibility that the child is being abused. Many workers with disabled children have not had child protection training (as it is believed that disabled children are not abused, and therefore that training is not necessary). So when any signs of possible abuse occur, workers do not know how to make sense of them and attribute them automatically to behaviour stemming from impairment. (Kennedy, 2002: 159–60)

But, of course, we should be aware too of the opposite possibility: that apparent symptoms of abuse may indeed be the consequence of impairments. And we should also be mindful that 'when alleged "neglect" is an aspect of abuse, difficult questions arise concerning the balance between parental protectiveness and the acceptance of the child's needs to take risks' (Burke and Cigno, 2000: 105). The same difficult balance must of course also be struck by the parents of non-disabled children, as I discussed in the previous chapter, but in the case of disabled children, overprotectiveness can sometimes amount to a sweeping denial of personal autonomy.

Different professional systems

I have already alluded to the different systems that characteristically deal with 'children with disabilities' as one category, and 'child protection' as another. 'Children with disabilities' services tend to operate by trying to provide a variety of services, including respite care, to help families to cope – and no doubt they help to prevent a great many families reaching the sort of breaking point where abuse might occur. But one downside of this is that arranging for children to be looked after elsewhere can be used as a way of sweeping family problems under the carpet. Jenny Morris gives the example of a young woman, 'Suba', who 'had been rejected by her mother at birth and experienced emotional and physical abuse throughout her childhood'. Suba was sent away to boarding school, and as an adult 'feels angry that the professionals who were in contact with her did not confront the abuse she experienced, but instead saw sending her away to school as a solution', to the point that

> when it became clear that she continued to experience ... abuse during the holidays, various arrangements were made so that she did not go home but stayed at school or in adult residential establishments, or went on special holidays organized for disabled children. (Morris, 1999: 98)

I think it is much less likely that such an arrangement would have been seen as a 'solution' for a non-disabled child. It may have prevented Suba from being exposed to abuse from her mother, but it denied her the possibility of any sort of secure family life, either with her mother or with a substitute family. And this, in its own way, is also a kind of abuse.

Working with disabled children

In one sense, the issues involved in doing child protection work with disabled children are exactly the same as those involved in work with any other child. As with any child, the child protection worker must find an appropriate way of communicating that will allow the child to convey what she needs to say and the worker to provide the child with the information she needs to have. As with any child, the worker must be sensitive to issues of power, divided loyalties, and so on.

For disabled children, however, the power issues may be much more acute than they are for other children. Some disabled children may be dependent on adults to meet even their most basic needs, and options that are available to non-disabled children simply are not practicable. Kennedy (2002: 157) makes the point that the advice offered in preventative programmes designed for non-disabled children may be irrelevant for disabled children, because of the different options that are available. A child with a visual or motor impairment cannot simply run away from a situation that she finds threatening or uncomfortable, for instance. On the other hand, advice that disabled children particularly do need may be absent. Children who are necessarily subject to invasive medical procedures, or who require intimate personal care, for example, may need particular help on the distinction between appropriate and inappropriate touching.

Communication with disabled children may involve a range of very specific skills, over and above the skills that are required in any case to work effectively with children. Morris found that, in one of the areas she studied, 'only 27% of the children on the caseload of the Children with Disabilities team ... used speech to communicate, while another 25% used limited speech' (1999: 100). Children who are unable to speak as a result of motor impairments may use a variety of technological aids. Children with learning difficulties may communicate using sign systems such as Makaton. The first language of deaf children may be British Sign Language – or American Sign Language in North America – and these sign languages are not visual representations of English, but different languages with their own grammatical systems. This means that, as Kennedy (2002: 153) points out, even if deaf children can write in English, the English they use may be a second language.

Attempting an investigative interview, or therapeutic work, without being familiar with the child's preferred means of communication, is equivalent to trying to work with a French child without being able to speak French. Child protection professionals whose brief includes disabled children either need to be familiar with the relevant communication systems, or need to develop close working relationships with other professionals who do have the necessary skills and are able to act as interpreters.

The communication challenge does not end there. Working with people from other countries requires not just a way round the language difference, but also an understanding of the cultural differences. In the same way, effective communication with a child with disabilities requires not just a familiarity with the particular communication system she uses, but also a familiarity with the particular circumstances and lifestyle of the child, who may attend a different kind of school, use different services and have different experiences of adult professionals than other children.

Exercise 6.3

Rodney French is a boy of 13 with Down's Syndrome. He lives with his mother and older sister. He occasionally visits his father, who is separated from his mother. Rodney has minimal language, consisting solely of single-word utterances. These utterances are also very hard for others to understand, as he is barely able to articulate consonantal sounds at all. ('Mum' would therefore be something like 'Uh'. 'Dad' would be something like 'Ah'. His sister Holly is 'Oyee'.) He is receiving assistance from a speech therapist, with whom he has a very good relationship according to both his family and his school. Attempts are being made to help him to supplement his spoken language with Makaton signs, but so far he has made little progress with this.

Mrs French, Rodney's mother, is very protective of him, and anxious about his safety. For example, she is anxious about Rodney's contact visits with his father, as she feels that his father's flat is not a safe environment, and that his father does not supervise him closely enough.

Towards the end of the summer holiday, Mrs French reports the following to a duty social worker. Rodney seemed distressed and agitated at the prospect of returning to school, even though in the past he has always looked forward to school. Trying to establish why, Mrs French asked him to make a drawing, at which Rodney produced a picture of two figures (circles with lines sticking out of them), one of which she says represented Rodney and the other Mr Fleet, who is a learning support assistant at the school, a single, openly gay man of 55. She says that Rodney told her the picture represented Mr Fleet putting his finger into Rodney's anus. Mrs French says that she cannot allow Rodney to go back to school while Mr Fleet is there.

With Mrs French's permission, the duty social worker speaks to the head mistress of Rodney's school, Mrs Teal. Mrs Teal says that she is extremely sceptical about this allegation because (a) Mrs French has always been antagonistic to Mr Fleet's personally and opposed

(Continued)

his appointment because she believes it is not appropriate for a homosexual man to work with children *(although in actual fact there is no reason to suppose that homosexual men pose any more threat to children than heterosexual ones)*. Mr Fleet is in fact very popular with the children, including Rodney; (b) Rodney is not capable of drawing a recognizable object or person; and (c) Rodney is not capable of making an allegation of this kind verbally, except by being asked a series of yes/no questions – and he is prone to respond in whatever way he thinks will meet approval.

If you were responsible for following this up, how would you proceed?

Comments on Exercise 6.3

There are several different initial 'gut reactions' that one might have to the information so far presented. You might wonder, for example, whether the whole thing is really a manifestation of Mrs French's anxiety about separation from Rodney and of her homophobia – and that she is simply projecting these feelings onto her son. This seems to be the view of Mrs Teal. But whatever your initial reactions, these are serious allegations that are being made, which need to be looked into. It is important not to use the difficulty of communicating with Rodney – and the existence of a half-way plausible alternative explanation for the allegation – as a pretext for not trying to establish what Rodney himself has to say.

It might have occurred to you that one way forward would be to obtain the collaboration of Rodney's speech therapist, whom Rodney apparently knows and likes, and would seem to have some expertise in communicating with him. The speech therapist may not have much experience in child protection matters, however, so that any interview with Rodney would need to be planned collaboratively. Some care will need to be given to the questions that are put to Rodney, so that he is not led into either confirming or denying that Mr Fleet abused him. Thought should also be given to the venue and context in which he is interviewed, so as far as possible Rodney would feel comfortable and able to say whatever he wants. (The inter-agency strategy discussion, discussed in Chapter 2, is intended precisely for the purpose of thinking through these types of issues.)

Naturally one hopes that, by planning the interview carefully, and ensuring that it is conducted by someone with the appropriate communication skills and a good relationship with Rodney, it will be possible to determine whether there is any basis for believing that Rodney may have been sexually abused by Mr Fleet (or indeed by someone else). However, there is a real possibility that, even after such an exercise, it may still not be clear whether there is a basis for the allegations or not. It is a fact of life in child protection work that some investigations are inconclusive, and this is true of investigations involving non-disabled children as well as disabled ones. This would leave very difficult questions to be decided by the inter-professional system and by the family. But careful planning of the investigation, and appropriate expert help, should at least ensure that the chances of obtaining useful information are maximized.

Opinions on this allegation are rather polarized between Mrs French, who is convinced that Mr Fleet has abused Rodney, and the school, who are convinced that this is a figment of Mrs French's imagination. The views of others – Rodney's father, the family doctor, the speech therapist – may help to give a more rounded picture.

Assessing families

In Part III of this book I will discuss why some parents mistreat or neglect their children. I look in Chapter 7 at how stressors of one kind or another can precipitate abuse and/or preoccupy parents and carers to the point where they neglect their children. And I will argue that families are most vulnerable when stress factors in the here and now ('horizontal stressors') touch on areas which a family finds difficult for reasons connected with its own history ('vertical stressors'), or the history of its particular community or society.

All the stressors – horizontal and vertical – that can occur in families whose children are not disabled, can, of course, equally well occur in the families of disabled children. But the presence of disabled children is itself commonly a stressor, (a) because the child's impairments commonly present the rest of the family with additional challenges, but sometimes also (b) for more complex reasons to do with hopes and expectations, which I discussed earlier. The cultural context, as well as the family history and the history of its individual members, will all influence the ability of the family to cope with the challenges facing them in the here and now.

In any assessment of a family where there are child protection concerns, it is important to try and get a sense of the relationships between the child and her family. In the case of disabled children, we perhaps also need to look at the relationship between the family *and the disability*. One starting point for this might be Minnes' (1988) categorization of factors affecting a family's ability to cope with disability into:

1   The child's own characteristics.
2   The 'internal resources' of the family.
3   The 'external resources' of the family.
4   The family's perception of the child.

Minnes was looking specifically at the families of children with *learning* disabilities, but these categories seem to me to be valid for the families of other disabled children too (and indeed they could be applied to the families of non-disabled children).

The child's own characteristics

Different children present very different challenges. For example, the families of children with Down's Syndrome seem to cope better – on measures of stress and depression – than those children with some other kinds of intellectual impairment (Hodapp, 1996). This is probably due in part to the fact that Down's children tend, on average, to be affectionate and sociable, and to be less prone to difficult and challenging behaviour patterns than some other learning-impaired children. But it is perhaps also because the syndrome is relatively common and well known, and there are well-developed support networks.

Some physical disabilities may make very large demands on families in terms of physical care. Children with autistic spectrum diagnoses (as in Exercise 6.2) may be incapable of the normal give-and-take of human communication and make exceptional demands on the patience of adult carers.

No child should be seen as being so difficult and demanding that abuse or rejection is inevitable, but any realistic assessment should consider the demands that are made by the child on her carers and on other family members.

The 'internal resources' of the family

This refers to the personal characteristics of the family members and of the family as a whole, and to the way they deal with challenges. In this area, as in others, coping strategies based on practical problem-solving seem to be more adaptive than 'emotion-focussed' ones. 'In virtually every study, mothers who were focussed on actively solving problems seemed better off than those focussed primarily on their own emotional reactions' (Hodapp, 1998: 81). It is possible to learn new coping strategies, however, and in some cases this might be the focus for an 'intervention'.

The 'external resources' of the family

'External resources' include such things as the family's financial resources, accommodation, and the services and support networks available to them, so these are important factors in any assessment. An obvious method of intervention in cases where parents are in danger of not being able to cope, is to improve the support network by providing services, or assisting them in recruiting additional support. But, as discussed above, this kind of intervention poses the danger of simply 'plastering over' a deeper problem such as emotional rejection. This is one reason why any assessment should pay close attention also to the family's attitude towards the child.

The family's perception of the child

Abuse can simply be the result of stress brought about by a particular situation. This is as true in relation to children with disabilities as to those without. (Most parents will admit to having, at some time or another, taken out angry feelings on their children, even if this has only taken the form of unnecessarily harsh words.) If an abusive incident is the result of a problem of this kind, then helping to alleviate the stress may well be a solution.

However, if the abusive incident is part of a long-standing pattern of abusive behaviour, or reflects long-standing negativity or ambivalence towards a child, then the picture is rather different. Sending a child away for more respite, for example, may in these circumstances only confirm a child's feelings of rejection and abandonment. Any assessment should therefore explore the feelings of parents and other family members towards a child, and the child's towards them. Are the feelings predominantly positive or negative? Is the child's presence welcomed or resented? If the feelings are predominantly negative is this temporary, or is it the long-term view?

We all tell ourselves different 'stories' to give some sort of meaning to our lives. Parents of disabled children, and disabled children themselves, will come up with different narratives with which to deal with the question of 'Why us?' or 'Why me?' Some might view it as a special responsibility placed upon them, or a kind of challenge. Others might view the additional demands of a disability as being 'unfair', a burden, a distraction from the real business of their life. Some might view it as a punishment. (There may be cultural differences here: Westcott and Cross, 1996: 2–3, suggest that many religious traditions include the idea that disability is a punishment for the past actions of the parents.)

Some parents may end up viewing the disability as an affliction placed upon them by the child (the parents in Exercise 6.1, perhaps). Others may view it as something that they align themselves with the child against, battling on behalf of the child to overcome the obstacles that the world places in the way of those who have impairments. Some may be so pre-occupied with overcoming the disability that they forget the child herself. We need to understand the context in which abuse or neglect takes place, to understand its severity and meaning. It is always with these nuances, as much as the actual practical facts, that any child protection assessment, whether with disabled or non-disabled children, needs to grapple.

Chapter summary

In this chapter I have looked at the special case of disabled children and considered:

- the particular vulnerability of disabled children to maltreatment for a variety of different reasons. I discussed in particular the role in this that is played by family factors, widely held assumptions about disabled children, and the fact that there may be different professional systems dealing with 'child protection' and 'disability'.
- the particular issues that arise when working with children with disabilities, including issues of power and, in particular, issues to do with communication which arise for children with a variety of disabilities. I suggested that trying to interview a child without the relevant communication skills is akin to interviewing the speaker of a foreign language without an interpreter.
- the need to assess the families of disabled children and how they deal with the disability, suggesting that for each family it is important to consider the characteristics of the child, the family's internal and external resources, and the family's attitude to the child.

The next chapter will return to children in general, rather than specifically disabled children, and will consider the long-term consequences of child maltreatment.

7 | Harm

- Physical harm
- Psychological harm
- Effects of physical abuse, emotional abuse and neglect
- Effects of sexual abuse

Stopping and, if possible, undoing, harm done to children by their carers is the purpose of child protection work. In fact, preventing 'significant harm' is in English and Welsh law the sole justification for the intrusion into family life and privacy that child protection work entails. Similar laws apply in the US and elsewhere. Unless there is evidence that significant harm is being done to a child, or is likely to be done, then there is no legal justification – nor, I think, moral justification – for insisting on professional involvement, though of course it continues to be perfectly appropriate to offer professional services to those who want to use them.

Child protection workers need some understanding first about what kinds of harm are caused by child maltreatment and secondly about what precisely it is about a carer's behaviour that causes the harm, otherwise they would not know what it was that needed to be changed. Sometimes the harm we are concerned about includes the possibility of physical injury. But even in cases of physical abuse, the injury is only part of the harm caused, with psychological and emotional harm often being much longer lasting than the injury and much more profound in its effects on the rest of a person's life.

Exercise 7.1

The following are two imaginary scenarios involving physical abuse. Which one seems to you to be the most abusive? What kinds of harm might they do?

1   A nine-year-old boy ('David') is seen at school with scratch marks and bruises on his neck and hand-print bruises on his legs. Questioned about it, his mother admits to grabbing him by the neck and then smacking very hard around the legs. 'I love him to bits,' she says, 'but my husband has been away on business for the last two weeks and David has been driving me nuts.' Yesterday, she says, she had been walking back from a park with David, pushing his two sisters, one aged two years and one aged six months, in a double buggy, when he demanded to be allowed to go to the sweetshop across the road to spend his pocket money. She had refused. He had then stepped straight into the road causing a car to make an emergency stop to avoid hitting him, and another car to nearly run into the back of it. Very frightened, angry and embarrassed, she had grabbed David very roughly by the neck to drag him back off the road and had slapped him several times. 'I've never hit him before. I don't even *believe* in smacking kids. But I'm afraid I just lost it.' David is a boisterous lively child at school, and seems much the same today as other days. 'He's never run out into the road before though,' his mother says.

2   A nine-year-old boy ('Peter') is very well-behaved and hard-working at school, very attentive to the teachers and always well turned-out. He is the adopted only child of a professional couple. One day in school, he does uncharacteristically badly in a spelling test, getting nine marks out of 15. He is very distressed and agitated about this. His teacher takes time to explore this with him. Eventually he tells her that when he has a spelling test in school, his mother always asks him how he got on. And, if he obtained less than 100 per cent, she makes him stand in a corner until his father gets home, perhaps an hour later. His father then sends Peter to fetch a ruler and smacks him on the back of the hand with it – one smack for each incorrect answer – before setting him some revision work to do, which he will be tested on later. 'We will not allow you to degenerate into an idle good-for-nothing illiterate like your real mother,' is what he says his parents tell him. No visible injury has ever been seen at school.

Comments on Exercise 7.1

In reality, you would need to consider all the evidence carefully and it could well be that the picture that would eventually emerge in either one of these cases would be very different from your first impression based on the above brief accounts. However, on what we have so far, I would suggest that there look like being much more serious child protection issues in Peter's case than in David's, even though David has visible non-accidental injuries and Peter does not.

Peter's treatment by his adoptive parents seems calculated to deeply undermine his confidence and his sense of self-worth in ways which might well have negative consequences for his mental well-being across his entire life. It looks like emotional abuse, and raises questions for me as to whether Peter should be in this family at all.

In David's case, if this really is a one-off incident, I would suggest that the harm done to him is probably negligible, and that it would probably be counter-productive for the child protection system to remain involved at all, provided that it could be reasonably satisfied that this was indeed an uncharacteristic event.

Physical harm

The following are some of the forms of physical harm that can result from child mal-treatment:

Death and serious injury

The most extreme physical consequence of child abuse and neglect, though also a rare one, is of course death. Death occurs as a consequence of violent assaults such as punching, hitting and (in the case of small children) shaking, but parental neglect is almost as common a cause of death as actual physical assault. In rare, extreme cases neglect can result in children dying from starvation, or cold. More commonly, neglect kills by resulting in fatal accidents such as drowning, falling, burns and road accidents. In the US, in 2002, 38 per cent of child maltreatment deaths were associated with neglect alone (NCCANI, 2004). I would suggest, though, that such statistics be handled with caution, because the line between a purely accidental injury and one that is the result of parental negligence can sometimes be a debatable one.

Exercise 7.2

Simon, aged seven, suffered fatal burns when he attempted to cook chips for himself and for his younger brother, aged five, and ended up pulling up the hot chip-pan over himself. This occurred at about 11 a.m. and it would seem that Simon's parents were upstairs in bed at the time.

Is this a case of neglect?

Comments on Exercise 7.2

You will probably agree that for the children to be left unsupervised in this way does sound negligent. If I added, though, that both parents had flu at the time, that the father had given them breakfast and been up with them most of the morning and that, when the incident happened, he had just got back into bed with his wife to drink a cup of tea with her, having left both of the children downstairs apparently engrossed in a cartoon on TV, it might seem more like very bad luck.

On the other hand, if I added that the children had, say, been the subject of repeated complaints and referrals to police and social services because they were regularly seen by neighbours playing unsupervised next to a busy road – and if Simon's school had been concerned that Simon often arrived late to school wearing inappropriate clothes, and that he often seemed to have had no breakfast, a different picture emerges, of children whose parents for whatever reason are really not very focussed on their safety or their needs.

Physical abuse, neglect and some kinds of sexual abuse can also result in long-term physical injury. Shaking a baby, for instance, can cause brain damage which, if not fatal, may cause paralysis, blindness and permanent, profound intellectual impairment. (However, it is important to note, in recent years, there have been challenges in the medical community to the idea that the presence of certain retinal injuries are *necessarily* symptoms of so-called Shaken Baby Syndrome [for example, Lantz et al., 2004].)

Failure to thrive

Failure to thrive (FTT) can be seen in children who have grown up in institutional environments where they have suffered extreme deprivation, which may include both psychological/emotional elements and physical ones such as poor nutrition. Rutter et al. (1998) looked at the long-term effects of early life experiences in the grossly deprived environment of orphanages in Romania prior to recent reforms of the Romanian childcare system. Such children can show marked delay in physical and intellectual development and a range of abnormal behaviours. The Rutter study found that early psychological privation appeared to be a more important predictor of long-term developmental problems than poor nutrition.

FTT does not only occur in an institutional context however. Sometimes babies fail to put on weight, or even lose weight, without any apparent organic cause. This has in the past been identified as a symptom of emotional abuse or neglect, but it is not an assumption which we should make too readily. Some babies are extremely resistant to feeding in spite of their parents' best efforts. Batchelor (1999: 35–6), discussing research in this area, concluded that 'a small number of children with an inborn constitutional predisposition will, in the face of stress or neglect, develop growth hormone deficiency which results in stunted growth. However, this is a very rare condition which affects perhaps three to five children per 10,000'.

Psychological harm

Children who have been abused or neglected suffer long-term psychological harm which may continue into adult life and which may include some or all of the following:

- low self-esteem
- depression and suicidal impulses
- difficulties in relating to others
- difficulties as parents – including, in some cases, becoming abusers themselves
- mental health problems, including drug or alcohol problems
- low educational attainment
- restlessness and difficulty in concentrating

These consequences do not occur inevitably. A proportion of the victims, even of very serious abuse, appear to emerge relatively unscathed. Summarizing 26 studies of college students, Bagley and Thurston come to the conclusion that 'about half of those who experienced long-term intrusive abuse by a trusted family member or authority figure do not have psychologically abnormal outcomes as a young adult' (1995: 140). Nevertheless the likelihood of all these outcomes is certainly greatly increased by abuse and neglect in childhood.

All the consequences listed above can follow on from all the different varieties of maltreatment so that, while I will discuss the different categories of abuse in turn below, you will see common themes running through all of them. One of these is that abuse or neglect is much more harmful when it is chronic and long-lasting, and that isolated incidents – however distressing at the time – do not on the whole result in long-term harm. Another is that the relationship in which the abuse takes place is an important determinant of the outcome.

But why is it, if no long-term physical harm has been done, that the mental consequences are often still apparent, and still suffered, long after the abuse or neglect itself has stopped? There are a number of different types of explanation – not necessarily mutually exclusive – which may account for this.

Critical periods

There are known to be certain periods in child development during which certain neurological structures are laid down. If normal development is interfered with in those periods, then irreversible harm may occur which cannot fully be put right at a later stage. We know, for example, that there is a certain critical period during which the visual cortex of the brain develops, and that if a developing animal is deprived of visual stimulation during this period, it may never acquire normal vision (Rutter and Rutter, 1993: 12). Are some kinds of psychological harm similarly irreversible if they occur at particularly sensitive stages of development? There is some evidence of this.

For example, the study I mentioned above of children from Romanian institutions adopted in Britain (Rutter et al., 1998) found that children entering Britain from Romania at under six months, having previously been cared for in institutions, appear to have caught up cognitively with their peers by age four. Children entering Britain when *over* six months of age also showed substantial cognitive catch-up, but were nevertheless delayed compared to children who had not experienced an institutional upbringing. The differences between the children who were removed from the institutional environment at under six months, and those who were removed at an older age, suggest that there may be a critical period at which psychological/emotional privation has long-term consequences which may be hard to completely undo.

In fact, most of us probably know from personal experience that early life experience has long-term and deep-seated effects that continue long after the original circumstances have ceased to apply. Even if we are lucky enough not to have experienced serious abuse or neglect, most of us can surely identify aspects of ourselves dating back to childhood which are just not readily amenable to change, even if we would like to change them.

Internalized working models

One way of looking at the harm that is done as a result of abuse or neglect in childhood, is to see it as 'bad information' which becomes part of a person's view of the world. The term 'working models' comes from John Bowlby (1980), the originator of attachment theory, though it is an idea that has counterparts in other psychodynamic models. According to Bowlby, during early childhood, we each construct a working model of the world and our position in it. The elements of this model will include ideas about our own value relative to other people, and ideas about what we can expect from other people and how best to relate to them.

A child who is neglected by her carers is in a situation where the person on whom she relies to respond to her needs and provide her with security is not actually available. A child who is physically, sexually or emotionally abused by her carers may find herself in a position where the person she relies upon for safety and protection is simultaneously her main source of threat and danger. These are 'no win' positions. The child has no means of resolving them and can only resort to various defensive strategies, such as 'splitting' which, in the short run, help to reduce anxiety but in the long run 'distort reality and lay down partial, incomplete memories and dysfunctional behavioural sequences which become reactivated whenever similar situations are met' (Howe, 2005: 46). Instead of building up an accurate picture of the world, the child develops a 'faulty working model', excluding from consciousness information that increases anxiety but which she can do nothing about, a process Bowlby called 'defensive exclusion', though it is similar to what psychoanalysts call repression and denial.

Faulty working models are very resistant to change and indeed may be impossible to change unless the person concerned can be made aware of the distorted nature of her own thinking and the defences that she has put in place to protect her against new information. The long-term emotional harm – low self-esteem, difficulty in relating to others – that we can often see in people who have been abused or neglected as children, is thus the result of faulty working models of the world which that person is continuing to apply long after the original reason for it is past.

The following exercise attempts to illustrate this process.

Exercise 7.3

William, aged four, lives with his mother. There is no one else in the family and William has very little contact with anyone else. William's mother is subject to extreme mood swings which are sudden and unpredictable. Sometimes she treats him kindly, but at other times she flies into frightening rages and threatens to abandon him, or kill herself, and tells him that it would all be his fault. On occasion she has followed up such threats by cutting herself with a knife. On other occasions she has gone out and left him alone in the flat, sometimes for hours on end.

At the age of four, William cannot deal with this situation as an adult could. He has no way of knowing, for example, that his mother's behaviour is abnormal and no life experience to tell him that it is unreasonable of her to blame him for her distress. He is probably not aware of any possible outside source of help. He cannot remove himself from the situation or find someone else to live with.

His mother may be terrifying, but she is also his only source of comfort, nourishment and safety. In many ways, she is his world.

How would William try to cope with this?

Comments on Exercise 7.3

It seems to me that William cannot defend himself in any real way from what is happening, so all that is open to him is to resort to various psychological defences.

(Continued)

One psychological defence that we all use when faced with an unavoidable fact which we find intolerable (such as the news of a bereavement, for example) is to tell ourselves: 'This isn't really happening', 'This isn't real'. In short, we 'go into denial' – or 'defensively exclude' – the thing that we can't cope with. This is a normal and necessary response to a shocking new event, but in most cases it is followed by a period of adjustment to the new reality, a gradual coming to terms with what has happened.

For a child in William's situation, however, there can be no coming to terms with something that cannot be consigned to the past but will recur over and over again. He can't really afford to come out of denial and is therefore likely to attempt a whole series of psychological manoeuvres to hold reality at bay.

He could tell himself that the mum who mistreats him is a different person from the mum who is kind to him – and that the kind one is his real mum – or he may even split his idea of himself into two, so that when things are relatively calm, he can dissociate himself from the memory of the bad times by seeing them as things that happened to someone else.

He could agree with his mother that everything is his fault, and that he deserves the treatment that he gets from her. Although this does not sound a very comfortable position to take, it may well be less frightening to think of himself as bad, than to think of the adult who controls his whole world as being capricious and dangerous.

He could tell himself that he doesn't really need his mother anyway.

He might try to find means of comforting or distracting himself, rather like the baby monkeys in the cruel experiments conducted in the 1950s and 1960s by Harlow and his collaborators (Harlow, 1963), who clung to crudely-made monkey dolls covered in terry cloth. (I think a persuasive argument can be made that this pattern of seeking external sources of comfort and distraction may lead in later life to addictions of one kind or another: see Flores, 2004.)

And perhaps these patterns and habits of thought – and these means of self-comfort – may become so entrenched over time that even when he has grown up and left home, William will still use the same strategies to deal with the world: excluding what is painful from consciousness, holding contradictory stories in his mind at the same time, blaming himself for things that are not his fault (or perhaps being unable to distinguish between the things that are his fault and the things that are not). Meanwhile, under the surface, would still be all the feelings that he has tried so hard to deny – anger, fear, longing – ready to erupt unpredictably at moments when the effort of containing them becomes too great.

Post-traumatic stress

The characteristic group of symptoms labelled as Post-Traumatic Stress Disorder (PTSD) include recurrent recollections of the event which intrude into everyday life, recurrent dreams about the event and 'flashback' phenomena in which the event itself seems to be recurring. They also include intense psychological distress and actual physiological reactions (for example, sweating and trembling) to situations which remind the sufferer of the original traumatic event and a general reduction of the sufferer's ability to focus on other aspects of life (see Kanel, 2003: 202–39). These symptoms were described as 'shell shock' in the First World War when they were found to be characteristic of soldiers traumatized by their experiences in the trenches, but similar symptoms are found in people who have been exposed to other kinds of events such as train crashes or terrorist incidents, whose horror is simply too much for the brain to be able to process.

If one imagines a young soldier cowering in a trench during a bombardment which he is unable to prevent or control or predict, it is not hard to see parallels with the experience of children living in perpetual dread of the next incident of sexual abuse or the next eruption of adult violence. But for children there is the added factor that the trauma occurs 'during crucial developmental years, when basic capacities for emotion regulation and identify formation are taking shape' and where 'children must cope, often by themselves, with the overwhelming nature of abuse in the context of limited cognitive and psychological resources' (Stovall-McClough and Cloitre, 2006: 219). Many researchers have confirmed the presence of characteristic PTSD symptoms among survivors of childhood abuse (for example, Feerick and Snow, 2005).

Feedback loops

Another way in which the effects of maltreatment can become entrenched occurs when the victim's initial response to maltreatment causes her to behave in a way that provokes further negative responses from others, which in turn makes the victim generate more of the same behaviour – and so on. This would be an example of a 'feedback loop' – a pattern that is often found in biological systems that try to maintain a steady state in relation to their environment. In mutually satisfactory parent–child relationships, in which both parties reward each other for their attention, such loops are beneficial, but there can also be 'vicious circles', which lock all of those involved in a dysfunctional relationship.

Children from abusive or neglectful backgrounds placed in foster-homes will often behave in ways that seem calculated to provoke rejection or hostility from their new carers. The following describes a ten-year-old victim of neglect, now in a long-term foster-home:

> Bobby always set himself up for rejection. He inevitably asked for attention when the foster mother was tied up with someone else. For example, if someone was injured or crying, Bobby would demand her focus when she was busy bandaging or cuddling. On the other side, whenever she attempted to give Bobby positive attention, he rebuffed her. Bobby, whose history showed him to be sorely neglected, compulsively re-enacted that history within the foster home. (Delaney, 1998: 50)

Many of the psychological effects of maltreatment – such as low self-esteem, lack of trust in others and so on – are qualities that tend to be 'self-fulfilling prophesies'. A person whose fear of rejection makes her very withdrawn and uncommunicative, for example, may well find that people avoid her company. The 'vicious circle' is therefore one of the ways in which 'internalized working models' can perpetuate themselves.

In order to break the vicious circle it is necessary not only to stop the abuse or neglect from happening, but to address the *patterns* of thought and behaviour which the abuse has established – patterns which may not only distort the thinking of the abused person, but may also provoke negative responses from others. This is a point which can easily be forgotten. People sometimes assume, for example, that by removing a child from an abusive situation and placing him in a caring one, or by changing the abusive situation *into* a more caring one, the effects of abuse and neglect ought to be undone. In fact, children who have been maltreated often can't respond to any amount of caring unless they are also given specialist help aimed at addressing the 'faulty working models' that they have internalized while living in the abusive and neglectful situation.

Effects of physical abuse, emotional abuse and neglect

'We have certainly not found any evidence that physical abuse of *itself* (except in the most severe cases) causes long-term harm' was the perhaps surprising conclusion of one large British study of the long-term effects of physical abuse (Gibbons et al., 1995: 53). Gibbons et al. looked at a group of 170 children who'd been put on a child protection register ten years previously under the category of physical abuse. The children had been aged 0–5 at time of registration. The study tried to control for other factors such as social deprivation by selecting a 'Comparison group' of children who were matched to the 'Index group' by age, gender, social class, and by the fact that they lived in the same neighbourhood and attended the same schools. The interviewers who talked to the children and their parents did so 'blind': they did not know whether the children and parents they were assigned to interview were in the Index group (the children who had been on the register) or the Comparison group (the children who had not been on the register). The people who scored the interviews likewise worked 'blind'.

Various developmental measures were used to assess the children ten years on from the time when the Index group children had been on the register. The measures used included:

- Growth – height, weight, head circumference.
- Behaviour – using standard questionnaires filled in both by teachers and parents.
- Emotions – these were assessed using the child's own self-reports. Children were interviewed on their current circumstances and these interviews included questions to do with *fears* and *depression*. The interview transcripts were rated 'blind' and given high or low scores for 'fears' and for 'depression'.
- Problems with peers – again using the children's own self-reports on issues such as friends, bullying and social isolation.
- Cognitive ability – using standard tests.

The researchers then looked at whether there was any significant relationship between these developmental measures and whether children were in the Index group or the Comparison group. In other words: were their scores on these developmental measures affected by whether or not they had been on the register for physical abuse ten years previously? The measures were also compared with other factors, some of which related to the original abuse episode, some of which related to family history, and some of which related to current circumstances.

The main significant differences between the groups were in the areas of behaviour and problems with peers. Reports from both teachers and parents were more likely to say, for instance, that Index children were 'not much liked', 'often disobedient', that they 'often tell lies', that they could not settle 'for more than a few minutes' and that they were 'squirmy/fidgety' as compared to children in the Comparison group. Index children themselves reported significantly more problems with peers than Comparison children. All these differences, however, though statistically significant, were not large, and there was a large overlap between the two groups.

A statistician, 'blind' to whether the children were in the Index or Comparison groups, sorted all the children into three outcome categories:

- Poor outcome (in terms both of behavioural and emotional problems and of school performance).
- Good outcome (in terms both of behavioural and emotional problems and of school performance).
- Low performance (good outcome in terms of behavioural and emotional problems, but low in terms of school performance).

Of the Index children, 42 per cent turned out to be in the Poor Outcome group, as compared to 19 per cent of the Comparison children, while in the Good Outcome group were 22 per cent of the Index children and 48 per cent of the Comparison children. In other words, about one-fifth of the Index children seemed not to show any long-term developmental problems, while about one-fifth of the Comparison children *did* display such problems. These differences could still be found when factors like economic disadvantage and household type were adjusted for.

Having sorted the children into these 'outcome' groups, it was then possible to use statistical analysis to see whether, and to what extent, these outcomes were linked to a variety of different factors.

One factor looked at was severity of injury. In the Index group, about 16 per cent of the injuries leading to registration were classified as serious: i.e., fractures, head injuries, internal injuries, severe burns, poisoning. Others had more minor injuries or had been registered because they were thought to be at risk of injury. But severity of injury had no significant link with outcomes, except in four cases where permanent physical damage had been done.

But, while severity of injury did not turn out to have a statistically significant link to outcome, a range of factors associated with registration *did* show a statistical link. The following are a few of them:

- When neglect, as well as physical injury, had been an issue at time of registration, this was found to have a significant link with poorer outcomes in terms of behaviour at school, and depression. Higher depression scores were also associated with marital violence having been an issue at the time of registration.
- Children who'd been registered because of *risk* of injury, rather than actual injury, were also associated with higher depression scores than the other Index children. (For professionals to identify a risk of physical injury, they would have to have picked up a strong sense of threat in the home. My suggestion would be that this *atmosphere of threat*, which would also, of course, be picked up by children in the family, may be the harmful element here.)

The study also identified a number of statistically significant associations between children's reports of *current* parental style and outcomes:

- Difficulty in peer relationships was associated with a punitive style and use of physical punishment.
- Behaviour problems at school were associated with parental criticism and a punitive style.
- Cognitive attainment related positively with parental strictness and good relationships between parent and child, and negatively with parental criticism.
- Depression was linked to a child's rating of parental relationships.
- Problems with peers were associated with parental criticism, with punitive parental style and recent physical punishment.
- Poor outcomes were associated with parents reported by their children as being unpredictable or prone to shouting, making threats, smacking or hitting.
- Poor outcomes were associated with children who reported few shared activities with their mothers and who enjoyed activities with their mothers less.
- Poor outcomes were associated with children who disagreed with the statement that their mother usually kept her promises – 57 per cent of the Poor Outcome group, as against 91 per cent of the Good Outcome group. For fathers the respective figures were 71 per cent and 84 per cent.
- Poor outcomes were also more likely for children exposed to marital problems and domestic violence, and for children whose carers reported themselves to be lacking in support from the wider community.

What I take from studies like this, and from my own experience, is that physical abuse should be regarded as one of the *indicators* of an abusive parent–child *relationship,* but that it is the abusive relationship itself that mainly causes long-term psychological harm. As Geraldine MacDonald puts it: 'psychological maltreatment is increasingly recognized as the mechanism whereby other forms of abuse bring about adverse developmental outcomes' (MacDonald, 2001). In order to minimize the harm, therefore, it is necessary not just to prevent incidents of physical abuse from occurring, but also to change the relationship which underlies those incidents.

Given that this is the case, we should perhaps not be surprised that emotional abuse and neglect, even if not accompanied by physical abuse, can do as much psychological harm as physical abuse. For example, citing six different pieces of prospective and retrospective research, Gaudin (1999: 100) concludes that neglect results in cognitive and academic deficits in older school-age victims, and that 'these negative developmental effects have been found to be far more enduring for neglect than for any other kind of maltreatment'. In Chapter 11 I will have more to say about the way in which exposure to adult violence, which is a form of emotional abuse, has severe long-term effects on children which can be similar in kind and severity to those suffered by children who are themselves the direct victims of violence.

Effects of sexual abuse

'It is now well-established that up to a half of both men and women who experience long-term sexual abuse in childhood will have chronic mental health problems in adulthood', according to Bagley and Thurston (1995: 148). Long-term effects of sexual abuse include self-destructive behaviour, anxiety, feelings of isolation and stigma, poor self-esteem, substance abuse, eating disorders, sexual problems and mental illness. The emotional and psychological effects of sexual abuse seem to be likely to be especially severe when the abuse is by the father or a close family member (see, for example, Beitchman et al., 1992), when it involves genital contact and when it involves the use of force. The severity of long-term psychological effects is also related to the response received by the victim when the abuse came to light, for example, whether she is believed and supported.

Although PTSD symptoms, as discussed earlier, are found among many survivors of sexual abuse, David Finkelhor (1988: 61ff) pointed out that PTSD does not describe *all* of the typical psychological consequences of sexual abuse, which may include cognitive disturbances such as 'distorted beliefs about self and others, self-blame, sexual misinformation and sexual confusions'. Finkelhor proposed four 'Traumagenic [i.e. trauma-*causing*] dynamics' that are at work in sexual abuse, which I will now list. Although his model is now some 20 years old, I think it continues to be a helpful way of separating out the different ways in which sexual abuse causes long-term harm. It seems to me too that all but the first of these four dynamics are applicable not only to sexual abuse but to physical abuse, emotional abuse and neglect.

Traumatic sexualization

Sexual abuse occurs under conditions which shape the sexuality of a child in inappropriate and dysfunctional ways:

- Children are often rewarded by abusers for sexual behaviour that is inappropriate for their age and as a result they can learn to use sexual behaviour as a strategy for manipulating others. In fact, sexually provocative behaviour by children is one of the ways in which it comes to light that they have been, or are being, sexually abused.
- Children also learn to give a distorted amount of importance to sexual parts of their bodies. Sexually abused children may become highly preoccupied with their genitals.
- Sexually abused children are commonly given highly inaccurate information by abusers about sexual behaviour and what is normal and appropriate.
- Sexually abused children may commonly learn to associate sex with frightening and disturbing memories. For example, they may learn to associate sex with violence or threats.

Here is an instance of a child developing a 'faulty working model' which includes ideas about the role of sex in human relationships that in the long run are likely to be harmful. The long-term implications of the distorted thinking and behaviour that may result from traumatic sexualization might include some of the following:

- A preoccupation with sex and compulsive sexual behaviours, or, on the other hand, an aversion to sex, reflected in avoidant or phobic behaviour.
- Involvement in prostitution. Silbert and Pines (1981) found that 60 per cent of a sample of San Francisco prostitutes had been sexually abused.
- 'Revictimization'. Russell (1986) found that women survivors of sexual abuse were nearly twice as likely as other women to be victims of rape or attempted rape, and more than twice as likely to have been subjected to physical violence from husbands or partners.

- Sexual performance problems.
- Difficulties as parents. Survivors of sexual abuse may inappropriately sexualize their children, and may themselves become involved in sexual abuse of children.

Betrayal

Sexual abuse in the family – and, in different ways, other kinds of child abuse – involves a betrayal. Someone on whom the child relies for protection becomes a source of distress and fear. Someone on whom the child relies to look after her interests is found to place other things before her most basic needs. Even family members who are not directly involved in the abuse may be seen to have betrayed the child, by failing to notice the abuse, or in some cases by tolerating it.

The effects of this dynamic might include difficulties in trusting others or in accurately judging the trustworthiness of others. Difficulties might include clinginess or isolation, marital and relationship problems, vulnerability to abuse and exploitation, failure of the survivor to recognize threats of abuse to her own children, or failure to protect them. (It may at first sight be surprising that some survivors of abuse are not good at protecting their own children from abuse. One might expect them to be exceptionally vigilant, as indeed many are. But we must remember that among the survival mechanisms of victims of abuse are 'dissociation' and 'defensive exclusion'. Thus a victim of abuse may become very skilled at blocking out the evidence of abuse.)

Stigmatization

Victims of sexual abuse (and victims also of violence) tend to report feelings of worthlessness, shame and guilt. As Finkelhor writes, children pick up these messages about themselves in a variety of ways:

> Abusers say it directly when they blame the victim … or denigrate the victim … They also say it indirectly through their furtiveness and pressures for secrecy. But much of the stigmatization comes from the attitudes the victims hear or the moral judgements they infer from those around them … [S]imply the fact of having been a victim is likely to impel the child to search for attributions to explain 'why it happened to me'. (Finkelhor, 1988: 70)

Steel et al. (2004) found that the longer the abuse persisted the more likely it was that victims would attribute blame to themselves. Quas et al. (2003) find that self-blame is more likely when the abuser was known and trusted by the victim.

The implications of stigmatization for adult life might include isolation, drug or alcohol abuse, depression, suicide and self-harm.

Powerlessness

Utter powerlessness and helplessness in a frightening situation is the stuff of nightmares. In sexual abuse (and again, in various ways, in other forms of abuse also), the sense of being invaded and of being powerless to resist becomes reality at the most basic of levels. In some instances it is quite literally the child's own body that is being invaded. In all instances it is her privacy, her status as a child, her expectations of protection, that are violated.

Some forms of sexual abuse involve violence or threats of violence and even threats to life. For a small child to be repeatedly threatened with abandonment, for example, may simply be too much to bear, so that the victim has to resort to the psychological defences discussed earlier in this chapter, such as 'splitting' or 'dissociation', whereby she tells herself, in effect, that 'this is not happening to me'. (It is worth noting that these kinds of psychological mechanisms are also present in *abusers,* who are able to split off their abusive activity from the rest of their lives.)

Long-term effects of this dynamic of powerlessness might include things like nightmares, phobias, eating disorders, depression and revictimization, or various behaviours which are to do with trying to regain a sense of power, such as manipulative behaviour or even abusing others. Finkelhor suggests that powerlessness may be exacerbated by experiences of attempting to escape from abuse but failing. He also makes the following very important point, which should be carefully noted by social workers and other child protection professionals:

> children often experience an enormous, unexpected, and devastating increase in powerlessness in the aftermath of abuse, when they find themselves unable to control the decisions of the adult world that may visit upon them many unwanted events – separation from family, prosecutions, police investigations – in addition to the termination of abuse. (Finkelhor, 1988: 72)

Exercise 7.4

Suzanne, aged 14, lived with her mother, step-father and younger sister (aged ten). She had been showing signs of unhappiness for some time in school (weeping, poor concentration, isolation, truancy) and a particular teacher, Miss D, had spent a lot of time with her trying to establish a relationship with her and to encourage her to talk about whatever was on her mind.

Then, in one of her sessions with Miss D, Suzanne burst into tears and said something bad was going on, but she couldn't tell Miss D for fear of the consequences. Miss D tried to reassure her, and eventually Suzanne said that she would tell Miss D if Miss D could assure her that she would keep it secret.

Miss D said that she would tell no one. Suzanne then told her that over the past few months, her step-father had been coming into her room, feeling her under her bedclothes and masturbating. He had told her to keep it secret, that her mother would never believe her, and that if she told her mother, she would be put into care.

Having been told this story, Miss D became very anxious. She had promised to respect Suzanne's wish that this be kept secret, yet unless she took some action, the abuse would continue, and indeed not only Suzanne but also her little sister would continue to be at risk. Miss D discussed this with her head of year, who told her to go back to Suzanne and tell her that this would have to be reported to the social services.

Suzanne was angry and distressed, but Miss D went ahead and phoned social services who, in turn, contacted the police. A joint investigation was carried out. Suzanne reluctantly repeated her allegations. Her sister was also interviewed but did not make any allegations. The step-father was arrested and put on bail with a condition that he should move out of the family home.

(Continued)

The next day, Suzanne's mother contacted the police and said that Suzanne wanted to make a further statement. At the police station, Suzanne made a statement retracting all of her previous allegation and stating that she had made it all up to get back at her step-father after a disagreement.

There was no evidence other than Suzanne's now retracted original statement (no medical evidence, no witnesses, no corroborating evidence of any kind). The police could take no further action. The family indicated they wanted no involvement from social care. No further action was taken, even though Miss D was firmly convinced that Suzanne had told the truth about the abuse and had retracted because she saw the situation getting out of her control and having outcomes that she did not want.

What went wrong here? What could have been done differently?

Comments on Exercise 7.4

You probably observed that it was a mistake on Miss D's part to promise to keep Suzanne's secret (although one can understand why she did it). If she had been clear that she couldn't guarantee to keep a secret, it is possible that Suzanne would not have told her what was going on. But Miss D probably could have guessed what kind of thing might be going on, and would have been able to discuss possible scenarios and to consider what might happen if Suzanne decided to talk.

If Suzanne had a chance to think through in advance what might happen, who would be involved and how she would have handled it, then perhaps, when and if she did decide to make an allegation, she would have been more likely to go through with it. If she had thought in advance about the implications and made her own decision as to when to take the next step, then she would not feel so powerless in the face of the professional system and would not have to feel that the professional system (in the person of Miss D) had betrayed her or lied to her.

It could be objected that this approach might have resulted in delay, or in Suzanne never making an allegation, so that she (and perhaps in the future her sister) would have gone on being abused. This might be so, but we need to remember that if the system makes people feel so powerless that they are reluctant to disclose abuse, then that too will result in it being unable to protect these children.

Chapter summary

In this chapter I have looked at the nature of the harm that is done to children – and to the adults they become – as a result of child abuse and neglect.

- I discussed the physical harm that can occur as a result of physical abuse, neglect and sexual abuse

(Continued)

(Continued)

- I then considered the psychological harm that commonly occurs as a result of maltreatment in children, and considered the ways in which such harm may come about
- I discussed the impact of physical abuse, suggested that it is the psychological element of physical abuse which tends to result in long-term harm and noted that neglect and emotional abuse can result in psychological harm of similar severity to that caused by physical abuse
- I discussed different ways of conceptualizing the often devastating psychological impact of sexual abuse.

This chapter concludes Part II of this book. In Part III I will move on to consider the reasons that abuse and neglect occur, beginning in Chapter 7 with an overview of the causes and contexts of child maltreatment.

Part III

CAUSES AND CONTEXTS

8 | Origins of Abuse and Neglect

- Risk factors
- Patterns of maltreatment
- Premeditated abuse
- Absence of love
- Stress-related abuse and neglect
- Competence-related abuse and neglect
- Abuse by children

Having considered the signs and consequences of abuse and neglect in Part II, I will now consider the question of when and why abuse and neglect occurs. In this chapter I will consider the range of external factors that are associated with abuse and neglect. I will then consider the different ways in which, in particular cases, parents and others may end up abusing or neglecting children and consider what the best response is in each case. In the following four chapters I will look more closely at some specific contexts.

Risk factors

Just as we must have some understanding of how maltreatment affects a child's development if we are to know how to intervene and change things for the better, so we need some understanding of what factors may make it more likely that people will maltreat children so as to be able to make the right decisions about how to respond to particular situations.

One way of approaching these sorts of questions is to look at families where abuse or neglect has occurred and to compare the characteristics of these families with those of other families where there has been no concern about maltreatment. It is then possible to identify 'risk factors', characteristics that occur more frequently in situations where maltreatment occurs than they do in other situations.

Fatal abuse

Cyril Greenland (1987) produced a list of risk indicators based on studies of 107 actual child deaths in the UK and Canada. The risk factors which Greenland came up with are listed in Table 8.1. Exercise 8.1, below, invites you to consider their implications.

Exercise 8.1

In the inquiry report into the death of Jasmine Beckford (London Borough of Brent, 1985) it is suggested that such tragedies might be avoided by using findings such as those of Greenland as an assessment tool to identify high-risk families. Look through the list in Table 8.1. What difficulties can you see in using it in such a way?

Table 8.1   Indicators associated with increased likelihood of child death through non-accidental injury

Characteristics of parent
Themselves abused or neglected as a child
Aged 20 or less at the birth of their first child
Single parent/separated; partner not biological parent of child
History of abuse/neglect or deprivation
Socially isolated; frequent moves; poor housing
Poverty; unemployed/unskilled worker; inadequate education
Abuses alcohol and/or drugs
History of violent behaviour and/or suicide attempts
Pregnant, or post partum (i.e. has recently given birth); or chronic illness

Characteristics of child
Previously abused/neglected
Under five years old at the time of abuse or neglect
Premature or low birth weight
Birth defect; chronic illness; developmental lag
Prolonged separation from mother
Cries frequently; difficult to comfort
Difficulties in feeding/elimination
Adopted, foster or step-child

Source: Greenland (1987).

Comments on Exercise 8.1

What probably struck you is the broadness of the categories. For example, being a single parent is one of the nine characteristics of parents, but obviously most single parents do not abuse or neglect their children. Their presence on this list merely reflects the fact that there were a higher proportion of single parents among the parents of the 107 children in Greenland's sample of child death cases than there are in the general population. Likewise, not all premature or adoptive babies are abused, and their presence in the list simply reflects the fact there were higher proportions of premature babies and of adoptive babies among the 107 than there are in the population in general.

Lists like Greenland's may tell us something, in a general sense, about the different characteristics of abusive families, but they are very little use in predicting abuse in any given individual instance, since clearly it would not make any sense to treat every lone parent, or every parent who was under 20 when her first child was born, or every parent of a premature child, as a high-risk case. It *is* true that if a number of these factors were present in a single case the situation would certainly look more risky than the average family. For instance, if a mother of 17, who had been physically abused herself as a child, was a heroin user and had convictions for violent offences, was caring on her own for a premature baby who was ill and cried a lot, then this would certainly be a situation in which there was a well-above-average risk of abuse or neglect of some kind occurring, but then again, you might have guessed this even if you hadn't seen Greenland's list or read this book.

The type of methodology used in studies such as Greenland's is known as *actuarial,* because it is essentially the same as that used by actuaries, the people employed by insurance companies to calculate the statistical likelihood of different kinds of accidents for different groups of the population. Actuaries, for example, have worked out that young men are more likely to have car accidents than older men or women, and as a result young men have to pay higher car insurance premiums. In this sense, being a young man is a 'predictor' of traffic accidents – or a risk factor – but this does not mean (a) that most young men will have traffic accidents, or (b) that other people will not have traffic accidents, or (c) that being a young man is, of itself, a *cause* of traffic accidents.

In relation to child protection work, there is a lot of muddled thinking about this sort of thing, which leads to many people having quite unrealistic ideas about the ability of professional agencies to predict abuse. I will return to this in Chapter 14. For the moment I simply make the point that there is no assessment tool that will tell you for certain which situations are dangerous and which are not and that, while risk factors or predictors such as those listed by Greenland do help to suggest in a general way what kinds of situations *may* result in abuse, none of them should be seen as an inevitable (or even necessarily a probable) *cause* of abuse.

Sexual abuse

Child sexual abuse does not have the same link with socioeconomic status as exists in the case of physical abuse and neglect. 'A growing number of studies have reported weak or no association between measures of family socioeconomic status and risks of CSA' (Fergusson and Mullen, 1999: 37–8). There are, however, statistical links between sexual abuse and marital dysfunction, the presence of step-parents in the family, parental alcoholism and parental criminality, though once again I emphasize that this does not mean that most step-parents or alcoholics are sexual abusers. The victims of sexual abuse are more likely to be female than male – the risk for girls being 'two to three times higher than the risk for males' according to Fergusson and Mullen (1999: 36) who, by combining the findings of a variety of studies, also arrive at the following 'weighted average' figures:

- Abusers of girls are 97.5 per cent male, while abusers of boys are 78.7 per cent male.
- Some 10.4 per cent of child sexual abuse involved close family members, including parents, step-parents and siblings.

- 'The most frequently reported perpetrators were acquaintances of the victim.' On average 47.8 per cent of perpetrators were described as acquaintances.
- 'CSA perpetrated by parent figures is relatively uncommon … with the weighted average estimate suggesting 3.3 per cent of CSA incidents were perpetrated by natural fathers.'
- The weighted average for step-parents was 2.7 per cent, but 'the fact that rates of perpetration by stepparents are similar to rates of perpetration by natural parents, suggests that stepparents are more likely to commit CSA, since there are far fewer stepparents in the population than natural parents.' Anderson et al. (1993) suggested that step-parents were roughly ten times more likely to sexually abuse than parents.

(List compiled from Fergusson and Mullen, 1999: 45, 47. These weighted average figures should be treated with some caution, since the studies they are compiled from often came up with widely divergent findings.)

Statistical associations and causality

As I have already warned, the fact that a certain factor is associated in a statistical sense with abuse, does not mean that abuse is inevitable, or even necessarily likely, when that factor is present.

Another important point to note is that an association between abuse and a given factor does not necessarily mean that this factor is or can be a *cause* of abuse. A statistical association between A and B, whatever A and B might be, tells you only that A is more common when B is present. This could mean that A is caused by B, or that B is caused by A, or that both are caused by another factor. Very commonly in complex human systems there is 'circular causality': A and B *cause each other*. (Imagine A is a thermostatic switch and B is the temperature of a room: each one controls the other.) These points may seem rather academic at this point but I will come back to them in a more concrete and specific way in later chapters. For the moment I am simply cautioning you against coming to simplistic conclusions about causation on the basis of statistical associations.

Patterns of maltreatment

Another way of approaching the question of what causes some parents to abuse or neglect their children is one that, in a medical context, would be described as 'clinical'. A clinical approach is based, not on actuarial calculations, but on observation of actual cases and of patterns that recur, and on a process of learning what helps and what does not, which allows tentative models to be developed as to what is going on. Adopting more of a 'clinical' than an 'actuarial' approach, I would suggest that, as an alternative to dividing up child maltreatment into physical abuse, sexual abuse and so on we could instead classify it according to the kinds of context in which it occurs, on the lines of the following:

1 *Premeditated abuse* in which the abuser is drawn towards some sort of abusive behaviour in order to meet some need or desire of his or her own, and in which the abuse is deliberate, planned – and fantasized about – in advance. The main instance of this sort of abuse is sexual abuse, but it could also be said to apply to some cases of feigned or induced illness as discussed

in Chapter 5, in which parents deliberately make their children ill, or get them diagnosed as ill, in order to meet psychological needs of their own. These kinds of behaviour are difficult to understand for those who are outside of it. Most adults probably cannot imagine *wanting* to sexually abuse a child, let alone acting on it. As a result, these premeditated abusive patterns are probably the least amenable to a 'commonsense' approach.

2   *Absence of love.* Even very abusive parents often love and are loved by their children but it can happen that emotional abuse or neglect is linked to the fact that a child is simply not loved, wanted or valued by the parent. This may be a temporary phase (many people have times when they just can't *feel* love for another person) but it can happen that there simply *is* no love.

3   *Stress-related abuse and neglect.* A good deal of abuse and neglect is linked to stresses of one kind or another, to which different individuals are more or less vulnerable. This kind of maltreatment is probably the easiest for most people to understand. Any parent who has ever snapped at her children after a difficult day at work has, in a small way, 'been there'. Under stress-related abuse and neglect we might also include abuse and neglect that occurs in situations where parents have drug and alcohol or mental health problems, but I will leave discussion of these situations to the next chapter.

4   *Competence-related abuse and neglect.* Some maltreatment of children is related to ignorance about children's needs. In most cases this sort of problem should not come under the umbrella of child protection at all, but it sometimes does, especially when issues of competence overlap with other issues.

Reality is always more complicated than any attempt to classify it. These categories do in fact overlap and shade one into another, but I hope that by using them in the following discussion I will highlight the fact that child abuse and neglect is not a simple unitary phenomenon, but something that can occur in many different ways for many different reasons.

Premeditated abuse

What makes an adult set out to deliberately abuse a child? Why do some adults become sexually preoccupied with children? One factor that is common to a significant proportion of sex abusers is that they themselves were sexually abused as children: 'estimates of the percentage of CSA perpetrators who report being sexually abused in childhood typically range from 20% to 30%', according to Fergusson and Mullen (1999: 49). But these figures still mean that the majority of sexual abuse perpetrators are not themselves victims of sexual abuse. Similarly, and it is important to note this in order to avoid unfairly stigmatizing abuse survivors, most victims of abuse do not become perpetrators.

However, if you look back at the discussion on the psychological effects of sexual abuse in the last chapter, you can see how some of these effects – such as 'traumatic sexualization' and the habit of 'dissociation' – could result in some individuals:

(a)   learning to view children and childhood as 'sexual',
(b)   coming to view closeness, intimacy and power in extremely sexual terms,
(c)   being able to 'dissociate' from normal inhibitions and taboos,
(d)   developing difficulties with forming normal relationships and finding closeness and intimacy in that way, and
(e)   developing a sense of powerlessness and a need to compensate for this by obtaining power over others (see, for example, Finkelhor and Browne, 1986; Erooga and Masson, 1999).

But sexual abuse in childhood is not the only developmental route through which an individual can grow to have children as his primary objects of sexual interest. Emotional immaturity, fear of adult relationships, a preoccupation with power and control and fear of rejection are all overlapping factors which may lead an individual down this pathway. Being sexually abused is just one of a number of experiences that may predispose him to have these particular characteristics.

As well as trying to understand sexual abuse in terms of its historical origin in a person's life, we can also look at it as a behaviour that sustains itself in the present, asking ourself the question as to what is it about this behaviour that is so powerfully self-reinforcing. Wolf (1984) proposed that offenders are typically individuals with low self-esteem who get into a cycle in which they retreat into isolation, using sexual fantasy and masturbation to make themselves feel better and to obtain an illusion of being in control. Fantasy then leads on to planning and carrying out actual abusive acts. Dawn Fisher summarizes the rest of Wolf's cycle as follows:

> Once they have committed the offence, itself a highly reinforcing event, the diminished sexual excitement following ejaculation (either as part of the abuse or subsequently through masturbation), is followed by a period of transitory guilt ... In seeking to reconstitute his self-image the offender typically uses further distorted thinking to alleviate his guilt and anxiety, by minimising or justifying the abuse and promising himself that he will not do the same again. However, underlying this he is left with the knowledge that he has committed a sexual offence, resulting in further damage to his self-esteem, bringing him back to the feelings he had at the start of the cycle. (Fisher, 1994: 19–20)

Once a person is on the pathway of sexual abuse it is very difficult to get off it and there are many striking parallels between the behaviour and thinking of sexual offenders with that of people addicted to drugs. Distorted thinking is characteristic of addictions of all kinds. This allows the addict to carry on doing something which he knows to be wrong – and harmful even to himself – by somehow denying to himself what he is doing. Interestingly these mental contortions closely resemble some of the defence mechanisms by which *victims* of abuse cope psychologically, by telling themselves 'this isn't happening to me', and it is worth noting that a significant proportion not only of sex offenders, but also of alcoholics and drug addicts, are themselves victims of childhood abuse.

Sexual abusers of children, like other addicts, become extremely skilled at minimizing and rationalizing their conduct. They get very good at concealing from themselves and others the extent of their problem and at releasing themselves from responsibility for their own behaviour by (a) blaming others and (b) mental compartmentalization, or 'splitting'. And, as the lives of other kinds of addict can become increasingly organized by their habit, so also can the lives of sexual abusers of children become organized around finding opportunities for more abusive behaviour. Interactions with others can then become essentially manipulative, not pursued for their own sake, but aimed at making new opportunities for abuse. Sexual abusers become highly skilled at manipulation, at identifying vulnerable children (typically children who are short of adult attention, and are perhaps already the victims of neglect or abuse), and 'grooming' them for abuse. They may also become adept at identifying vulnerable adults who will give them access to children (as in the novel *Lolita*, by Vladimir Nabokov).

These skills of manipulation, deception and self-deception, built up by constant practice, can make sexual abusers highly plausible. *It is not safe or sensible to make judgements about the dangers posed by such people, or their responsiveness to treatment, unless you have specialist training and have a sufficiently specialized role to allow you to accumulate a lot of experience in this area.*

Although the parallels between the behaviour of sexual abusers and other kinds of addict is, I think, striking (and I will return to them in the next chapter) there are of course also differences. There is, for one thing, a moral difference, in that drug addiction does not involve making another human being into an object of gratification in the way that sexual offenders do, even though it can often result in the needs of others being unnoticed or disregarded. Another factor found in sexual abusive behaviour but for which there is no exact parallel in the case of other addictions, is the way in which fantasy and masturbation (and often pornography) become part of the cycle, fuelling the sexual obsession and allowing the offender to not only 'groom' his victim for abuse but also, as it were, to *groom himself* for further offending.

Implications for assessment and intervention

Protecting children who have been sexually abused is generally a matter of ensuring that they have carers who are capable of preventing the abuser (or abusers) from being given further opportunities to abuse them. This often entails assessing, and trying to support and strengthen, the ability of other adults around the child to stand up to the abuser, and to recognize and resist his attempts at manipulation.

Of course, where the abuser is an important figure to the child, the ideal intervention entails helping the abuser to give up abusive behaviour, but the treatment of sexual offenders – and assessment of the risks that they continue to pose – is a difficult and complex area, and is not something that should be undertaken by professionals who do not have specialist knowledge and experience. In the absence of clear and compelling evidence to the contrary from an authoritative source, child protection plans need to be based on the assumption that a sexual abuser continues to present a high risk indefinitely if he is allowed unsupervised contact with a child.

Absence of love

> Not feeling loved by your parent is deeply painful. Your attachment figure is the person to whom you instinctively turn at times of need, but all you find is indifference, or in more extreme cases, loathing… But of course it is not just hurtful to feel that your well-being and safety are not uppermost in the mind of your carer, it is also frightening. If a parent rejects you, particularly when you are in a state of need or distress, then where might you find comfort or understanding? (Howe, 2005: 90)

It is important to acknowledge that some parents simply do not care about their children and deeply resent that child's existence and all the inconvenience that this causes. Some too feel this way about a specific one of their children, perhaps because of the circumstances of the child's birth or conception, or because the child is a disappointment in some way, or a reminder of someone or something that the parent would rather forget, or because of some aspect of their own childhood experience. It is a mistake to simply assume that, at some level, deep down, parents – and perhaps particularly mothers – *always* love their children. But a huge amount of shame and guilt is attached to admitting, even to yourself, that you do not love your own child. Indeed the idea is so shocking – remember the discussion on child protection and deep taboos in Chapter 4 – that it can be hard for professionals to hear such an admission even when it is made. ('You don't really mean that, surely!' is the sort of response that professionals may be tempted to make.) It is important to listen to what parents say about this and to help them say it because a great deal of courage is required on the parent's part.

Step-parents sometimes find it impossible to care for children who are not their own. Another situation in which love sometimes fails to happen is in adoption. Like the grafts which gardeners attempt between one plant and another, adoptions sometimes just do not 'take'. Adoptions of older children, in fact, may break down in as many as 40 or 50 per cent of cases (PIU, 2000) though of course most do so without becoming child protection cases, and I do not wish to suggest that in every case, the problem is a failure to learn to love the child.

Stress-related abuse and neglect

In order to think about the ways in which different kinds of stress may push adults towards physical abuse, emotional abuse or neglect, I find it helpful to draw upon the notion of *horizontal stressors, vertical stressors* and *system levels,* which I take from Betty Carter and Monica McGoldrick (1989). *Horizontal stressors* refer to challenging events that occur as we move through life, some of which are predictable, some of which are not. An illness, for example, would be a horizontal stressor, as would a car accident, or the birth of a child, or a school examination. *Vertical stressors,* on the other hand, are areas of difficulty that we carry from the past. Life becomes particularly stressful when horizontal and vertical stressors intersect. For example, a difficult exam is moderately stressful for most people, but may be far more stressful for a person from a family background in which a person's worth is measured by academic achievement. *System levels* are the different levels at which both horizontal and vertical stressors operate. Each individual encounters her own unique challenges and carries her own unique legacy from the past, but so does each family, community, or even nation.

Taking this simple model back into the arena of child abuse and neglect, you will see that some of the risk factors identified by Greenland (1987) could be seen as horizontal stressors – a child who is sick or cries a lot, for instance, or a parent's own illness. A parent's history of having been abused or neglected herself as a child, on the other hand, would be a vertical stressor. As in the example I gave in the previous paragraph, danger points are likely to arise when horizontal and vertical stressors interact. Thus a screaming child is a stressor for any parent, but if the parent was himself habitually ignored or shouted at when he was in distress as a child, he may well find a screaming child much more difficult to cope with than would a parent whose own parents consistently responded to his distress. For a parent whose own screams of distress were ignored, the sound of a screaming child may bring up powerful – even overwhelming – feelings of loneliness, impotence and rage. It is not difficult to see how such feelings may sometimes translate themselves into physical abuse. Sometimes they result in children being battered to death.

The risk factors in Greenland's list also describe stressors that operate at several different system levels. Each individual carries her own unique history. But stressors such as poverty, poor housing and unemployment may affect whole communities. And whole communities, too, may carry vertical stressors (such as, for instance, an awareness that the area where they live is seen by the rest of the town as a 'sink estate'). It is a very serious limitation of the inter-professional child protection system that it is largely powerless to address factors such as poverty, poor housing and unemployment, even though these clearly and demonstrably have a very direct impact on the ability of parents to cope. (I will return to this topic in Chapter 12.)

But one system level, other than the individual one, that it *is* possible to address at the casework level, is that of the family. It is important to remember that vertical stressors can be carried and reproduced by families over many generations, and that changing the way an individual operates may require changes to be made by those around her too, and for the whole family to operate in a different way.

Exercise 8.2

The following case is an instance of neglect, though I suspect that the British professional system would deal with the case as a 'child in need' rather than a 'child protection' case. What vertical and horizontal stressors are present in this situation?

Robert, aged 14, is picked up by the police at 2 a.m. with some friends in a disued lock-up garage, where they have been drinking and inhaling solvents and seem to intend to spend the rest of the night. It transpires that Robert has been away from home for two days, although his mother, Janice, a single parent, has not reported him missing.

Janice says he does what he likes and when she tries to stop him going out he shouts abuse at her and pushes her out of the way. He is taller and heavier than she is. He regularly stays out all night, and misses school nearly 50 per cent of the time. He also helps himself to money from his mother's purse. Janice is resigned and seemingly indifferent to this. Asked why she does not report him missing, she shrugs and says 'What's the point? Even if the police do find him he'll only go out again the next night.' She says he should be in care, because she can't do anything with him.

Janice is 42. Her own father walked out of the family home when Janice was six and did not maintain contact. Her mother remarried and Janice was abused by her step-father, sexually and physically, until her mother and her step-father separated when she was 12. Her mother could not cope with her, and at the age of 13 she entered the care system, after which her mother only had intermittent contact with her. She had several moves within the care system and suffered further abuse there at the hands of a male residential social worker.

The family live on state benefits. She has a younger son, John, aged ten, by a different father. John attends school and is presenting no difficult behaviour problems for Janice, or his school, as yet, though she says he is starting to copy Robert.

(Continued)

(Continued)

Comments on Exercise 8.2

The most obvious current – 'horizontal' – stressor in this situation is surely adolescence and the challenging behaviour associated with adolescence. Most parents find this difficult to cope with at times: it typically involves having to insist on certain boundaries against constant pressure to drop them. Janice seems to have abandoned any attempt to hold this line, and as a result her son is putting himself in some danger, apart from creating problems for himself in the future. Coping with this task alone as a single parent is probably harder than doing so with the support and reassurance of another parent, so being alone is another horizontal pressure. Another is poverty and its practical consequences.

Among the vertical (historic) stressors are, I suggest, the following:

- *Janice's history of abuse by men, and therefore her experience of powerlessness in relation to men. This must make it harder to stand up to a son who is now, physically, a young man.*
- *The fact that Janice's own mother felt unable to parent her after the age of 13. This must make it feel harder to parent a child who is older than that age.*
- *Janice's rejection by her own parents. This will make her vulnerable to feelings of rejection and prone to employ various psychological defences to ward off the anxiety and pain that rejection evokes. I suggest that Robert's angry defiance of her will feel like rejection and that a common defensive strategy would be to (a) give way to him to avoid his anger, and (b) shut down her own positive feelings for him so as to make his rejection of her less hurtful.*

You will see that the three examples of vertical stressors that I have suggested are, in the current situation, interacting with the horizontal stressor of Robert's adolescent transition, making it far harder to cope with than it would be for another parent who was not carrying the same baggage from the past.

I would suggest that an approach to this case that is based simply on demanding that Janice takes more responsibility for her son, is not likely to work, because she already has her answer: 'Take him away. I can't cope.' But taking Robert into care is unlikely to work either. To really address the difficulty would require addressing the patterns of behaviour and emotional response which they have got into as a result of their particular family history.

Parenting children is a stressful activity at times for all parents, but most parents manage to get through it without lapsing into seriously abusive behaviour. (I do not think that many parents could claim *never* to have behaved in an abusive or neglectful way.) My suggestion is that abusive or neglectful behaviour becomes more likely when the stresses of parenting are combined with other horizontal stressors from other sources, and/or with vertical stressors that are the legacy of the past.

Implications for assessment

Looking at the problem in this way, assessment becomes a matter of trying to identify the horizontal and vertical stressors, at various levels, that are contributing to the abusive or neglectful behaviour. The more difficult part of this is identifying the vertical stressors, which are of course invisible, and which individuals and families may not themselves be consciously aware of. But some of the patterns which might suggest the presence of powerful vertical stressors might include:

- Extreme distress/anger caused by a child crying or making demands.
- A preoccupation with order, tidiness or control, within which childish behaviour becomes a nuisance and a threat.
- A preoccupation with academic achievement. In my experience this is a not uncommon cause of abusive behaviour when children fail to meet parents' expectations. It may be more common in middle-class families, and more common in some cultures than others.
- An inability to say no to a child, or to set boundaries, resulting in a child becoming more and more demanding. This may result from feelings of powerlessness on the part of the parent which may well date back to childhood experience.
- Very negative and rejecting messages directed towards a child. Sometimes these simply reflect the fact that the child was never wanted.
- Particular children being singled out either for positive or negative attention as against other children in the family.
- Children being strongly identified with a particular parent, or with particular grandparents or other family members, suggesting that feelings about that family member are also being projected onto the child.

Implications for intervention

In a minority of cases, the conclusion of such an assessment may be that a parent simply does not have the emotional resources to cope adequately and safely with the demands of a child on top of the other things – both in the present, and from the past – that she has to deal with. More commonly though, such an assessment will identify stressors in the present and from the past which have contributed to abusive or neglectful behaviour. Sometimes a child protection plan may be able to actually reduce or remove some of the present (horizontal) stressors. If part of the problem is that child and parent never get a break from each other, for instance, it may be possible to arrange for the child to have some day care. If part of the problem is overcrowded housing, then it may be possible to negotiate a move to a bigger place. Some horizontal stressors – lack of money for instance – may not be within the scope of child protection professionals to tackle, though, and a child protection plan may be able to offer no more than opportunities for parents to discuss different strategies for dealing with their situation.

In the case of vertical stressors, the best approach varies from individual to individual and family to family. Some people find it helpful to develop a clearer understanding of 'where they are coming from' and why they are distressed by particular things. Some may need help to move on from painful events in the past, which they have never acknowledged or grieved, and which therefore have become volcano-like sources of unpredictable distress. Some may respond better to a more pragmatic approach, aimed less at understanding the past and more at finding different ways of behaving in the future, which will allow them to leave past patterns behind them. Opportunities to talk, reflect and be listened to are important for any of these approaches.

Work on such matters does begin to cross over into the realm of what would be called 'therapy', and child protection professionals need to consider, in consultation with family members, whether they are the best placed people to do it. Do they possess the necessary skills and experience, or the time? Would family members prefer to work on these difficult issues with someone who was not also involved in the policing and administrative aspects of child protection work? It is difficult in a child protection climate that is much preoccupied with information gathering and information sharing, but I would suggest that one issue that needs to be considered when entering this sort of area of work is how people's privacy is going to be protected.

Professional intervention as a stressor

For most families intervention by child protection agencies is a considerable source of stress in its own right. In many cases it will interact with, and activate, vertical stressors. For poor families, social work intervention may be yet one more instance of humiliation at the hands of the state. A parent who was herself in the care of social services as a child, and who was unhappy there – or even abused there, as in the example given in Exercise 8.2 – might find the intervention of a social worker into her family life particularly difficult. If an intervention has the effect simply of adding to the stressors on a family, then it is likely to actually *increase* rather than decrease the risk of child maltreatment.

The implications of this are that, first, as I discussed in Chapter 2, it is sensible as far as possible not to use the 'child protection' route as a way of helping children, if there are other, less intimidating ways of providing help. Secondly, if the child protection route must be followed, it is essential that something is actually offered to the family, and that their difficulties and their efforts to cope are acknowledged.

Competence-related abuse and neglect

It sometimes happens that behaviour appears at first sight to be neglectful or abusive but seems in fact to be the result of genuine ignorance about the needs of a child or the role of a parent. Some adults may have lacked appropriate role models while growing up; some are very isolated and have little access to sources of advice. Some parents have wildly unrealistic expectations of what a child should be capable of at a given stage of development, or simply do not know what children need in terms of diet, or physical care, or stimulation. Some have no idea as to how to set boundaries to keep them safe. Occasionally even cases of sexual abuse may have a competence component, if the perpetrator is a child or has a learning disability and seems to have a genuine lack of understanding about appropriate sexual behaviour.

When there seems to be a lack of knowledge or of parenting skills, an appropriate form of intervention is education: the provision of advice, information, instruction or role models. In my experience, however, it is seldom the case that apparent abuse or neglect is *purely* competence based. If a parent was consistently dressing a child in ways which were inappropriate to the weather, for instance, I would be hesitant to conclude that this was the result of simple ignorance, since observation alone would indicate that a child was too cold or too hot. Failure to notice the child's discomfort would therefore seem to me to indicate that the parent was not very 'switched onto' their child's needs, perhaps because of the existence of other stressors which were taking away a great deal of the parent's attention.

Another reason why a parent might not pick up on a child's needs is lack not of competence but of *confidence*. Some people have learnt not to trust their own judgement or commonsense, perhaps as the result of consistently receiving negative messages. A purely educational approach, aimed at imparting factual information about child-rearing, may sometimes be counterproductive in such cases, since it may have the effect of further 'deskilling' the parent: confirming that they do not know what to do and cannot trust their own judgement. As Tucker and Johnson (1989) put it, support offered to parents should be 'competence promoting' rather than 'competence inhibiting'.

Tucker and Johnson's comments were addressed in particular to those working with mothers with learning difficulties. In families where parents have learning difficulties, issues of competence are particularly relevant, and often contentious, and I will separately discuss this area of work in Chapter 10.

Abuse by children

I will conclude this chapter by noting that child abuse can be perpetrated by other children and teenagers as well as adults. In fact, in the case of sexual abuse, abuse by children and young people constitutes a very substantial proportion of all detected abuse. Looking at criminal statistics for England and Wales, Erooga and Masson (1999: 1–2) found that 'children and young people aged between 10 and 21 years accounted for 47 per cent of all cautions for sexual offence; and 13.5 per cent of findings of guilt as a result of a court process'.

Adolescence is the time when a large proportion of adult offenders report having started out on their abusive careers: as many as 50 per cent, according to Abel et al. (1985). This means that identifying cases of abuse by children is important not only for the sake of the current victims but also as a means of 'nipping in the bud' abusive careers in which perhaps hundreds of children might subsequently be abused by a single, persistent offender. As with other kinds of abuse, however, no infallible checklist exists that would allow us to recognize in advance those individuals who will go on to become abusers, but among the factors associated with sexually abusive behaviour by children and young people, are the following:

- Abnormal sexual environments, including families where sexual boundaries were too rigid or too relaxed.
- Sexualized models of compensation, where sex is seen as a comfort in difficult times.
- A parental history of sexual or physical abuse.
- History of drug or alcohol use in the family.
- Parental loss.
- Social isolation, lack of confidence, lack of social skills and maladaptive coping skills. (Summarized from Calder et al., 1997: 51.)

Chapter summary

This chapter has looked at the reasons that child maltreatment happens – the when and why of child maltreatment – including the psychological origins of abusive behaviour. I have looked at:

- 'risk factors' or 'predictors' of abuse, what they are, and what their limitations are in predicting specific instances of abuse
- different ways in which abuse or neglect can arise – I divided these into 'premeditated abuse', absence of love, 'stress-related abuse and neglect' and 'competence-related abuse and neglect'
- 'premeditated abuse' and sexual abuse in particular; its possible origins, both in terms of the past experience of abusers, and in terms of the ways that abusive behaviour reinforces and maintains itself in the present
- absence of love as a factor in some cases of abuse and neglect
- the ways in which stress, both in the 'here and now' and from the past, can be a factor in abuse
- the extent to which some forms of neglect and abuse may arise from lack of competence
- abuse by children and adolescents.

In the next chapter I will move on to look at two particular contexts in which child protection issues can arise: families where one or more parents abuses alcohol or drugs, and families where one or both parents have mental health problems.

9 Parents with Substance Use and Other Mental Health Problems

- Substance use and parenting
- Direct effects on children
- Direct effects on parenting
- Social effects
- Distorted thinking and family systems
- Parental substance use: assessment and intervention
- Parents with other mental health problems
- Good enough parenting
- Supporting families

Parental mental health problems and drug and alcohol problems are present in a substantial proportion of all families referred to child protection agencies. Kearney et al. (2003) concluded, on the basis of interviews with social workers in childcare teams, that 'at least 50% and in some teams up to 90% of parents on their caseload had either mental health problems, alcohol or substance misuse problems' (2003: 8), though one should bear in mind that such statistics are dependent on how terms such as 'mental health problem' are defined. In this chapter I will consider first the issues involved in working with families where the parents have drug and alcohol problems and then those involved where the parents have other mental health problems.

Substance use and parenting

I am sure that most readers of this book use alcohol, a substantial number use nicotine and a considerable number use or have used various illegal substances (not to mention prescribed drugs). I am guessing however that only a small proportion of these would choose to identify their substance use as a problem. How precisely we *define* 'problem use' or 'abuse' of alcohol or drugs is, of itself, problematic. There is also a great deal of controversy about the nature of drug 'addiction' and 'dependency'. See Davies (1997) for instance, for a challenge to conventional notions about 'addiction'. Or look at Kroll and Taylor (2003: 57–84) for a discussion on different ways of conceptualizing substance misuse and the pros and cons of viewing it as an 'illness' on the one hand, or as an act of choice on the other.

From the point of view of the child protection professional, though, drug and alcohol use become problem behaviours if they impact on a person's capacity to parent. They seem to be factors in a significant number of cases. Cleaver et al. (1999) quote studies which suggest that substance use problems (i.e. problems with drugs or alcohol) are identified as a feature of 20 per cent of initial child protection referrals. This proportion rose to 25 per cent of all cases where follow-up interviews occurred. Summarizing research on the effects on children of problem drinking by their parents, Velleman (2001: 36) concludes that 'many children experience very negative childhoods, often experiencing high levels of both violence and inconsistency ...' and that

> many children show very negative effects of these experiences, having problems in a variety of areas, showing higher levels of behavioural disturbance and anti-social behaviour, or emotional difficulties, of school problems, and a more difficult transition from childhood than do children who have not had this upbringing. These effects are frequently worse if both parents have alcohol problems, or if the problem drinking occurs at home. (Velleman, 2001: 36)

While violence can be associated with alcohol abuse in particular, neglect is the most common form of child maltreatment associated with drug abuse:

> Neglect of children, rather than physical or sexual abuse, is the most likely reason for intervention by social services in families where one or both parents have drug problems. (Barnard and McKegany, 2004)

I don't want to imply that all adults who use illegal drugs or who have problems with alcohol are poor parents. It is important *not* to make this assumption. Actually the vast majority of parents in the UK and most other Western countries use alcohol, illegal drugs or both and still manage to be good parents. Even those who use drugs or alcohol heavily and at the expense of their own health, may still manage to meet their day-to-day responsibilities and act as caring and responsible parents.

Labelling all drug users or drug addicts or alcoholics as 'bad parents' not only does an injustice to all of these people and to their children, but also discourages people with substance misuse problems from seeking help, for fear that their children will be taken from them. An American study of cases coming to court (Murphy et al., 1991) found that drug misusing parents were half again as likely to have their children permanently taken away from them by the courts as alcohol misusing parents, and that drug misusing parents were less likely to take up services offered to them than people identified as having alcohol problems. Discussing this finding, Velleman (2001: 39) comments that there are 'major implications here for care services ..., with the obvious point needing to be re-made very often: that the issue is whether or not parenting ability and actual behaviour is satisfactory, not whether one or more parents use or misuse hard drugs.'

On the other hand it *is* the case that a wide range of studies show a statistical association between drug use and child maltreatment, and especially child neglect. If parents use drugs it does not automatically mean they are bad parents, but (for whatever reason) people with drug and alcohol problems seem considerably more *likely* to have parenting problems than the population at large (for example: Chaffin et al., 1996; Forrester, 2000; Barnard and McKegany, 2004). We should, however, bear in mind the following:

- The causal link between substance abuse and child maltreatment is a two-way one. Cohen and Densen-Gerber (1982) found that, of patients being treated for drug or alcohol addiction, 84 per cent reported having experienced physical abuse or neglect as children. Drug use may be seen as an attempt to 'self-medicate' in order to alleviate anxiety and distress, which may be the result of such experiences. It may also be seen as an attempt to establish a sort of control over one's environment and one's state of mind – not unlike eating disorders, self-harming and a whole range of other 'obsessive' or 'addictive' behaviours – which is particularly attractive to people with early childhood experiences of finding themselves in frightening situations over which they had no control.
- Rather than either one causing the other, both drug use *and* poor parenting may be the result of poor childhood experiences. 'Many substance-abusing parents say they had loveless childhoods, believing that their parents either had little time for them, or actively rejected them' (Howe, 2005: 184). Philip Flores proposes that addiction can actually be viewed as an attachment disorder in which 'the vulnerable individual's attachment to chemicals serves both as an obstacle to and as a substitute for interpersonal relationships' (Flores, 2004: 4).
- Poverty is another factor known to be implicated both in child maltreatment and in substance abuse:

    Put simply, addiction fills voids. These voids can be psychological, social, emotional, spiritual and temporal. Mass unemployment is a most efficient way of creating these voids and heroin addiction comes along to fill them. The symbiotic relationship between unemployment and heroin addiction in the UK started in the early 1980s and has been maintained to this day. (Gilman, 2000: 23)

- Substance abuse and parenting problems may be linked in a 'vicious circle' (an example from Howe, 2005, is given shortly), where each exacerbates and perpetuates the other.

Drug use and poor parenting are linked in a complex, multi-directional web that includes other factors such as poverty, mental health problems and family history. But there are a number of ways in which parental drug use – and the lifestyle which may be associated with it – can impact very severely on the well-being of children.

Direct effects on children

The use of alcohol, heroin and other opiates and cocaine during pregnancy can result in impaired growth. Alcohol use in particular can result in permanent physical harm. Foetal Alcohol Syndrome can result in delayed development, permanent learning impairment, facial abnormalities and long-term behavioural effects (Robinson and Rhoden, 1998: 81–2).

A common result of the use of heroin during pregnancy is that babies become addicted to opiates *in utero* and display withdrawal symptoms at birth. Withdrawal symptoms can make babies extremely difficult to manage, even for experienced foster-carers: they may show chronic distress and seem impossible to settle or comfort. Neonatal Abstinence Syndrome, as this is called, can produce a range of effects including: irritability, hyperactivity, abnormal sensitivity to touch, accelerated cardiac action, an increased respiratory rate, changes in the sleeping/waking rhythm, wild sucking at fists, shrill and long phases of screaming tremors, shivering, sneezing, perspiration, fever, vomiting, diarrhoea, inhibited feeding and, in some cases, convulsions (Leopold and Steffan, 1997).

Apart from these *in utero* effects, there are also some other health risks to which children of substance misusing parents may be exposed after birth. They can be at risk of accidental overdosing if drugs are not safely stored. They may also be exposed to illnesses associated with drug use, including – in the case of users of intravenous drugs – HIV and hepatitis.

Direct effects on parenting

Specific behavioural changes resulting from drug use can affect the quality of the parent–child relationship. The use of amphetamines can result in anxiety, paranoia and even psychosis (SCODA, 1997: 12). Alcohol is a disinhibitor, which can reduce an individual's ability to control violent impulses.

More generally, the effects of the use of drugs and/or alcohol on the functioning of users can make parents less available to a child. It is worth bearing in mind that drugs and alcohol affect parental functioning both while the parents are actually intoxicated by the substance and during the times in between when they may be tired, have poor concentration and little energy and feel unwell. A parent's functioning will be adversely affected by drink, for instance, both while drunk and while hung over.

However it is important to note too that some people claim to be *better* parents on drugs (see Kroll and Taylor, 2003: 113) since drugs lift their mood and enable them to cope. After all, doctors commonly prescribe drugs for depression, anxiety or inability to sleep and it is a curious fact that while society tends to try and discourage people from using mind-altering drugs, it frequently actively encourages – and sometimes even *compels* – people with other types of mental health problems to accept mind-altering drugs as treatment.

Parental unavailability and attachment

I've already noted that the direct effects of drugs and alcohol on parents' functioning can result in lack of physical availability of the parent. Substance abuse can also result in a lack of emotional availability if a parent's primary focus becomes their drug habit, rather than their children's needs.

This lack of physical and emotional availability of drug-using parents can cause poor supervision of children and resulting accidents. It may also explain why a variety of research studies have 'consistently found impaired attachment patterns in substance-abusing mothers and their infants, including decreased maternal responsivity and disturbances in infants' attachment behaviours …' (Guterman, 2001: 118). The development of a secure attachment requires parental responsivity to the needs of a child. The child's attachment to the parent cannot be fully reciprocated if the parent's primary attachment and first priority is in fact their habit – and if the habit itself represents an attempt by the parent to cope with distress arising from the parent's own unmet attachment needs as a child.

Imagine, for instance, the case of a baby who is demanding and hard to please as a result of Neonatal Abstinence Syndrome and has had to spend some time in a special care unit:

> When these infants eventually do return home to their mothers and fathers, they are in urgent need of maximum high-quality care. They are likely to make heavy demands on their parents' caregiving capacities. And yet it is the very intense nature of these attachment needs that is likely to frighten and dysregulate the parent. A vicious circle sets in. The greater the child's needs, the more helpless and hostile is the parent likely to feel, and the more likely it is that he or she will turn to drugs and alcohol … (Howe, 2005: 187)

Role reversal

Coleman and Cassell (1995) observe that in some cases children of substance misusers

> may be put in reverse caring roles in which they have to look after their parents instead of their own needs being met. For example, a 6 year old girl regularly brought her [alcoholic] father to his psychiatric appointments because he could not always find his way and needed prompting about time. (Coleman and Cassell, 1995: 187)

This type of role reversal can result in an attachment between parents and children which in a sense is very strong, but is nevertheless not secure or helpful to the child:

> Although parents' emotional attachment to their children was assessed as 'mostly very high' in relation to both mothers and fathers … in the sense that parents talked about their love and devotion to their children … this was not always indicative of the rounded attachment required for healthy development … Indeed, this high level of emotional 'attachment' often resulted in a degree of intense dependency which was unhelpful to the child. In other words, the child was seen as a therapeutic presence and a source of comfort, to help the parent through a difficult time. (Kroll and Taylor, 2003: 50, discussing research by Klee et al., 1998)

Stress, anxiety and unpredictability of care

Non-availability of parental figures is difficult for children, but so too is unpredictability. Robinson and Rhoden (1998: 82), in a book on the children of alcoholics, discuss psychosomatic symptoms – headaches, nervous tics, upset stomachs – shown by children who are having to contain constant anxiety about a situation at home where they do not feel psychologically or physically safe. They include the following account by one of the authors of his own personal experience of growing up with an alcoholic father:

> Weekends were difficult for me as a young adult because, as a child, that's when the crises with my father would erupt. Anytime there was quiet, it was the calm before the storm, and the rapid-fire jolt of my father's inebriated outbursts would hit me like a jackhammer. Waking up on

Saturday mornings or holidays with nothing to do make me panic stricken. I felt out of control and that something terrible could happen during those idle hours. (Bryan Robinson, in Robinson and Rhoden, 1998: 87)

Social effects

Problem use of illegal drugs and alcohol has a number of social consequences which can impact on family life. In particular the cost of maintaining supplies of addictive drugs drains financial resources to the extent that daily life for the addict can be dominated by activity – including criminal activity – aimed at obtaining money to buy more. This can impact on the addict's children in a very direct way if insufficient money is left over for food, clothing, fuel and so on. It is also yet another way in which problem substance use can result in the parent being unavailable for the child.

Children may also be drawn into the business of obtaining drugs in various ways. They may have to accompany a parent trying to obtain supplies of drugs, or in some instances they may become more actively involved, acting as couriers, or becoming involved in crime aimed at funding the habit. The issues are slightly different in the case of alcohol, since alcohol is legal, easier to obtain and, relatively speaking, cheap compared with drugs such as opiates and cocaine, but alcohol use too may place an intolerable financial burden on a family (as indeed can other, non-chemical addictive behaviours such as gambling).

The financial burden of substance abuse can undoubtedly result in standards of care that fall quite clearly into the categories of neglect and emotional abuse. But it is worth noting here that this is a more acute problem for *poor* families. The children of a rock star with a drug dependency are clearly not likely to go hungry as a result of their parent's habit.

The lifestyle of an addict also carries with it risks of imprisonment and/or hospitalization with the resulting impact on children as the result of separations. Children may also be exposed to an environment in which drug use and/or drug dealing is normal. They may also be exposed to frightening events, such as overdoses, police raids or bizarre behaviour. Normal daily routines may be impossible to maintain.

Distorted thinking and family systems

Alcoholics and drug addicts engage in distorted thinking which in some ways is similar to that of paedophiles. They can become adept at rationalizing behaviour which is harmful to themselves and others, at minimizing that behaviour, at 'splitting' themselves – for example simultaneously sincerely believing that they are going to stop the habit while at the same time actively working on plans to obtain more drugs – and at presenting a plausible front to the world. And, not unlike paedophiles, they may become skilled at co-opting others in support of their habit. These mental manoeuvres can amount to a radical distortion of reality, in which feeding the habit becomes in practice more important than feeding the children, even while in theory the addicted person insists and believes that the opposite is true.

Exercise 9.1

Tommy (four months old) is the child of Frank (21) and Wendy (29). The family are known to the social services department because of concerns on the part of health professionals at the time of Tommy's birth that Frank's heroin addiction might affect his parenting capacity, but the health professionals agreed to offer support and to refer back to social services if necessary – and up to now there have been no concerns about the standard of care offered to Tommy. According to the family doctor, Frank dotes on the baby, and says being a father is the best thing that has ever happened to him.

Last night, the police arrested Frank attempting to break into a shop. Frank then told the police that he was concerned for his son, who he had left at home on his own. The police went round to Frank's house to find Tommy in a cot in front of an electric fire, very overheated and screaming. In the room around him were syringes and other signs of drug use. A piece of clothing hanging on the fireguard had started to singe and smoke. Frank told the police that Wendy had gone out to see a friend, leaving him in charge of Tommy. He says he knows he should not have gone out, but he was desperate to buy heroin and had no money to do so.

A woman police officer waited at the house for Wendy's return. She reported that Wendy seemed drunk or possibly under the influence of drugs on her return, but seemed to be capable of caring for Tommy. Wendy seemed annoyed at Frank for going out when he was supposed to be looking after Tommy but, in the opinion of this officer, she was not seriously upset about what had happened and did not seem to see its seriousness.

Police records show that both Frank and Wendy have been charged before with minor drug-related offences and other offences such as shoplifting. On one occasion a year ago, the police were called out to a domestic dispute. Wendy had alleged that Frank had punched her and she had a black eye coming up, but when the police arrived she seemed to want to shrug it off and did not want to press charges.

What child protection issues are raised by the information given so far?

Comments on Exercise 9.1

Tommy does not seem to be immediately at risk in the care of Wendy. No one is alleging that Wendy (or indeed Frank) have acted in a way that was deliberately intended to harm Tommy. But this incident falls clearly into the category of neglect. In pursuit of his own needs, Frank has placed Tommy both in physical danger and in the situation of no one on hand to come to him if frightened or distressed.

Could this be a one-off incident (as Frank may possibly maintain)? Well, the evidence so far suggests that Frank's drug use, at any rate, is not simply a one-off. There is evidence of drug use in the flat, there are previous drug offences. But in particular the fact that he was apparently so desperate to get money to buy drugs there that he was not even able to wait until Wendy was back seems to me to suggest that Frank may have difficulty in making even the physical safety of his child a higher priority than maintaining his drug habit.

But perhaps, now that she knows the risk of Frank abandoning him, Wendy may be relied upon to make sure that Tommy is not left alone again. Again, this is something to look at, but it does appear that such a conclusion should not be drawn too readily. We have the police officer's observation that she seemed not to grasp the seriousness of what happened. We have evidence in the past she was resigned to accepting violence from Frank. There are also reasons to believe that she is also a drug user.

An added layer of complexity occurs when we consider the possibility that drug addiction may serve a purpose for the functioning of a family as a whole:

> Frequently the addiction serves a purpose in maintaining family stability. Remove the addiction and the unmentioned fear of the family is that it will fall apart … Therefore, while the family may protest loudly about the misery of addiction, giving up their roles in this and accepting a temporarily unbalanced and addiction-free family, while developing new roles, may be too difficult for them to deal with. This would result in family members having to address underlying issues that remain unresolved all the time that an addiction exists. (Watts, 2000: 98)

If 'addiction fills voids' it follows that breaking an addiction will leave a gap in the life of an individual, a feeling of emptiness. The feeling of emptiness is unpleasant and people feel a strong need to fill the gap somehow. The point I am now making is that this gap may not only be experienced by the individual, but by a whole family, which may have effectively organized itself around the maintenance of an addictive pattern. The family's social networks, its daily routines, its dramas and excitements, its identity, may all have been constructed around obtaining and using drugs. Not only for an individual but also for a family, breaking an addiction may not be the 'solution' that it might seem to an outsider. It may present new and difficult problems.

Parental substance use: assessment and intervention

Some people are able quite successfully to separate out their substance use from their parenting. Rosalyn Coleman and Diana Cassell give the following example:

> A 35 year old mother of three young children had been using methadone for 5 years as a treatment for heroin dependency. During the day she only used methadone to 'keep her straight' (i.e. so that she would not have withdrawal effects), but on some evenings, or after a row with her husband, she used heroin, which made her drowsy. When this occurred, she would ask her husband to be available for the children. (Coleman and Cassell, 1995: 187)

This demonstrates that an assessment of a family cannot look simply at *whether* a parent uses drugs, but must examine *how* the drug use fits into the broader picture. In those cases where substance use does impact on parenting, though, assessment will need to include the motivation and ability of the parent to stop or modify their pattern of substance use, and any intervention would need to include steps to address and monitor the drug and alcohol use, as well as to deal with whatever specific aspects of parenting are placing the children at risk. The workers involved need to be mindful of the difficulties for substance users themselves, and for their families, in the early stages of recovery from an addiction, and need to ensure that both individuals and families receive adequate emotional and practical support.

One of the challenges of working with drug-using families is that the work spans not just several agencies but two different multi-agency systems (child protection systems and substance abuse systems) with different traditions, rules and priorities. Michael Murphy and Fiona Harbin propose that:

Two different assessment processes, that would normally be completed by practitioners in both systems, need to come together as a three-stage process that measures both substance misuse and its subsequent impact on the child. (Murphy and Harbin, 2000: 3)

The three stages they propose are (with my own comments and interpolations added):

1 The use of the substance

Addressing these questions will fall more in the area of expertise of the drug and alcohol service professionals, rather than the child protection professionals:

- What substances are being used – and what are their effects?
- The extent and context of drug/alcohol use. Is it recreational use only or an addiction?
- What are the cost implications of use, and what does this leave the family to spend on other things? How is the habit funded? (Drug dealing? Other crime? Prostitution?)
- What are the lifestyle implications of using, and maintaining supplies of, drugs/alcohol? (Who with? Where? When?)

2 The effect on substance use on parenting

These questions need to be addressed both by the drug service and child protection service professionals:

- What are the parents' own experiences of being parented, and what are their expectations of themselves as parents?
- How available are the parents to the children as a source of protection, care, support, attention and control – and to what extent is this availability affected by substance misuse?
- Do the parents protect the children from exposure to their drug/alcohol use?
- Do the parents involve the children in any way in the business of obtaining drugs, or obtaining funds for drugs (for example, by acting as couriers)?
- Do the parents place the children at physical risk from drug/alcohol use (for example, by leaving used needles where children might pick them up)?
- Are the parents able to prioritize the children's needs over drug/alcohol use – and if so at what level (needs for food, needs for physical safety, needs for attention)?
- Are parents willing to stop or modify their drug/alcohol use, if this is necessary to improve their care of their children?

3 The child's needs

These questions would be addressed mainly by the child protection agencies but require an understanding of the drug use itself, and its relationship to stress and anxiety:

- What are the child's current needs, taking into account his developmental stage and individual history?
- What other sources of support and help are available for the child?
- What sort of demands is the child making on the adults? (Has the child got a disability, for instance, or is the child presenting difficult behaviour problems?)
- Are the child's demands such as to become a stressor which may impact on the parents' drug/alcohol use?

Parents with other mental health problems

In the view of Sylvia Duncan and Peter Reder (2003: 200), substance misuse is 'the most worrying of parental mental health problems' and is 'particularly identified as a risk factor for child abuse'. However, other types of mental health problem are also commonly present in families where there are child protection issues, and I will now move on to look at these. 'Mental health problem' or 'mental illness' are terms which can be defined in many ways. Various statistics are commonly cited about the incidence of mental health problems in the population (MIND, 2006, for instance quotes figures suggesting that between one in four and one in six people is suffering from some form of 'mental distress' at any one time in the UK), but such figures depend on how broad or narrow a definition is used. Most of us experience *some* problems with our mental health (just as most of us make *some* use of alcohol or drugs) but people diagnosed as having more extreme mental health problems such as schizophrenia or bipolar disorder are in fact relatively rare (according to MIND, 2006, the UK incidence of each is around 1 per cent of the population).

I will not attempt a definition of 'mental health problem' or 'mental illness' here. My position, as with drug and alcohol problems, will be a pragmatic one: some people experience problems with their mental functioning to a degree that this impacts upon, or threatens to impact upon, their ability to protect and care for their children. Sometimes these problems are the result of symptoms which are generally recognized and defined by a particular psychiatric label such as 'depression', 'schizophrenia' or 'personality disorder'.

Like drug and alcohol problems, other adult mental health problems such as depression have a two-way relationship with childhood abuse. Like substance abuse problems, they are commonly linked to the sufferer's own experience of childhood abuse or neglect. They also impact on the sufferer's ability to parent in somewhat similar ways to those discussed previously in relation to drug and alcohol problems, as will be apparent in the following discussion.

'There is no doubt that mental illness in parents may represent a risk for their children', comments Amy Weir (1999: 2), citing research showing a high incidence of depression, anxiety and personality disorders among the parents of abused children. David Howe, writing specifically about depression, concludes that:

> Severe and chronic maternal depression predicts increased rates of poor self-regulation, poor peer relationships, negative self-image, behavioural problems, problems with sleep, a proneness to inactivity, weak academic performance, and mood disorders in children. Some children are socially withdrawn. Many have problems of concentration and deficits in attention. (Howe, 2005: 192)

This does not mean that every parent who has depression or some other mental health problem is incapable of parenting a child: this is very far from this case. However, there are a number of ways in which mental health problems can impact severely on the quality of a parent's relationship with a child.

Non-availability or unpredictable availability of parents

A parent who is depressed – or one who is preoccupied with her own internal state – may not be available to a child, physically or emotionally. 'Being emotionally unavailable to others, including one's children, is strictly limited if you are depressed', as Howe puts it (2005: 191) and this can be devastating because children rely on their carers not only for practical care but for feedback, encouragement and comfort. As I discussed earlier in the chapter, parental non-availability can have several consequences, including the physical dangers associated with lack of supervision but also the emotional harm that is done by the absence of a secure attachment figure.

Unpredictable availability of a parent can be particularly difficult for a child to cope with. It is hard to know how to approach somebody when their responses could be either extremely positive or extremely negative, and not knowing can result in anxiety about relationships in general. This can particularly be difficult for children whose parents suffer from bipolar depression:

> Depressed caregiving might result in extreme withdrawal, gross understimulation and disengagement. In other cases it can produce hostile, intrusive, excited, over-stimulating, grandiose, yet inconsistent and distracted parent–child interactions. Parents who suffer bipolar depression can display both types of caregiving as they swing from manic euphoria to depressed withdrawal. Mothers with bipolar depression put infants at greatest risk of forming insecure disorganized attachments … Underlying both types of parenting, however, is insensitivity and a lack of attunement. The caregiving lacks spontaneity. It is not child-centred or child-minded. (Howe, 2005: 190)

Parental non-availability can be a consequence of mental health problems other than depression, for example if a parent is preoccupied with delusional ideas, obsessions or irrational anxieties to the extent that this prevents the parent from being able to attend to the child. Amy Weir points out that drugs given as *treatment* for mental illness, such as some major tranquillizers, may also impact on a parent's availability (Weir, 1999: 2).

Distorted thinking and inappropriate or frightening behaviour

Apart from affecting the *availability* of the parent, parental mental illness can affect the quality and content of the parent–child relationship. Schizophrenia can result in paranoid delusions, for instance. For a small child, dependent on her parents to explain and interpret the world, this can be profoundly disturbing. (Imagine being three years old and living with parents who believe that alien invaders are coming into the house through the television set.) Schizophrenia and other conditions can also result in highly inappropriate behaviour, which, as Sandra Lancaster observes, can be confusing and damaging for a child struggling to make sense of it:

> The usual process of attending to cues in interaction with the child may not be present in parenting by a mentally ill mother. Instead, the parent may respond with inappropriate affect. If a child is distressed and his or her mother responds with laughter or stares blankly at them, the child will need to make some interpretation of this experience. Without knowledge, or the cognitive capacity to understand such knowledge, the egocentricity of the young child will mean that they are more likely to take some responsibility for the parent's response. (Lancaster, 1999: 16–17)

Lancaster goes on to comment that a child 'is particularly at risk for developing later disorders (including psychosis) where the mother's interpersonal boundaries are blurred and the mother has incorporated the child into her delusional system' (Lancaster, 1999: 17).

A parent whose mood and behaviour are unpredictable or inexplicable is frightening because a parent is the very person on whom the child relies to provide a safe, secure environment, even more so if the behaviour includes threats of violence or self-harm.

Role reversal

I have already discussed role reversal, in which the child parents the parent, as it sometimes occurs in relation to the children of parents with drug or alcohol problems. It can also occur in relation to other mental health problems. Weir quotes the following comment of a 14-year-old girl trying to cope with her mother's bipolar depression:

> The worst part is when you're not sure how ill she is and if you should call the doctor or a friend. Sometimes she just cries and cries. My sister had to do lots of housework when mum was ill. She didn't hate mum but she got a bit mad and felt she was the mum, and mum was the child. (Weir, 1999: 3)

I do not wish to imply here that it is necessarily inappropriate for children to care for their parents because in many respects and in many situations this is entirely appropriate. A child may provide physical care to a disabled parent and still receive from that parent warmth, guidance and emotional support. The harm comes, though, when all the care flows in that same direction and the child is required to put her own childhood and her own needs in abeyance in order to meet the needs of a parent:

> This compulsive caregiving strategy helps children avoid feeling there is nothing they can do to increase their feelings of security, but it comes at a developmental price ... Parentified children might be good at recognizing other people's emotional states, but they are poor at understanding their own. (Howe, 2005: 194)

Acute dangers

Occasionally, parental mental illness results in an acute threat to a child's physical safety, when the parent's delusional system and/or emotional state leads the parent to feel compelled to kill or harm the child in some way. It is very rare for children to be killed by their parents, but parental mental illness is implicated in a substantial proportion of cases where this does occur.

Parents may kill their children as a result of delusional ideas: 'I killed her by pushing her head under water, my hands were round her neck – I had to do it before the Mafia got to her', said a parent cited by Falkov (1996: 2). One scenario that can occur is that of 'a severely depressed parent [who] may... talk about their child as though they were an extension of themselves, posing the risk of an altruistic murder of the child as well as suicide by the adult' (Duncan and Reder, 2003: 206). This pattern seems to be particularly common in Sweden where one study of child homicides found that over 60 per cent had occurred in the context of the suicide or attempted suicide of the killer (Somander and Rammer, 1991).

Adrian Falkov conducted a survey of 100 child deaths reviewed in the UK under Section 8 of the *Working Together* guidelines (Department of Health, 1991), and found that 32 contained 'clear evidence of parental psychiatric morbidity' (Falkov, 1996: 8): 25 of them involved mentally ill perpetrators, ten involved mentally ill partners. The most common method of killing by mentally ill perpetrators was asphyxia (in 23 per cent of cases), followed by the use of implements (17 per cent) and poisoning (17 per cent).

Good enough parenting

I have suggested that parents with mental health problems can do serious harm to their children's development and well-being and I have gone on to note that parents with mental health problems constitute a substantial proportion of all parents who kill their children. You might well be feeling by now that I am being far too negative about parents with mental health problems. 'Surely having a mental illness is hard enough,' you might argue, 'with all the misery, loneliness and stigma that this entails, without adding to the suffering of people with mental health problems by accusing them of mistreating their children?'

I repeat the point, therefore, that the above discussion is not meant to imply that all parents with mental health problems harm their children, or that anything more than a *tiny* fraction of them represent a threat to their children's lives. But this is a book about child protection, so I necessarily focus on the fact that in some cases adult mental health problems *are* implicated in harm to children. Sometimes (as I have noted elsewhere in this book) even when parents' problems are not in any sense of their own making, it is necessary to intervene to protect their children. While this often seems very unfair on the parents – 'kicking them when they are down' so to speak – sometimes it would be even *more* unfair on the children to leave them in an environment which was not meeting their needs, in order to avoid distressing their parents. Children are people in their own right, and not their parents' possessions.

Having said this, though, I do want to emphasize that we need to try to avoid an overly narrow 'child protection' perspective. The fact that parents with mental health problems are disproportionately represented among child protection cases does show that poor parental mental health is a risk factor, but could equally well be used to argue that parents with mental health problems are being failed by the system and are not being given the support that they and their children need to prevent things getting to the point where children are being harmed (a point made, from an American perspective, by Park et al., 2006).

There are a small number of families where parental mental health problems really do preclude a parent from being able to care adequately for a child: families where a child is physically in danger, or families where a child is persistently given such negative or distorted messages about herself and the world as to seriously threaten her healthy development. But there are many more cases where, with appropriate back-up, families where a parent has a mental health problem can still provide a home in which a child can flourish. Children do not need perfect families, even if such things existed. Some challenges and adversity in childhood, after all, do contribute to learning and growth.

How do we distinguish between these two different situations? Weir points to the 'chronicity and severity of the mental illness' (1999: 2) as factors which help to determine the impact on the child. The outlook for the child is poorer when the parent's disturbed behaviour is chronic so that their child's needs are neglected not just sometimes but persistently over long periods, and in situations where 'the child has become incorporated into the parent's psychotic delusions or hallucinations … [which] will become apparent in what the parent says, does or threatens to do, such as talking to the child as though they are a dead relative, or accusing the child of hating them' (Duncan and Reder, 2003: 206), or where children have themselves come to share their parent's delusional beliefs. The outlook is better where the parent's mental health problems are intermittent:

> Several research studies have found that parents who have discrete episodes of illness and who are able to function well in-between with good relationships with their children, have far less difficulty in caring for their children. When the illness of parents is chronic and persistent, there is no respite for the children and they may be continuously exposed to difficult and damaging parental behaviour. (Weir, 1999: 2)

Sylvia Duncan and Peter Reder, however, caution against an automatic assumption that episodic mental health crises are not so harmful to children:

> In some instances, a child's age, resilience and support from the other parent indicates that their development will not be significantly compromised by the episodes of disturbed parental behaviour, even though they inevitably suffer emotionally [an important distinction]. With other families, it becomes evident that the 'good' times are really not so, since the child is primarily struggling with uncertainty and a fear that the 'good' times will eventually end … [and] detailed accounts of the parent's behaviour during the periods of remission may also reveal that they are unable to focus adequately on the child's needs or empathize satisfactorily with their experiences. (Duncan and Reder, 2003: 207)

Exercise 9.2

Gary, aged nine, lives with his mother Annabelle (aged 32), who suffers from severe depression. Gary is a quiet child in school. He does not present any difficulties to his teachers, and is compliant and polite, but his academic achievement is low and he often seems distracted. He is isolated. Teachers have noticed that when children invite their classmates to birthday parties and so on, Gary is often excluded from the list.

Annabelle is a quiet, gentle woman, who appears to teachers to be devoted to Gary. When she is seen by teachers, she is always very appreciative of everything that the school is doing for him. However she never responds to letters and requests that the school sends home and is very rarely seen at the school gate (Gary lives about a mile away and makes his own way home). Recently he has been coming to school late, sometimes in dirty clothes, and seems to be paying very little attention in class at all. Then he misses two days at school without explanation. Annabelle's telephone has been cut off. Gary's class teacher visits their home to discuss this.

(Continued)

Their home is a first-floor flat which is usually in a somewhat chaotic state and almost invariably, at any time of day, has all its curtains drawn. The teacher observes that Gary is very attentive to his mother, sitting beside her, stroking her hand and looking at her to check her reaction to everything that is said. She speaks very quietly, almost in a whisper, and tears frequently come to her eyes. She speaks very warmly of Gary, his kindness to her, his gentleness, his maturity. She refers to him as 'the man of the house', 'more like a brother' and says 'I don't know where I'd be without him'. She says that the family doctor and others have all been very helpful, but the main thing is 'we've got each other'. The teacher discovers that Gary normally sleeps in his mother's bed.

Gary is persuaded to come into school the next day. But when he gets home, Gary finds his mother unconscious on her bed having taken an overdose, and has to go round to a neighbour's flat to ask her to summon an ambulance.

What thoughts do you have about the way forward in this case?

Comments on Exercise 9.2

It is difficult to see situations of this kind as being abusive, because Annabelle is very positive about Gary, and there is no sense of malice or absence of love. (Some might wonder if sexual abuse was a factor in a case of this kind, given the shared bed and the very tactile relationship, but I do not think that these are indicators of sexual abuse in the absence of other evidence: it is actually not unusual for single mothers to share a bed with a child.) Nevertheless you probably agree that a huge amount of responsibility is being placed on Gary's shoulders at the age of nine. The overdose attempt will surely confirm his fears, already evidenced by his distractedness at school, about his mother's ability to cope on her own. His own needs – to progress at school, to join the community of his peers – are sacrificed in the service of her needs. His mother's comments about him, while flattering and doubtless sincere, also have the effect of continually denying him the right to be a nine-year-old child: she has effectively promoted him to her own generation.

Yet he is loved, and his devotion to his mother is real. Annabelle for her part is finding it hard coping with life at all, let alone with additional demands that might be made upon her by child protection professionals. Nevertheless Gary does need to be released from some of the responsibility he feels towards his mother, and needs to have some source of support for himself, and some respite from the intense closed world of the family flat. Annabelle's overdose may possibly provide an opportunity to look afresh at these things. If she has a period in hospital for instance, other arrangements will need to be made for Gary in the short term and, with each of them separately cared for, it may be possible to start thinking of other sources of help and support for each of them.

Supporting families

The job of the child protection professional is not simply to stand outside a family looking in, deciding whether the parenting is 'good enough'. It is also – or it should be – to try and provide services that will assist parents in providing good enough care.

Real mental health services

If parents are to manage their mental health in such a way as to be able to provide care for their child, they need help in their own right from mental health professionals and facilities, with whom they need to work in an atmosphere of trust and privacy. I suggest that a good child protection professional – and a good child protection system – needs to respect this, and should resist the temptation to try and co-opt the adult mental health services as a kind of listening post within their surveillance system. If people are denied the opportunity to talk in confidence, they will often simply keep their problems to themselves. (If you were a parent, would you wish to talk about your own inner fears and doubts to a person who reported everything you said to the child protection services?) The pressure group AIMS believes, for example, that 'mothers lie when they are asked questions about post-natal depression: they are afraid to tell the truth in case they are reported to social services and their babies are taken. So they are not getting help' (AIMS, 2004).

Support to children

Having parents with mental health problems can be both frightening and isolating. Amy Weir comments:

> Children may be embarrassed and insecure about their parent's illness and find it difficult to involve themselves fully in school and other activities with friends. They also tend to have very little information about their parent's mental illness, and can be vulnerable to bullying and social isolation as a result of negative remarks made about their parent's behaviour or characteristics. (Weir, 1999: 2)

Weir goes on to describe a 14-year-old girl seeking information from the local library about mental illness under the guise of a school project. One way of mitigating the effects on children, therefore, is to provide services to the children themselves. Cathy Styles and Melissa Knight (1999), for instance, describe an after-school group for children of parents with diagnosed mental illnesses which aimed to provide the children with opportunities to talk about their experience, provide them with support and information about mental illness and provide them with strategies for coping.

Respite care

Pressured child protection professionals often long to 'fix' the problem, one way or the other, so they can close the case and move on to others. But sometimes the best solution for a child is not Plan A or Plan B, but a recognition that Plan A will work some of the time but that Plan B needs to be held in reserve and made available at difficult times. Children whose parents have episodic mental health problems can often be best helped by respite care arrangements which allow them to live with respite carers during a difficult period, and then return home when their parent's condition stabilizes. If this can be with the same set of carers on a regular basis, the arrangement is far more satisfactory, than a succession of strangers. Members of the extended family often fill this role very well – and of course families often make these arrangements for themselves informally without going through the professional system – but it is important to be sensitive to the role that the grandparental generation may have played in the parent's mental health problems.

Knowing when 'support' is not enough

In the course of my career I have encountered situations where more support to parents and children, given at an early stage could have prevented the break-up of a family. These situations are tragic and it is important that child protection professionals remember that they are not simply there to demand change of parents (who, if they are in the throes of a mental health crisis, are not likely to be helped by additional demands being made upon them), but to provide help, difficult though this may be when resources are limited and the demands constant. Hard-pressed agencies are resistant to long-term involvement with families, but often, as I noted above, long-term support may be the best solution. (And in fact, as I will discuss further in Chapter 13, apparently 'tidier' alternatives, such as 'permanent' fostering or adoption are not necessarily as secure or permanent as they might appear.)

On the other hand I have encountered situations where a multitude of support services have been provided but where these have really served to mask the absence of a viable parent–child relationship, with the result that children are left for long periods in harmful emotional environments, with the possible result that they miss the opportunity to experience a secure caring family anywhere. These situations too can be tragic.

Here, as in other areas, child protection professionals have to steer a difficult middle path which may feel wrong whichever course they take. The British local authority social worker quoted below is describing the experience of having her work scrutinized in court by 'children's guardians' (court-appointed social workers). She is not specifically describing work with parents with mental health problems, but she does clearly illustrate the difficulty I am describing:

> Sometimes they say 'We can't believe it took you this long to get this case to court, the chronology's been so bad'. And you think, if I came in two years ago when the chronology wasn't so long you'd have said 'Why are you here now? You haven't given the parent a chance.' (Beckett et al., 2007: 57)

Chapter summary

This chapter has looked at the issues that arise when a parent has a problem with drugs or alcohol or has some other kind of mental health problem. The areas covered have been:

- the relationship between substance abuse problems and parenting problems
- the direct effects on children of parental substance abuse (for example, Foetal Alcohol Syndrome)

(Continued)

(Continued)

- the direct effects that drug and alcohol use can have on an adult's capacity to parent
- the effects on children of the lifestyles associated with substance abuse (for example, parents being preoccupied with obtaining money to fund the habit)
- the way that addiction can distort the thinking both of individuals and family members
- issues to be covered in assessment and intervention of families where there is a drug or alcohol problem
- the impact of other parental mental health problems on children
- how to decide whether parenting is 'good enough' to meet a child's needs
- supporting families with mental health problems.

The next chapter will look at another group of parents facing formidable challenges in their own lives – people with learning difficulties – and consider the particular child protection issues that arise in that context.

10 Parents with Learning Difficulties

- What do we mean by 'learning difficulties'?
- Intelligence and parenting
- Two viewpoints
- Society, parenting and learning disability
- Assessment of parenting
- Appropriate intervention
- The rights of children

For most of the twentieth century, in Britain and elsewhere, adults with learning difficulties typically lived in large institutions where the sexes were segregated and relationships between them controlled, with the explicit aim of preventing them from having children. It was only in the last two decades of the century that there was a major shift away from institutional care towards living 'in the community'. Not surprisingly there has been a corresponding increase in the number of people with learning disabilities forming sexual relationships and having children. But official concerns about learning disabled people as parents do not seem to have gone away. Tarleton et al. (2006) report research both from the UK and across the world, suggesting that something like *half* of all parents with learning disabilities have their children removed from their care.

In the UK, at the time of writing, there has recently been a heated public debate about this. In 2005, one national newspaper accused 'the social work establishment' of needlessly breaking up loving families by removing children from parents solely because the parents had learning disabilities:

Today in the Daily Mail we reveal the profoundly disturbing details of how decent people can be caught up in a nightmare they don't understand, how happy, cared-for children can be torn from their mothers and given to strangers and how a remorseless administrative machine insists it's all for the best.

No, this isn't a story from the dark days of Soviet dictatorship. This is happening in civilised, liberal Britain, where parents have no rights at all if they don't measure up to the standards of intelligence deemed appropriate by social workers.

And it doesn't matter if your children are loved, well-nourished and properly clothed. It does-n't matter if they are content and cared for in a stable, hardworking environment.

They are still liable to be snatched from you and put into the cold 'care' of the local council if you happen to have learning difficulties or a lower than average IQ, whatever your other quali-ties. (*Daily Mail* Comment, 2005)

The British tabloid press is not always strong on factual accuracy. Actually no legal provi-sion exists in Britain under which children could be removed from those parents *solely* on grounds of a parent having a low IQ and there is no means by which social workers could make these decisions alone. Courts can only make orders which allow children to be removed from their parents if they are satisfied that the children would otherwise suffer significant harm as a consequence of the care offered by the parents. But the fact remains that, rightly or wrongly, judges, magistrates and the child protection professionals on whom courts rely for information are coming to the conclusion that there are serious child protection or child welfare issues in around 50 per cent of families where children have learning disabilities, such as to justify removal of the children. But why are they coming to these conclusions and is there an alternative?

What do we mean by 'learning difficulties'?

The debate is not helped by a frequent lack of clarity in the literature about what is meant by 'learning difficulties' (or 'learning disability' or 'intellectual impairment') and about what level of learning difficulty is being discussed at any particular moment. McGaw and Sturmey (1993: 104) note that some programmes which 'claim to be addressing the needs of parents who have learning disabilities' turn out to be actually aimed at adults whose IQ is above the threshold that is generally recognized as defining a learning difficulty. Obviously it would be a mistake to generalize about the needs or parenting capacity of people with learning diffi-culties on the basis of such programmes. Likewise it would be a mistake to make general-izations about people with learning difficulties in general, on the basis of studies of people at one or the other end of the range of abilities. Many studies of learning disabled parents focus on parents at the upper end of the ability range. (Feldman et al.'s study [2002: 316], for example, looked at a group of mothers who 'were living independently in the commu-nity, could talk coherently, handle money, take public transport and shop'.)

Intellectual ability, like height or shoe size, is something which varies widely across the population, with the largest number of people being in the middle of the ability range, and increasingly small numbers towards the two extremes. At the above-average end of the spec-trum there are people who are recognized as being sufficiently distinctive from the norm that we sometimes apply terms to them like 'exceptionally gifted'. For people at the other end of the ability range words like 'mental retardation' and 'mental handicap' (not to mention 'imbecile', 'idiot' and 'moron') were used in the past, but are now widely seen as derogatory so they have been replaced with terms like 'learning difficulty', 'learning disability' and 'intellectual impairment'. But, whatever words we use, the fact is that where we draw the line between 'not very bright' and 'having a learning difficulty' is, in the end, arbitrary.

Wherever we choose to draw this line, the group that falls within that line will still include a wide range of abilities. People with learning difficulties are not at all a homogeneous group in terms of ability (let alone in terms of other attributes, in which they are of course just as diverse as the rest of the population). At one end of the ability range they include people who lack the cognitive skills to develop language or to use a knife and fork, while at the other end of the range they include people who can read and write, cook, keep house, manage money and go out to work.

The traditional measure of intellectual ability is the IQ test, in which average intelligence is given a score of about 100. There are a lot of problems with using a unidimensional measure of this kind to capture something as complex as intellectual ability (even measures of shoe size, after all, have two dimensions!) but I will not go into these here. If we accept the concept of IQ for the purposes of the present discussion, a working definition of learning impairment, given by Anthea Sperlinger, includes the following: 'significantly sub-average intellectual functioning (i.e. a composite score of two standard deviations below the mean on an accepted assessment of intellectual functioning) ... a score of, or below, IQ 74 for the UK population'. Her definition of *severe* learning disability includes a 'score below IQ 50 on standardised tests of intelligence' (Sperlinger, 1997: 4–5), and she writes that approximately '20 people per 1,000 in the UK have learning disabilities. Within this group, some 3–4 per 1,000 of the general population have severe or profound learning disabilities' (Sperlinger, 1997: 5).

The arbitrary nature of these categories, though, is illustrated by the fact that Dowdney and Skuse (1993: 26) define 'mental retardation' as an IQ of below 70, *mild* learning difficulties as an IQ of 55–70 and *severe* learning difficulties as below 40.

Intelligence and parenting

At the beginning of the twentieth century, the main concern about people with learning disabilities having children was that they would pass on their disabilities through their genes. At the beginning of the twenty-first century, these concerns have been replaced by new ones:

> The eugenic fear that people with intellectual disability will pollute the gene pool by reproducing large numbers of genetically defective offspring has since been discredited ... However, concern about the consequences of people with intellectual disability becoming parents is undiminished. 'Nurture' rather than 'nature' is now the primary cause for concern. Parents with intellectual disability are often presumed incapable of providing the stimulation children need to develop 'normally'. (McConnell et al., 2003: 122)

If the concerns of contemporary child protection professionals about parents with learning difficulties are no longer about eugenics, nor in fact are they primarily about abuse.

Tarleton et al. conclude that 'allegations of abuse by parents with learning difficulties are rare; children are more likely to be removed on the grounds that they are at risk of harm due to neglect, including lack of stimulation' (2006: 7). Maurice Feldman and Laurie Case, reviewing the available research, write:

> Typically, when parents have intellectual disabilities, the primary (but not exclusive) concern is protecting the child against physical and psychological neglect related to parental incompetencies ... Children of parents with intellectual disabilities are at-risk for developmental delay, psychosocial retardation, and behavior disorders. (Feldman and Case, 1999: 28)

But are these problems actually the result of the learning difficulties of the parents or is this merely a dangerous prejudice on the part of social workers and others, as the *Daily Mail* article implied? My suggestion is that the truth lies somewhere between: there can be a link, but there also can be prejudice. What is more, there are also other factors, such as social isolation, which are implicated in the parenting problems of many people with learning difficulties. (It is much harder to do the difficult job of being a parent when you do not have the support of others around you.) The problem in many cases may not simply be the learning difficulty, but the lack of adequate support.

Having a learning difficulty does not automatically result in a person being a poor parent. However, I think it is misleading also to suggest, as Tim and Wendy Booth do, that 'there is no clear relationship between parental competency and intelligence' (1993a: 463). At the low end of the intelligence spectrum there are people who lack the cognitive ability to meet their own basic needs, let alone the needs of others, and could not conceivably be competent parents, and it surely must follow that there is a somewhat higher level of cognitive ability below which ability to parent, even with generous support, begins to be in doubt.

What research *does* seem to show though – and what I imagine the Booths' comment refers to – is that, *above a certain minimum level,* parenting competence is not related to IQ. In other words, a minimum level of intellectual ability seems to be required to carry out the tasks of parenthood, but above that level, increased intelligence does not result in better parenting. Tymchuk and Andron (1994) suggest that there is no clear correlation between parenting competence and IQ until it falls below 60. And Dowdney and Skuse write that:

> There is general agreement that IQ does not relate in any systematic way to parenting competence until it falls below 55–60 ... Below this level, less competent parenting has been reported ... above it successive increments within the retarded range are not associated with increased parenting competence. (Dowdney and Skuse, 1993: 33)

A decision about a person's capacity to parent should *never* be made on the basis of an IQ measurement, of course, but what these findings suggest is that it is only as we approach the more 'severe' end of the very broad spectrum of abilities encompassed by the term 'learning difficulties' that intellectual ability *per se* begins to present difficulties for adequate parenting.

Doing the job of a parent may not be 'rocket science', but it does require some basic reasoning skills. As Glaun and Brown put it,

> it would be simplistic to assume that competent parenting depends primarily on love. It also involves cognitive abilities, such as exercising judgement by weighing up situations or options, anticipating the consequences of actions, using forward planning and organisational skills, remembering routines, understanding the developmental capabilities and limitations of the child, and demonstrating flexibility of thinking. (Glaun and Brown, 1999: 102)

These authors go on to note that intellectual functioning is 'mediated by emotional status'. This reminds us that parents of average, or above-average intellectual abilities can also have difficulty with weighing up options, forward planning and so on, if they are preoccupied with other things, or they are under stress, or their thinking has been distorted in some way by their own experiences or circumstances, and that learning disabled people may be able to do these things adequately if the stresses upon them are reduced.

Two viewpoints

When there are concerns that children are being inadequately cared for by parents with learning impairments, two different groups of agencies may find themselves approaching the problem from very different angles. On the one hand, modern learning disability agencies rightly see themselves as operating on behalf of the person with learning difficulties, and attempting to remove or mitigate the obstacles between that person and the life opportunities enjoyed by people without disabilities. They see themselves as advocates on behalf of people with learning impairments, and view their task in terms of fighting for the rights of a group of people who have historically been oppressed and denied human dignity to an extent unparalleled by almost any other group.

Those rights might include access to social and leisure facilities, to work, to housing, to political representation and to services which will enable them to offset their learning difficulties. Historically, people with learning impairments have often been characterized as permanent children ('He is 50 but he has a mental age of five'), so that fighting for the rights of people with learning difficulties can be seen as fighting for their right to be treated as adults. Over the past few decades, the right to be parents has come to be seen as an important part of this.

By contrast, while child protection workers may see themselves as working for the whole family, their primary responsibility is not towards the parents, but towards the child (the tone is set in England and Wales by section 1 of the 1989 Children Act, which states that 'the child's welfare shall be the paramount consideration' for courts making decisions about children). There is no absolute right to be allowed to continue to parent. The needs of the child, rather than the rights of the parents, should be the yardstick for decision-making.

Examples of the 'right to parenthood' perspective are provided by the many publications of Tim and Wendy Booth who believe that parents with learning difficulties 'too often receive rough justice from the child protection system' (Booth and Booth, 1996: 81).

Challenges and obstacles are placed in their way and the professional system then ends up 'blaming the victim by putting all the problems parents may be having down to their learning difficulties' (1996: 85).

On the other hand, Gillian Schofield considers that 'the approach which Booth and Booth appear to pursue fails to consider the welfare of the child or to see children in themselves as significant actors in the family situations in which they live' (Schofield, 1996: 87). She agrees that there are 'some cases which are inappropriately accelerated through the system because the parents have learning difficulties', but suggests that 'there are also situations where children of parents with learning difficulties are remaining at home and suffering significant harm because it was felt that the mother had learning difficulties and therefore could not be held responsible'. She cautions that:

> care needs to be taken about the ways in which parents with learning difficulties are treated as a special case. It cannot be disputed that the fundamental developmental needs of children are going to be the same whether parents have learning difficulties or not. (Schofield, 1996: 91)

These kinds of differences in perspective can, in my experience, lead to quite sharp disagreements between learning disability professionals and child protection professionals about the handling of particular cases. To some extent such disagreements are useful – a 'creative tension', which challenges the assumptions of all parties and promotes fresh thinking. But these disagreements can also result in a kind of gridlock, effectively paralysing decision-making.

But, as Tarleton et al. (2006: 2) argue, 'the polarization between upholding the rights of parents and those of the child may be artificial'. We can surely all agree that no one, whether learning disabled or not, has an *absolute* right to parent, regardless of how they actually function as parents, for children are human beings too with rights of their own, and not their parents' possessions. But equally, when parents do have problems providing adequate care to their children, no one could really dispute that we owe it to the children, as well as to the parents, to see if it is possible to find ways of providing support and guidance to those parents which will enable them to parent at an adequate level. Child protection professionals and learning disability professionals really ought to be able to advocate for their respective primary service users, without seeing each other as enemies.

Society, parenting and learning disability

Although many parents with 'mild' learning difficulties do have difficulties in providing adequate care for their children, this may be the result of factors other than the learning difficulties themselves (Tymchuk, 1992; Dowdney and Skuse, 1993). These sort of difficulties are faced by other parents too, of course, but there are particular obstacles in the way of parents with learning difficulties which are not the result of their learning difficulties as such, but are placed there by the rest of society. People with learning disabilities often have to deal with stressors such as poverty and childhood deprivation, and are often socially isolated. The professional system may also deal with them in ways that increase rather than reduce their levels of stress.

Labelling

Tim and Wendy Booth point out that the very presumption that people with learning difficulties cannot adequately parent can result in their children being removed from them in circumstances where other parents would not have had their children taken from them. The presumption is then in danger of becoming self-perpetuating because statistics about the high percentage of children of learning-impaired parents taken into care may then be used as evidence that such parents cannot cope (Booth and Booth, 1994: 41). 'Parenting behaviour rather than IQ should be the criterion by which parental competence is assessed', they quite rightly assert (Booth and Booth, 1993a: 463). (In the previous chapter I made the similar point that the competence of parents with substance-use problems should be assessed on their parenting behaviour, not their substance use.)

If we expect people to fail as parents, there is a danger that we will be on the look-out for failure, and will take any instance of less-than-perfect parenting, any problem that may occur, as confirmation of our view, even if we might tolerate the same parental behaviour in other families. Booth and Booth (1993b) quote the following comment from a father with learning difficulties. He had been concerned that his daughter might be being abused at a house which she and other girls were frequenting while truanting from school, and had expressed his fears to the family's social worker.

> You feel as though they're telling you you're inadequate as a parent. I mean there's about three or four girls involved with this sex thing, but how come our Ann always seems to be the one that's put into a home? The other girl she was with, she's still at home. We saw her the other day, she wasn't at school. (Booth and Booth, 1993b: 165)

In other words we may end up 'setting the bar higher' for people with learning disabilities than we do with other parents, which would be discriminatory towards both them and their children. This sort of selective perception on the part of professionals can occur not only in relation to parents with learning impairments but to other parents too who are 'labelled' or unusual in some way: parents with mental illness, drug users, people from ethnic minorities, gay and lesbian parents, even sometimes single fathers – and indeed *any* family who enters the child protection system, and is therefore labelled as 'having problems'. It is something to watch out for generally and child protection professionals need to keep asking themselves the following question: 'This parenting behaviour may not be ideal, but is it something that we would be concerned about in the same way if it happened in another family?' It is very important that struggling families are not expected to reach *higher* standards than other families, or different standards from those that are generally accepted as normal in the community in which they live.

What is particularly unfair about labelling families or expecting them to fail is that such expectations can become self-fulfilling prophesies. To be monitored and criticized – and to have the expectation of failure hanging over our heads – is a substantial stressor for any of us, which may actually prevent us from operating as well as we otherwise would have done.

Inappropriate help

Professionals 'must *never seek permanently to remove a child from home* for reasons of neglect, inadequate care or abuse by omission before every effort has been made to equip the parents with the skills they need to cope' (Booth and Booth, 1993a: 466, emphasis in original). This fundamental principle should of course apply to all situations where there are concerns about parenting, but particular issues arise in relation to learning-impaired people. A learning difficulty is not the same thing as an inability to learn. In fact 'many parents with intellectual disabilities are able to learn parenting skills and provide acceptable child-care if they are given appropriate training and support' (Feldman and Case, 1999: 28) but people with learning difficulties learn at a different rate than other people, and require teaching techniques which are designed to meet their specific learning needs. This is an area in which a child protection worker needs to enlist the skills and knowledge of professionals with experience in working with people with learning difficulties.

'Help' which is not in fact helpful serves no purpose at all. As we would use interpreters in work with a family who did not speak English, so we should obtain help in translating the concerns of the child protection system into a form which learning disabled parents are able to understand and act upon.

Assessment of parenting

Susan McGaw and Peter Sturmey propose a model for the assessment of the parenting skills of parents with learning difficulties (McGaw and Sturmey, 1994) that considers what they call *primary* and *secondary* indicators. Primary indicators of good enough parenting are:

- the child's development
- observable childcare skills of the parents, including physical care, affection, ability to provide security, taking responsibility, ability to offer guidance to a child and to take control.

Secondary indicators include:

- life skills, such as reading, language skills, social skills, work skills and home care skills
- family history, including such things as the adults' own experience of being parented
- resources and support available to the parents.

Where a child is healthy, happy and developing well, and the parents are able to demonstrate good parenting skills, there is no reason why the 'secondary' questions above should be any business of child protection agencies. Where the 'secondary' indicators do become important is when an assessment identifies primary indicators of weaknesses in parenting. There is then a need to be as clear as possible as to the reasons for those weaknesses. Are they the result of learning difficulties? Or are they the result of unhappy childhood experiences, or a childhood in institutional care with no parental role models? Or are they the result of social isolation or a lack of resources? In order to decide what action to take in any child protection case it is necessary not only to identify problems in parenting, but to have some understanding of the likely cause of those problems. In the case of parents with learning difficulties we need to be as clear as possible whether the problems with parenting are:

1   The direct result of the learning impairment on the acquisition of parenting skills
2   Related to social factors resulting from having learning difficulties (social isolation, for instance)
3   The result of other factors that apply also to parents who do not have learning difficulties (marital issues, poverty, mental health problems, drug and alcohol abuse, poor childhood experiences).

Exercise 10.1

Rosie King is two months old. Her mother Lucy (aged 23) has a moderate learning disability (her IQ has been assessed as 55–60). Lucy is supported by a health visitor and by the 'Community Learning Disability Service' (CLDS), who support adults with learning difficulties living independently, and by a care worker from the Children's Social Care service of the local authority, who visits daily to help with practical parenting skills.

Lucy is physically affectionate with Rosie, though she is inclined to become agitated when Rosie cries or is difficult to feed or settle. Lucy does however find it hard to plan ahead and deal with unexpected situations; she has difficulties with absorbing information; and she also finds it hard to see Rosie's needs as distinct from her own. (For example, she will take Rosie out with barely any covers on a cold day, even though she herself has put on a jumper and coat.) It is with these kinds of things that the family aide, the health visitor and the CLDS are trying to give support.

A recent episode has, however, sounded alarm bells, and resulted in the formal involvement of the child protection system. What happened was that an acquaintance of Lucy's visited Lucy and asked to 'borrow' Rosie for the night to show to her friends. (This acquaintance was a woman called Janet, who does not have a learning disability, but has a police record for drug offences and several violent offences against adults.) When the health visitor came the next morning she found that Lucy had no idea where Rosie was, or where Janet lived, or how to get in touch with her. Rosie was only found later that day when the police stopped a car speeding and crossing a red light, and Rosie was found to be in the back seat with two of Janet's friends, aged 14 and 15.

The health visitor feels that this episode shows that, however much support Lucy has, she simply is not capable of being a parent to Rosie. 'It's all very well the CLDS talking about Lucy's "right" to be a parent,' she says, 'but where are Rosie's rights in all this?'

Background on Lucy King: Lucy lives in a flat on her own, but she required support from the CLDS with tasks such as budgeting, planning meals and so on. Lucy herself was the unplanned child of a one-off encounter. Her mother considered having a termination at the

(Continued)

(Continued)

time. There were serious concerns for Lucy after her birth because her mother was depressed, very dismissive of Lucy and was unsupported by her own family. When Lucy's mother and step-father had two more children together, it would appear that Lucy became something of a Cinderella figure in her family. There were several occasions when professional agencies were concerned that she was being subjected to neglect or emotional abuse. At 14 Lucy became pregnant and had a termination. Soon afterwards her mother and step-father insisted that she was accommodated in a foster-home and she lived in three different foster-homes for the remainder of her adolescent years.

She has (in the view of professionals who know her) often been exploited by men because of her very trusting nature. She is not certain who is the father of Rosie.

As a child protection professional primarily concerned with the welfare of Rosie, what issues would you want to consider in an assessment of this family?

Comments on Exercise 10.1

You will probably agree that a problem that emerges from the above account is that Lucy seems to find it difficult to see Rosie as a person with needs of her own. Letting a friend 'borrow' her seems akin to treating Rosie as a kind of doll. (However, you would need to explore this incident with Lucy herself before coming to firm conclusions about what it meant. Many parents, after all, leave their children with friends at times.) Lucy's failing to realize that Rosie will feel the cold, just as she does, sounds like another instance of the same kind of thing.

One of the things that you would look at in your assessment, then, would be the extent that Lucy is capable of recognizing Rosie's needs, and/or the extent to which Lucy is capable of learning to do so.

But you would need to be careful not to assume that the cause of the problem is primarily Lucy's learning difficulties. People of average, or above-average intelligence, can also find it difficult to recognize or focus on their children's needs if their own unmet needs as adults are sufficiently pressing to preoccupy them. There is plenty of material in Lucy's history to suggest that she may indeed have many unmet emotional needs from her own childhood. It seems that she may have been made to feel unwanted through much of her childhood for a variety of reasons, and to have been made to feel an outsider in her own family. Low self-esteem, and the need to please others and forestall rejection, may have been behind the Janet incident as much as any specific cognitive problem resulting from Lucy's learning difficulties.

In your assessment you would need to try and tease out these different factors because they make a difference to any subsequent work. You cannot really expect to be able to offer help unless you have a sense of where the difficulty lies. If Lucy's problems as a parent were mainly to do with her learning impairment, then you would want to look at the possibility of using appropriate educational techniques to try and improve her ability to think about Rosie's needs. If, however, her problems are to do with her own childhood history and negative self-image, then you might want to look at ways of helping her to address these issues, though of course you would still need to do so in a way consistent with her level of understanding.

What you would also need to hold in your mind, though, is that however sad Lucy's history is, your first priority as a child protection worker is Rosie. Lucy's mistake was to fail to think about Rosie's needs. The professional system should be careful not to make the same mistake.

Appropriate intervention

As I have already noted, the main reason why parents with learning disabilities come to the attention of the child protection system is not that they are abusing their children (though obviously this can occur) but because they are failing to parent safely or appropriately. Looking at children of learning disabled parents subject to care proceedings, Booth et al. (2005: 11) conclude that 'neglect rather than abuse was the main threat to their well-being, and this more by omission rather than commission on the part of their carers'. Feldman and Case (1999: 28) mention problems like untreated nappy rash, malnourishment or gastrointestinal infections as the sort of problem that can occur as a result of a parent simply not knowing how to go about things. Or children may present behaviour problems at school because their parents do not know the technique of providing consistent discipline. These are all to do with parenting skills deficits and in many cases, with appropriate help, the necessary skills can be learnt. But people with learning difficulties may find it more difficult than others to absorb and apply information, to retain skills once learnt, and to use reasoning to anticipate difficulties and dangers and take evasive action. This means that teaching these skills to people with learning disabilities is *in itself* a skill. Booth and Booth (1994: 18–19) offer ten 'training points' gleaned from the research literature. Among these are the following:

- 'The acquisition of new skills is more likely and training more effective where clearly specified, individualized goals are set and presented in small, discrete and concrete steps.'
- 'Training is less effective when parents are having to cope with external pressures in their lives.'
- 'The maintenance and generalization of new learning is assisted by teaching in real-life settings rather than in the classroom or clinic.' (A point also emphasized by Susan McGaw, 1996: 25, who maintains that 'home based visits have proven to be the most successful mode'.)
- 'Training must be geared to parental learning characteristics – for example, their slower rate of learning, inability to read, low self-esteem, difficulties in organizing, sequencing and sticking to time schedules.'
- 'Periodic and ongoing long-term refresher support is needed to maintain learned skills.'

This last point is also emphasized by Susan McGaw, who argues that there 'is a need to move from an assumption that our purpose is always to help a family achieve totally independent functioning' (1996: 25). She goes on to say that:

> the permanent disability of the parent requires that support for the family needs to be available on a continuing basis. Crisis-driven, short-term services often result in frustration, burn-out and blame on the part of the worker and mistrust, despair and cyclical crisis episodes for families. (McGaw, 1996: 27)

It can be very demoralizing for all concerned when a family case is closed, only to come back to the attention of the child protection or family support services again and again when lack of support has resulted in family functioning deteriorating and crisis point being reached. I pointed out in the previous chapter that the inclination of child protection professionals to seek a quick permanent 'fix' that will allow them to close a case and move on to others, while understandable when workers are constantly pressured to respond to new crises, does not necessarily serve the interests of children. There is certainly a case for some families – and not only families whose parents have learning difficulties – being recognized as in need of long-term back-up by professional agencies, just as some individuals with chronic health problems require long-term support from doctors, and do not constantly have to come back and demonstrate this need again from scratch.

Susan McGaw also points out that, not only do some parents need support on a long-term basis, but some 'will always require instrumental assistance in areas such as money management, meal planning, or obtaining medical care' (McGaw, 1996: 25). In other words, there will be some parents who cannot acquire all the necessary skills themselves and will need the professional agencies to do some things *for*, or at least *with*, them. After all, every parent relies on others to perform some tasks for them. As a parent myself, I take responsibility for putting a roof over my children's heads, but I would have to ask someone else to come and fix it if the roof leaked. This does not mean, I think, that I am not a competent parent.

The rights of children

There is a difficult balance to be struck, though, between ensuring that learning disabled parents are not needlessly discriminated against and giving them every possible chance of succeeding, and not losing sight of the children and their own needs. Children have rights too, and the children of parents with learning disabilities have the right to the same standards of care as other children.

I suggest that there is a point after which 'instrumental assistance' offered to parents ceases to be merely assistance and begins to become doing the parenting *for* them, so that they end up acting as parents in name only. I would question whether it is in children's interests to stay in their parents' care if the only way that this can be safely sustained is for a whole team of professionals on a rotating basis to visit daily, plan the meals, take the children to school, see they are put to bed, and supervise every aspect of their parents' interactions with them. This could effectively deny the children themselves the real experience of *actually being parented*, even if it maintains a kind of fiction for the rest of the world that they are being cared for by their parents.

Also, while it is important that child protection professionals do not 'set the bar' higher for learning disabled parents than for other parents, something which is manifestly unjust and oppressive, and contrary to the interests of children, it is equally important not to lower the bar for them either, as some of their advocates sometimes seem to be suggesting. The standard of acceptable parenting should be based on children's needs, not on parental ability, or there is no point in trying to have a standard at all.

For this reason, I cannot agree with Susan McGaw (1996: 26) when she argues that it is wrong to set tight timescales for assessments to decide whether the children of parents with learning difficulties should remain in their care. 'A tension … exists', she writes, 'between the "No Delay Principle" [in England and Wales this is enshrined in section 1(2) of the 1989 Children Act] which stipulates that a delay in court proceedings is presumed to be prejudicial, and the rights of a parent which may be compromised by actions that lead to a swift termination of their parental responsibilities.' Obviously these hugely important decisions do necessarily take time but undue delay in court proceedings *can* be extremely harmful to children. It denies them security until the matter is settled, closes off options for their future and increases the likelihood that long-term placements will fail (Beckett and McKeigue, 2003). This remains true whether or not parents have learning difficulties, and should therefore be a matter of *equal concern* whether or not parents have learning difficulties.

I have a similar concern in relation to the following comment from Booth and Booth:

> several study families reported having been warned against smacking their children. Ever fearful of losing them ... they did as they were told. However, generally lacking powers of verbal reasoning, they were left with no effective method of discipline and began to encounter problems of control. These problems were then cited by social workers as evidence of parenting deficits. (Booth and Booth, 1993b: 169).

Smacking is still legal in the UK and the USA, though banned in Sweden, Finland, Germany and many other countries. It would therefore be wrong for child protection professionals to demand of parents who happen to be under the scrutiny of the professional child protection system that they give up a form of discipline which is widely, openly and quite legally practised by their neighbours.

But whether or not you believe smacking is acceptable, it cannot be used as a substitute for verbal reasoning and I would be seriously concerned about any parent for whom smacking was the *only* method of control. What will they do when smacking fails to have the desired effect? (Will they increase the severity of the smacking?) How will they maintain control when their children are teenagers and are as big as they are? How will they cope when their children demand an explanation for a rule that seems to them to be unnecessary or unfair?

It seems to me that, when considering a person's capacity to parent, we are entitled to think about the situations that that person is going to encounter and is going to have to deal with, and think realistically about whether they are going to be able to cope or not. A capacity for verbal reasoning may not be so necessary when a child is 18 months old, but it is legitimate to think ahead and ask whether a parent will have the necessary skills to cope when the child is a little older. These matters are rather more difficult, perhaps, than the *Daily Mail* would have us believe.

Chapter summary

In this chapter I have looked at some of the particular issues that arise in child protection work when there is a parent or parents with learning difficulties. I have discussed:

(Continued)

(Continued)

- the different perspectives of child protection professionals and of professionals who work to support adults with learning difficulties – and the potential for conflict between these two groups
- what 'learning difficulties' actually means and how it is defined; I also referred to other terms such as 'mental retardation', 'learning impairment' and 'learning disability'
- the relationship between intelligence and parenting ability
- the ways in which the attitudes of society at large can impact on parents who have learning difficulties; I mentioned unwarranted assumptions and inappropriate help as two particular problems
- what needs to be considered when carrying out a parenting assessment involving a parent who has a learning difficulty
- what might constitute an appropriate intervention where a parent has learning difficulties, including the specific training skills that are involved and some of the dilemmas that may arise
- the need to retain a focus on the needs of children as well as those of their parents.

The next chapter will consider another area of work where the needs of children and the needs of adults are sometimes hard to disentangle: families where domestic violence between adults is going on.

11 | Violent Homes

- Adult violence and child abuse
- Gender, violence and abuse
- Child protection pitfalls

If, in the early 1980s, the police reported an allegation of domestic violence to a British social work team with child protection responsibilities, that team might well have taken no further action, unless there was evidence that the children themselves were on the receiving end of violence, or looked likely to become so. Domestic violence *per se* was not really seen as a child protection issue then. It was assumed that other agencies – principally, in the UK, voluntary agencies such as Women's Aid – were there to provide help to the adult victims.

However, in recent years there has been a shift towards bringing adult domestic violence within the child protection arena, because of the harm that it does to children.

Adult violence and child abuse

There are several ways in which domestic violence relates to child protection:

Overlap

People who are violent in one context are more likely to be more violent generally. It is not *necessarily* the case that adults who are violent towards other adults will also be violent towards children, but they are more likely to be. There are many studies that confirm this.

(Hester et al., 2000: 30–2, summarize a number of them.) One US study, for instance, found that, in a sample of 775 women who had children and violent partners, 70 per cent of the children were also physically abused (Bowker et al., 1988).

So if a child protection agency receives a report that domestic violence is occurring in a given family, it should be aware that it is fairly likely – though not certain – that children are also being physically abused.

Emotional abuse

Even in situations where the children are not themselves being directly physically abused, they are likely to be harmed simply by being exposed to adult violence. An adult who violently assaults another adult in the home is really also emotionally abusing any children in the home who may see, hear or be aware of that violence.

I previously noted in Chapter 7 that most of the harm that is done even by *direct* child abuse, except in very extreme cases where permanent physical harm is done, seems to result from the psychological aspects of the experience and the feelings associated with it: terror, helplessness, betrayal, worthlessness, isolation, guilt … This being so, we should not be surprised to discover that long-term harm is caused to children by living in a seriously violent environment. Children in a home where one adult is physically abusing another may experience a similar range of unbearable feelings as those who are the direct victims of abuse themselves. If, for instance, their father regularly beats their mother, they are faced with the fact that, of the adults on whom they rely for safety, security and protection, one is incapable of protecting even herself and the other is capable of violently assaulting someone he is supposed to love and care for. They may experience helplessness and guilt at being unable to protect someone they love. They may even be implicated in the abuse themselves, coerced or encouraged by the abuser to 'support and/or participate in the abuse and degradation of their mother' (Kelly, 1994: 44).

In fact research into the effects on children of exposure to adult violence have identified a wide range of possible long-term consequences – similar both in kind and in severity to the long-term consequences of direct abuse – that can persist into adult life, including low self-esteem, depression, drug/alcohol abuse, violent behaviour. (See, for example: Straus, 1992; Silvern et al., 1995; Henning et al., 1996; Harold and Howarth, 2004.)

But the perpetrators of the abuse themselves often find it hard to accept that children are harmed by violence that is not actually directed *at* them. Dora Black observes that even a father who has *murdered* the mother of his children may still say 'I've never done anything to hurt them' (Black, 1995: 230). The adult direct victims of the violence sometimes also find it hard to see that their children are victims too.

Impact on parenting capacity

Calder (2004) makes the point that domestic violence impacts on the ability of both parents to provide care to their children:

> The physical demands of parenting can overwhelm mothers who are injured or have been kept up all night by a beating. The emotional demands of parenting can be similarly daunting to abused

women suffering from trauma, damaged self-confidence, and other emotional scars caused by years of abuse. An additional problem occurs when the abuser undermines her parenting as a means of control. (Calder, 2004: 74)

Male violence

Another way in which we could link domestic violence and child abuse is that *both* domestic violence against adults *and* violence against children are perpetrated mainly by men (and both, some would say, constitute manifestations of 'patriarchy'). Perhaps wife-beating and child-beating – and indeed also sexual assaults against both women and children – are all essentially the same thing: means by which men use violence (and their own physical size and strength) to assert their dominance over the family?

But to explore this further, we need to take a diversion away from the subject of adult domestic violence to consider the links between gender, violence and abuse.

Gender, violence and abuse

Most of the care and protection provided for children in families is still provided by mothers. The informal network which most children depend upon to keep them safe is therefore, in the main, provided by women. The same is actually also true of the *formal* child protection network, for the majority of child protection professionals in the UK are also women. (I have attended very few multi-agency child protection conferences where men were not outnumbered by women.) Of the professions closely involved in child protection work, teaching, nursing and social work are all predominantly staffed by women in the UK. In 2000, for example, 86 per cent of applications for places on social work courses were from women (Perry and Cree, 2003: 377).

Child protection therefore, both at the formal professional level and at the personal and family level, is a predominantly female activity in contemporary society. But is it possible to argue that, by contrast, child *abuse* is a predominantly male one?

Gender and child sexual abuse

Both the available research evidence and practice experience suggest that sexual abuse is perpetrated far more often by men and boys than by women and girls. In Chapter 8 I referred to findings that more than 97 per cent of sexual abusers of girls and 78 per cent of sexual abusers of boys are male. (We should, however, bear in mind that most sexual abuse of any kind went completely undetected in the past and that we therefore cannot completely rule out the possibility that there may still be whole areas of abuse, either by men or by women, which we are still simply not yet aware of.) Sexual abuse by women and girls can and does occur (for more on this see, for instance, Saradjian, 1996) and if you are one of the 3 per cent of girls or the 22 per cent of boys who are sexually abused by women or girls, the fact that the number of women abusers is much lower than the number of male abusers is not going to be any comfort to you. But the figures do undoubtedly suggest that, as with sexual offences against adults, it is men and boys who perpetrate by far the largest number of sexual offences against children.

Gender and physical child abuse

The picture is not quite so obviously one-sided when it comes to physical child abuse. Studies reviewed by Featherstone (1996) suggest that in fact something approaching half of physical abuse of children – including fatal physical abuse – is perpetrated by women. The case of Lauren Wright, the six-year-old child who died in Norfolk in 2001 following a blow to the stomach from her stepmother, is just one of a number of British instances of children dying as a result of a physical assault by a woman:

> A woman who systematically beat, starved and abused her six-year-old stepdaughter until she died from multiple injuries was yesterday convicted of manslaughter and wilful neglect.
>
> Tracey Wright, 31, was found guilty of causing the death of Lauren Wright at Norwich crown court after a four-week trial which revealed 18 months of physical and psychological abuse. (*The Guardian*, 2 October 2001)

A similar number of incidents of physical abuse by women and men should not, however, be interpreted to mean that women are equally as prone as men to physical abuse of children. When comparing the figures for abuse by women and abuse by men we are not comparing like with like because the majority of children continue to be cared for in the main by women. A non-custodial father who sees his children one day a fortnight, for instance, has comparatively few opportunities to physically abuse his children as compared to the mother who cares for them on the other 13 days. A more meaningful comparison would be to look at the number of violent assaults by men and women *relative to the amount of contact with children that they have.* Looking at it in this way, it is still possible to argue that physical abuse of children *is* more of a male problem than a female one, although we cannot really conclude that violence against children is exclusively or overwhelmingly a male phenomenon.

Gender and domestic violence

Returning now to the subject of adult domestic violence, it would seem that it is actually not uncommon for the woman in a relationship to initiate violence towards the man. Murray Straus, reporting on a number of studies including a large survey based exclusively on reports from women informants, concluded that the frequency of assaults by wives on husbands was actually about the same as that of assaults by husbands on wives (Straus, 1993).

But, as with the figures on physical child abuse, there are very important caveats. Straus also noted that assaults *resulting in injury* form a far higher proportion of assaults on women by men than vice versa, something in the order of *six times* higher, according to two studies he cites. An Australian study (Headey et al., 1999) likewise found similar numbers of assaults by women on men as vice versa but found a significant difference between genders as to the extent that victims felt frightened and intimidated: nearly twice as many women as men reported this. This study also referred to crime statistics which show that nearly four times as many women are killed by their partners as vice versa (Black, 1995, writing about the UK, suggests that the ratio is nine to one) and to injury presentation data which show that, of injuries presented to hospitals as domestic violence, nearly five times as many were injuries to women as compared to injuries to men.

So, while it may be hard to sustain the argument that almost all domestic violence is initiated by men, this should not be taken as meaning that women's violence and men's violence are equivalent. As I've just shown, male-on-female and female-on-male violence differ very considerably in *degree*. Equally importantly, I suggest, they may also have very different *meanings* for those involved. To understand these meanings, we would need to compare not just the incidence statistics but the context in which the violence occurs, the psychological effect violence has on the victims and the ability of victims to avoid it. The very fact that, in the average couple, the man is larger and physically stronger than the woman, surely does in itself mean that violence one way has a different meaning to violence the other way (just as violence by a child against an adult has a very different meaning to violence by an adult against a child). The fact that in many families, the woman relies on the man to provide an income both for herself and the children, may also mean that it is harder for women to escape violence. In some cultures norms and expectations about a wife's duties and a husband's rights may further aggravate the difficulties of women attempting to get away from violence.

Perhaps it is simplistic to see violence in the family as something that only comes from men, or indeed to see men as the only members of families who have any power. But this should not be used as a pretext for discarding feminist insights into the dynamics of gender and power that are closely entwined with the issue of domestic violence. We should remember that less than two centuries ago in Western countries, violence by men against both children *and* women was not only socially sanctioned but *actually specifically permitted by law*. Demie Kurz, for instance, refers to an 1824 ruling by the Supreme Court of the State of Mississippi permitting the husband 'to exercise the right of moderate chastisement in cases of extreme emergency' (Kurz, 1993: 90, citing Browne, 1987). And although this 'right' (in respect of chastising women) no longer exists in Western countries many would argue that, right up to the present, the law has been reluctant to intervene in cases of violence against women within the home in the same way that it would intervene in, for instance, violence in the street. Different norms and expectations may also still exist in other cultures. I understand that there is a debate in Islam, for example, about the precise meaning of the following verse in the Qur'an but it certainly would seem to me to sanction a level of male violence towards women:

> As to those women on whose part you fear disloyalty and ill-conduct, admonish them (first), (next), refuse to share their beds, (and last) beat them (lightly). (Surah 4, Al-Nisa': 34, *The Holy Qur'an*, translated by Yusuf Ali, 1989: 195)

A middle way
Brid Featherstone and Liz Trinder (1997) propose a middle way between, on the one hand, a particular kind of feminist account which sees violence as an entirely male problem and assumes a complete identity of interests between women and children, and, on the other hand, the approach of some domestic violence researchers, who more or less ignore the issue of gender and power differences between men and women:

> The challenge, as we see it, is to move beyond the dichotomized options of either gender-blind systemic approaches or theories of patriarchy. (Featherstone and Trinder, 1997: 156)

Historically – and in many respects even in the present day – men's voices have been louder and more influential than either the voices of women or children and this can lead to women being blamed and held responsible for the violence perpetrated against them, whether it be domestic violence or rape ('she provoked it'). However, Featherstone and Trinder point out that it would be a mistake to move from this position to its polar opposite: a position in which *only* women's voices were heard, with children simply assumed to have the same interests as women, and men simply assumed to be violent brutes whose perspective can be excluded altogether. Critiquing research by Hester and Radford (1996) they comment:

> The gender identities in this script [i.e. Hester and Radford's conclusions] are familiarly unitary, discrete and oppositional. Women are the victims of abusive men, always done to rather than doing, but nevertheless fierce protectors of their children. Men are represented as a coherent and fixed category, appearing only as woman/child abusers, as the sole perpetrator. Fathers never appear as nurturers or carers.
>
> Whilst children's interests are sharply differentiated from those of their fathers, they are seen as largely inseparable from those of their mothers. Children are presented as an undifferentiated category of vulnerable and largely passive victims, at risk not only of abuse but also of manipulation by their fathers. (Featherstone and Trinder, 1997: 153)

Questioning whether this 'script' adequately describes all domestic violence situations, they cite a paper by Janet Johnston and Linda Campbell (Johnston and Campbell, 1993), who suggest that domestic violence falls into several different patterns, each of which has different implications for the planning of contact between children and non-custodial parents:

> … domestic violence can derive from multiple sources and follow different patterns in different families, rather than being a syndrome with a single underlying cause. (Johnston and Campbell, 1993: 198)

(In much the same way, one might argue, physical child abuse falls into a number of different patterns and cannot necessarily be seen as all lying along the same continuum.)

The different kinds of adult domestic violence identified by Johnston and Campbell are given below. I'm not suggesting that this should be taken as the definitive categorization but it does have two merits. First, it recognizes that there are different types of domestic violence. Secondly, although it recognizes the existence of both male and female violence, it is not 'gender blind'. It recognizes differences in power between the genders and different, characteristically gendered patterns of violence.

- *Ongoing or episodic male battering.* Often compounded by drugs or alcohol, this pattern most closely corresponds to the stereotype of the brutal 'wife-batterer', with unprovoked male attacks occurring for no apparent reason other than a need to dominate and control. 'The origin of the violence in these cases seemed to be internal to the dynamics of the men, to their low tolerance of frustration, their problems with impulse control, and their angry, possessive or

jealous reactions to any threat to their potency, masculinity, and "proprietary male rights" '
(Johnston and Campbell, 1993: 193).

- *Female-initiated violence.* Physical attacks initiated by women as a result of 'their own intolerable states of tension and stress. Typically, these women became furiously angry … in response to the spouse's passivity or failure to provide for them in some way … In the early stages of the conflict the husband would try to prevent or contain the fight … In some cases the man lost control … eventually responding in kind to the woman's attacks' (Johnston and Campbell, 1993: 195).
- *Male-controlled interactive violence.* Domestic violence arising out of disagreements that escalated into physical fights. Either party might initiate it but 'the overriding response by the man was to assert control and prevail by physically dominating and overpowering the woman' (Ibid.: 195).
- *Separation and post-divorce violence.* Uncharacteristic acts of violence that occur as a result of the trauma of separation, or as a reaction to particular traumatic events arising from the separation, and were not present during the marriage itself.
- *Pyschotic and paranoid reactions.* Violence resulting from seriously distorted thinking in which perpetrators (male or female) imagined former spouses to be deliberating trying to harm or humiliate them.

The form of domestic violence that most commonly comes to the attention of child protection professionals is the first kind, 'Ongoing or episodic male battering', and it is the child protection response to this kind of violence that I will mainly be discussing in the rest of this chapter (a discussion in which, therefore, I will generally assume the perpetrator to be male and the direct victim to be a woman). But, as Cathy Humphreys and Nicky Stanley note, we should not allow our recognition that this is the 'dominant, gendered pattern' to blind us to the existence of 'minority patterns' (Humphreys and Stanley, 2006: 13).

Child protection pitfalls

The job of child protection workers is of course primarily to protect *children* not adults. In the context of a situation where domestic violence is occurring this translates into a responsibility to protect children from the harm that can be caused by *exposure* to domestic violence as well as from the risk that they themselves might become the direct victims of violence. But it is impossible to have a coherent strategy for doing this without thinking about the dynamics of the adult relationships.

I think child protection workers can make errors of several different kinds in such cases which could be described as follows:

Minimizing

It is easy to minimize the extent of domestic violence or the impact it has on a family or the effect it has on children. Society in general has been guilty of minimizing the extent of domestic violence in the past – and arguably still is. Child protection agencies have been guilty of both minimizing domestic violence and of minimizing – or even completely overlooking – the fact that exposing children to adult violence is itself a serious abuse of those children, as *well* as of the adult victim.

Catherine Humphreys (1999), in a research study looking at files of child protection cases, found numerous examples of domestic violence being minimized. For example:

- Reports for case conferences failed even to mention domestic violence although the social worker who wrote the report knew it was going on.
- Domestic violence was mentioned but was described using euphemisms such as 'fighting' or 'marital conflict'. For example: 'One conference chair referred to "an argument between the parents"... which on closer reading [turned out to be] a knife attack, resulting in the woman being stabbed while holding the baby' (Humphreys, 1999: 80).

Forgetting the children

It is easy to become so involved with the adults, particularly when one of them is very clearly a victim of oppression and violence, that the children in the case become secondary or are forgotten entirely. Featherstone and Trinder (1997) caution against making the assumption that the interests of children are *necessarily* identical to those of their physically abused mother, or that a mother necessarily always acts in the best interests of her children. This is manifestly not the case in the event that the violence is actually initiated by the mother, but I suggest that it is also not the case, for instance, if a mother repeatedly returns to a violent partner who the children do not want to be with. This is not to say that we should not be sympathetic to the reasons why she does so – everyone has their reasons and sometimes someone whose life has been full of violence and abuse simply cannot imagine attaining any other kind of life – but all the same we also cannot truly describe her as giving a high priority to her children's needs.

Exercise 11.1
Children: David, aged six, Michael, aged three
Mother: Susan Smith, aged 22

Susan comes into a social work office seeking financial help and help with accommodation. The children are observed to be unwashed and very agitated. They are all over the interview room, going through the interviewing social worker's bag, writing on the walls, attempting to make calls with the social worker's mobile phone, playing with electrical switches. Susan pays them almost no attention at all (no eye contact, no explanation as to what was happening) other than continuously giving them sweets from a bag.

The story Susan tells is that she is newly arrived in the area fleeing a violent partner in North City, called Vince. Subsequent enquiries show that she and the children had a room at a Women's Aid Refuge in North City, but they were evicted from there when Susan let Vince and another man into the refuge and into her room, against the refuge's strict 'women only' rule.

Information obtained from North City is that she arrived there saying that she was fleeing a violent partner in Steeltown. Further enquiries show that she was evicted from the refuge in Steeltown, again for letting men into the house, and she then lived briefly in bed-and-breakfast accommodation in that city, until she met a man called Rod who, she says, ended up beating her in front of the children ...

(Continued)

Both the refuges in North City and Steeltown report that their staff were concerned about the children, who were sometimes left alone in the room, sometimes taken out by their mother late at night, and (they think) regularly exposed by their mother to her contacts with violent men (several of whom are known to have criminal records for violent offences). Discussions with local child protection agencies, however, never came to anything due to Susan's constant moves between areas. (It seems there were other moves before Steeltown and North City.)

If you were the social worker interviewing her, what would your reaction be?

Comments on Exercise 11.1

As I have said repeatedly in this book, I do not want to give the impression that anyone should come to a firm judgement on the basis of as little information as this. However, on what we have so far, I would have real worries about the immediate safety of these two children as well as for their long-term well-being.

Susan does seem to be a victim of male violence, and her reckless, danger-seeking lifestyle, in which she seems almost to actively seek out violent men, suggests to me that she may have been a victim of male abuse from an early age. But this doesn't alter the fact that the children really are not being adequately cared for. She really does not seem to have been giving any sort of priority to their needs. Susan may be herself a victim, but her actions and decisions are harming and endangering her children. The question is whether, given appropriate services, she can provide some security and stability for them, or not.

Child abuse tragedies in the UK frequently involve families who move repeatedly from one area to another, with the result that information is lost and local agencies do not fully 'take ownership' of their case. I would therefore suggest that, while the immediate need for money and accommodation obviously needs to be addressed, the present agency needs to act quickly to ensure that information is pulled together on this case, and that the relevant local agencies do take up their child protection responsibilities immediately – and continue to do so until they can be confident that equivalent agencies elsewhere have done likewise.

Blaming the victim

Blaming women who were victims of male violence, instead of violent men, has a long history. As we've seen, at one time male violence was seen as legitimate and even necessary (and may continue to be seen in this way in some cultural contexts). Even when violence against women is no longer sanctioned by law, there continued to be a tendency to excuse violence on the basis that women had in some way 'provoked' it. Now that domestic violence has come under the lens of the child protection system, blaming the victim can take on yet newer forms. A woman who lives in terror of a violent partner may, for instance, find herself under additional threat from child protection professionals who demand that she demonstrate that she is able to protect her children, or risk having her children removed from her.

We should be clear that if a woman has done everything she can to remove herself and her children from a seriously violent man, but he persists in tracking her down, assaulting her in the street or trying to break into her home, then the child protection agencies should be trying to protect her *and* her children, not blaming her for things which are outside her control. If the police, with their cars, radios, truncheons and hand-cuffs cannot stop a man from tracking down and assaulting his former partner, then how can the woman herself be expected to do so? To place responsibility onto a woman for something which she cannot reasonably be expected to achieve does not in any sense constitute child protection.

In her study of child protection files mentioned above, Catherine Humphreys found that:

> Although there were varying degrees of support provided for these women and children, the bottom line was that ... women were warned that if the man returned then the children would be accommodated, an Emergency Protection Order made, or there would be an immediate return to conference at which decisions would be made about the future of the children ... For women in these situations who are already the subject of violence themselves, such strictures must be experienced as punitive, particularly when they are not followed through with effective strategies from police, the legal system and services within the interagency forum to assist her with this difficult and often dangerous task. (Humphreys, 1999: 83)

One of the dangers of this is that women may be afraid to disclose that they are victims of domestic violence to child protection workers:

> The study of child protection cases by Farmer and Owen (1995) reported that mothers deliberately concealed from social workers the violence they were experiencing. (Humphreys, 1999: 85)

To add to the unfairness, it often seems as if the man faces no consequences at all for his violent actions:

> Men are dropped from, and become invisible in, the child protection system ... Frustrated [female] workers in the lower rungs of the hierarchy can inadvertently project their dissatisfactions onto other women who they perceive as 'failing' in their responsibility towards children. In the process the focus on where the key responsibility for shaping these relationships lies becomes invisible. (Humphreys, 1999: 84)

This tendency to place all the responsibility on the woman, incidentally, is sometimes evident not only in cases of indirect abuse but also in cases of direct male-perpetrated physical or sexual abuse of children. Sometimes the child protection system can seem almost more critical of the woman for 'failing to protect' a child than it is of the man who actually *carried out* the sexual or physical abuse. Agencies with all the power of the state behind them need to be very careful not to accuse women in vulnerable and powerless positions of 'failing to protect' their children in situations where the failure to protect ought to be laid at the agencies' own door, or at the door of society at large.

Exercise 11.2

Children: Jenny, aged two, Libby, aged eight
Mother: Belinda, aged 30
Father of Jenny: Mickey, aged 20
Father of Libby: Jake, whereabouts unknown

When Mickey moved in with Belinda, he was just 16 and Belinda was 26. She had ended her relationship with Jake – a man 12 years older than herself who was regularly violent towards her – when their daughter Libby was still a baby. Initially her relationship with Mickey seemed easier and less threatening. Mickey had been rejected by his own parents and Belinda started out as more of a mother figure to him than a partner. But following the birth of Jenny, Mickey began to feel very threatened by the amount of attention the baby was getting and the reduction in the amount of time and energy that Belinda had for him. He began drinking heavily and beating Belinda on a regular basis. Although very immature, he is a heavily built young man over six foot tall, who can easily physically dominate Belinda, a very slight woman, who is only five foot two. Lengthy beatings, usually late at night and resulting in black eyes, multiple bruising and cracked ribs for Belinda, were followed by tears of remorse, and declarations by Mickey that she is the only woman in the world that he has ever loved or made him feel loved.

The situation came to the attention of the child protection system when Libby's teacher, concerned about Libby's withdrawn, exhausted appearance, and her inability to relate to other children or concentrate on her work, managed to get Libby to tell her what was going on at home.

Belinda immediately acknowledged that the situation was intolerable for herself and the children, but said that she had found it hard to end it (a) because she simply did not know how to go about getting away from Mickey and (b) because she felt sorry for him and could see that his violence was the result of his own childhood abuse. With professional support, however, she acted quickly, taking herself and the children to a refuge and from there getting herself rehoused in a different part of town and obtaining a court injunction giving the police powers of arrest to prevent Mickey from visiting her there.

However, some weeks after her move, Mickey found out her new address, came to her door at 11.30 p.m. and demanded and pleaded to be let in. Belinda tried to summon the police, but due to a serious incident elsewhere they lacked sufficient manpower to respond for an hour and a half, by which time, after Mickey had been ringing the doorbell, banging the door, and shouting and sobbing in the street for over an hour, Belinda had eventually let him in, on the promise of good behaviour, so as to allow the children some sleep. When the police came round she told them to go away again. Later, after a lengthy talk had degenerated into an argument, Mickey began to beat her again. There was about an hour of shouting, smashing household objects, punches and kicks, all overheard by the two children.

To what extent is Belinda responsible for this new exposure of the children to violence?

(Continued)

(Continued)

Comments on Exercise 11.2

What I have tried to do in the above exercise is imagine myself in the position of a woman who eventually concludes that it would be easier for herself and her children to give in than to hold the line. It seems to me that it is often quite unrealistic to expect women to be able to hold such a line unless appropriate professional support is forthcoming. The failure in this case was not primarily Belinda's but the police's. The police in turn would be perfectly entitled to point to limited resources and competing priorities, just as other professional agencies frequently do, in order to explain why it was not physically possible to respond more quickly. But if professional agencies can point to limited resources, then so surely can parents. I think professionals should be very careful about accusing mothers of failing to protect children in incidents which occurred in situations of extreme emotional pressure which perhaps few of us could withstand.

Denying agency to the victim

In trying to avoid 'blaming the victim', though, it is possible to fall into the opposite error of releasing the victim from having any responsibility at all. Some women do initiate violence. Some women do recklessly and needlessly return with their children to situations where violence will predictably occur (as I tried to illustrate in Exercise 11.1). They will have their reasons for this and we may well feel a great deal of sympathy for women for whom even a violent relationship seems preferable to no relationship. But in our desire not to 'judge' the woman, we should be careful not to end up condoning the exposure of children to yet more traumatic and dangerous experiences. Allowing our feelings for the adults to get in the way of protecting children is a mistake that can easily be made in quite a number of situations, and not just in the arena of domestic violence. In the previous two chapters I discussed the issues involved in working with parents with drink or drug problems, mental health problems and learning difficulties. All of these are situations where our concern for the parents, and our desire not to judge them unfairly for problems not of their own making, may make us prone to forget that the issue for the child protection professional is not in fact whether or not parents are to *blame* in some moral sense, but whether or not they are capable of acting to meet the needs of their children. As Judith Milner and Patrick O'Byrne observe:

> Judgementalism has become a dirty word in social practice to such an extent that we sometimes find practitioners tolerating harmful circumstances for some family members in their efforts to avoid appearing judgemental of other family members – usually the older ones. (Milner and O'Byrne, 2002: 169–70)

It is also worth noting that casting someone *entirely* in the role of victim, even if done for the best intentions, can sometimes be very unhelpful and disempowering for the *victim herself:*

> Challenging 'woman blaming' should not lead to exonerating women from any responsibility at all, as this would diminish women's sense of effectiveness and agency altogether. (Burck and Speed, 1995: 3)

Again this is something that human service professionals frequently have to grapple with, not only in the child protection arena but in other areas too. How do we acknowledge that people we work with are often the victims of misfortune, and of personal and structural oppression, without taking away from them their own agency, their own responsibility for their actions and the consequences of their actions, their own freedom to make choices and make mistakes? (In my own profession of social work, this is arguably *the* central dilemma.)

Excluding or demonizing the man

I have already mentioned the danger of 'blaming the victim' (in most cases the woman) and holding the victim rather than the perpetrator (in most cases the man) responsible for protecting the children. Focussing on the woman and excluding the man is a common pattern not just in the domestic violence arena but in many other areas. I've already noted the tendency for the woman to become the focus of work, *even if the problem behaviour being addressed is actually the behaviour of the man.* This can occur for a variety of reasons:

- If the man has a job and the woman does not, a child protection worker may have to work outside her normal hours to visit when the man is at home. It may be simpler from a purely practical point of view just to work with the woman.
- Child protection professionals, consciously or unconsciously, may make the assumption that domestic matters are not really the responsibility of the man.
- Men themselves may make this assumption and absent themselves, or they may feel uncomfortable about being present when 'women's issues' are being discussed.
- Violent, aggressive men may be intimidating not only to their partners and children, but to child protection professionals. This may make professionals further inclined to visit when they are not there, or to avoid confronting them when they *are* there. It is easier to confront the less intimidating partner and easier to placate or avoid the intimidating one.
- As an extension of the previous point, it is worth remembering the discussion in Chapter 4 about the so-called Stockholm syndrome: those who feel threatened by violence sometimes end up defending those they feel threatened by. (This applies to workers, as Stanley and Goddard, 2002, argued, but of course it applies even more to the direct and indirect victims, who sometimes really are in a position analogous to those in the Stockholm siege.)
- Professionals may be inclined to simply assume that men will be violent or intimidating on the basis of reports that they have received, or on the basis of their own preconceptions, and act accordingly, even if the reality is different to this.

As we've seen, this tendency to exclude men can result in blaming women who are actually victims themselves, and in men being able to evade responsibility for their abusive behaviour. However, at other times it can also work to the disadvantage of men, in that their views may be excluded from any consideration, they may simply be assumed to be unredeemable brutes, and their importance to their children may be discounted. If, as a result, children are denied a relationship with a parent who is important to them, this in turn can work to the disadvantage of children too.

Chapter summary

This chapter has looked briefly at a rather large subject: the child protection issues that arise from violence between adults in a home. The topics covered have been:

- the relationship between adult violence and child abuse: direct physical child abuse is more likely in homes where there is adult violence, but even when there is no physical child abuse, adult violence constitutes a form of emotional abuse of children
- the relationship between gender and both adult violence and child abuse: I discussed the extent to which both adult violence and child abuse could be said to be mainly male problems, while child protection could be seen as a predominantly female activity
- pointers for child protection professionals dealing with domestic violence situations, including the need to be wary of blaming the adult victim of abuse, while also not denying agency to the victim, and not simply assuming that the interests of children are automatically the same as those of their mother.

In the next chapter, I will look at the extent to which poverty and social exclusion are related to child abuse and neglect and consider the nature of that relationship.

12 Poverty and Social Exclusion

- Poverty as a risk factor
- Poverty, social exclusion, unemployment and homelessness
- Psychological consequences
- Poverty as stressor
- Intervention and oppression

In Britain and other English-speaking countries, the general public and its political representatives expect the child protection system to anticipate and prevent child abuse. Yet a major factor in many cases of child maltreatment is something that, except in marginal ways, child protection professionals can do very little about: poverty and social exclusion.

A cynic might go as far as to argue that the real function of the child protection system is not so much to solve the problem of child abuse, as to provide someone to take the blame for it and to deflect attention from the role played by structural and economic injustices. I actually think that this contains more than a grain of truth (public policy is sometimes as much about being *seen* to have done something about a problem, as it is about actually bringing about substantive change) but, as I have commented elsewhere, I also think that a purely negative and cynical position is, in its way just as naïve as an entirely positive view (Beckett, 2006: 183). The fact that the professionals involved in child protection work cannot do much about poverty and structural inequalities, does not mean that they can't do anything useful at all.

It is certainly important for child protection workers to be aware of the difficulties faced by parents in poor communities. Poverty is a source of stress – and stress, we know, can push people who otherwise would have coped quite adequately into abusive or neglectful parenting.

Poverty as a risk factor

There are, even in wealthy countries, large numbers of families who are very definitely poor, in the sense that they live lives which the majority of the population would regard, in material terms, as intolerably bleak. A substantial proportion of families on child protection caseloads are poor in this sense.

Poverty is a risk factor. Cyril Greenland (1987), whose work on predicting child abuse I discussed in Chapter 8, identified poor housing, poverty and unemployment among his predictors of abuse. In the USA, Neil Guterman, summarizing a number of different studies, writes that:

> families reported to child protection services are more likely to be single mothers, have unemployed fathers, receive public assistance, and/or live in poor neighbourhoods ... Several sets of studies, as pointed out by the National Research Council [1993: 133] ... have further found that child maltreatment is likely to be concentrated in the 'poorest of the poor'. (Guterman, 2001: 27)

In Britain, Gibbons et al. (1995) found that, of their sample of children who had been on child protection registers on grounds of physical abuse, 57 per cent came from families without a wage earner.

As I have warned several times, we do need to be careful about how we interpret such figures. For one thing, children on child protection registers, or children reported to child protection agencies, may not necessarily accurately represent the distribution of child maltreatment. More prosperous, articulate and powerful parents may be better able to conceal child maltreatment from the authorities than poor people, for the poor are typically subjected to 'greater scrutiny by public authorities' (Guterman, 2001: 27). One could also make out a case that forms of child maltreatment that might be more typical of well-to-do families are less likely to be defined as child abuse and neglect. For instance, the practice of sending children as young as six away to boarding school still exists in some sections of British society and, though many would argue that it is likely to cause 'significant harm', it does not result in intervention by child protection agencies.

Nor should we necessarily assume that a statistical correlation between poverty and child maltreatment necessarily means that poverty *causes* child maltreatment. (In Chapter 9 I cautioned in a similar way against interpreting a statistical link between drug misuse and child maltreatment as meaning that the former necessarily causes the latter.) Since the vast majority of poor people do not maltreat their children, and since a significant number of better-off people *do* maltreat their children, we need to be clear that, even if poverty is associated with an increased *likelihood* of child maltreatment, it certainly does not cause it in most cases. We should also bear in mind that different kinds of child maltreatment have different causes. Sexual abuse in particular is not as closely correlated with socioeconomic factors as physical abuse and neglect (see Chapter 8).

To the extent that there *is* a link between poverty and child maltreatment we should also consider the possibility of different kinds of causal relationships other than 'poverty makes maltreatment more likely'. Perhaps it's the other way round! Perhaps child maltreatment makes *poverty* more likely? (We know, for instance, that one of the consequences of chronic abuse and neglect on children can be a deterioration in school work and problems in relating to others, both of which might reduce the likelihood of a person obtaining well-paid employment.) Then again, perhaps both poverty *and* child maltreatment are made more likely by the presence of some other factor? (For instance, people with certain personality characteristics or life experiences may have difficulty both with holding down a job *and* with being adequate parents.)

When we are considering social systems, it is usually unrealistic to expect to find a primary cause of anything, rather in the way that it is impossible to say whether the chicken or the egg came first. There is a complex network of relationships between poverty, child maltreatment and a whole range of other phenomena including intellectual ability, mental health, physical health, family history, social isolation and educational attainment. But I do suggest that the application of a little imagination is all that is required to see that poverty must cause considerable stress to families. And since, as I discussed in Chapter 8, stress is a major factor in child abuse and neglect, it would be surprising indeed if we did not find that child abuse and neglect did not occur more frequently among those who are poor.

Poverty, social exclusion, unemployment and homelessness

Poverty can be seen in 'absolute' or 'relative' terms. People are living in absolute poverty when they are so poor as to be unable to gain reliable access to the things that they physically need to keep alive. A subsistence farmer in Africa, whose crop has failed and who has no other source of income or food other than his farm, is living in absolute poverty. But people may not be in absolute poverty but still be poor relative to the standards of the society in which they live. We humans are social beings and, to participate fully in a society, we need to have the resources to operate within the norms of that society. 'Poverty is not just about what is needed to stay alive, but also about the conditions that allow people to stay healthy and participate in society' (Blackburn, 1991: 152).

A relative definition of 'low income' in common use is 'a household income that is 60 per cent or less of the average (median) household income in that year' (Palmer et al., 2005: 9). In Great Britain 11.4 million people were living in households below this income threshold in 2004/5. 'This represents a drop of 2½ million since 1996/97. It is, however, still much higher than in the early 1980s' (NPI, 2006: 1). Poverty is not evenly distributed across the country, though, and it is borne disproportionately by people from ethnic minorities, two-fifths of whom live in low-income families as compared to one-fifth of white families (NPI, 2006: 3).

The family type that is most vulnerable to poverty is the lone-parent family: 'a half of all lone parents are in low income, two-and-a-half times the rate for couples with children' (NPI, 2006: 1). A number of studies have found a strong correlation between lone parenthood and male unemployment – worse unemployment opportunities in a given area of the country being 'associated with more childbearing outside marriage' – and between marriage breakdown and various indicators of relative poverty such as living in rented accommodation or remaining in the parental home (Howard et al., 2001: 89). This suggests more strands in the complex web that links material deprivation with the way that families are formed and the way that they function.

Environmental poverty

Exercise 12.1

Suppose you were walking in a city which you had never visited before. What are the signs that would tell you that you were entering a 'poor area'? What would your likely reaction be?

Comments on Exercise 12.1

The first part of the question seems so basic as to be rather patronizing. I apologize but that is really my point. Poverty and deprivation are obvious to all of us. You can doubtless think of others, but perhaps among the visual signs that would suggest to you that you were in a 'poor area' are:

- *A high proportion of public housing*
- *Buildings in a poor state of repair and/or cheaply constructed*
- *Parks and other public areas poorly maintained and perhaps vandalized*
- *Shops tending to be confined to small local stores; no banks or large supermarkets*
- *Graffiti, boarded-up windows, uncleared litter and other rubbish*
- *Often, though not always, a higher proportion of people from ethnic minorities than in other parts of the city (in the UK, as discussed above, people from ethnic minorities are twice as likely to be poor as white people)*
- *Small children playing in the street*

I obviously don't know what your reaction would be to finding yourself in such an area – perhaps you live in one yourself – but I would suggest that a common reaction for anyone not having any specific business in the area, would be to leave it as promptly as possible.

Poverty is not evenly distributed within a country. It is also not evenly distributed within any given town or area. Wherever you live, you are almost certainly aware of neighbourhoods or roads or groups of houses that are seen locally as 'poor' or 'deprived' or 'rough'. What is more, if you were to visit a city you have never visited before, you would have no difficulty in recognizing which were its 'deprived' areas. Indeed in many cities, there are areas which are so obviously 'deprived' that outsiders are reluctant to enter them at all for fear of crime. This sense of danger is not based on mere prejudice. People in poor neighbourhoods are much more likely to be victims of crime than people in other areas. Pantazis and Gordon (1997) found that poor people were more likely than others to feel unsafe walking in their own neighbourhood or being alone at home. The New Policy Institute reports that 'households with no household insurance are more than twice as likely to be burgled as those with insurance' and 'half of those on low income do not have any household insurance compared with one in five of households on average incomes' (NPI, 2006: 3).

Poverty is not just something that happens to certain individuals or certain families in isolation, then, but is often *an instantly recognizable characteristic of whole communities.* Part of the experience of being poor is living in a 'poor neighbourhood': a neighbourhood which other people might prefer to avoid even passing through, and quite possibly a neighbourhood which not only *feels* dangerous, but actually is.

Peter Townsend (1979) introduced the idea of 'environmental poverty' to encapsulate that aspect of poverty which is not to do with an individual's or a family's income, but with the circumstances in which they live. Under the heading of environmental poverty we might include, 'lack of access to, gardens, parks, play space, shopping facilities and health centres, as well as taking account of pollution such as noise and dirt' (Blackburn, 1991: 93).

Social exclusion, unemployment and homelessness

If we look at poverty as not just a matter of money, but as a matter of access to things which the population at large would regard as a normal part of life, it begins to shade into the concept of social exclusion, which can be defined as 'the inability to participate fully in society' (Family Policy Studies Centre, 2000: 11). People may experience social exclusion for reasons other than poverty, as a result of disability, for instance, or the fact that they are members of an ethnic minority which is discriminated against. Disabled people have a lower average income than the rest of the population but the social exclusion they experience is 'not solely material. It has a lot to do with society's attitude to disabled people' (Knight and Brent, 1998: 4).

One form of social exclusion is to be excluded from the workplace. Chronic unemployment has been a feature of Western economies for many years. Families with children under 18 and no employed parent, constituted 9.8 per cent of American families in 2005 (Bureau of Labor Statistics, 2006) while in the UK, in autumn 2005, 16 per cent of children lived in workless households (National Statistics, 2006).

Another form of social exclusion is not to have a home. In wealthy Western countries, large numbers of families are homeless. A survey of US cities in 2005 found that families with dependent children accounted for 33 per cent of homeless people, with families often being forced to break up in order to gain access to shelter (US Conference of Mayors, 2005). In England:

- 98,730 households were in temporary accommodation on 31 December 2005 ...
- 86 per cent of households were in self-contained accommodation, 4.5 per cent were in bed & breakfast hotels ... and the remainder in other forms of shared-facility units.
- 74 per cent of households in temporary accommodation included dependent children. (ODPM, 2006)

The latter is a small proportion of the population as a whole, which includes some 17 million families, but is a group that is likely to be experiencing multiple stresses and is proportionately much more likely than other families to come to the attention of child protection professionals. Panos Vostanis found that 50 per cent of homeless families become so because of domestic violence and 25 per cent as a result of harassment from neighbours. He adds that, among homeless families:

> Most families have histories of previous chronic adversities that constitute risk factors for both children and parents ... Mothers are more likely to have suffered abuse in their own childhood and adult life and children have increased rates of placement on the at-risk child protection register, because of neglect, physical and/or sexual abuses. (Vostanis, 2002: 463)

This illustrates rather well the complexity of the relationship between social exclusion (in this case homelessness) and other problems such as child abuse and mental health. It would be wrong to say that homelessness has been the *cause* of problems such as domestic violence and child abuse in these cases, since these things preceded the family becoming homeless, yet it would be perverse not to recognize that homelessness is likely to greatly aggravate many of these problems. Anyone who contemplates for a moment the prospect of coping on their own with children for any length of time in a bed-and-breakfast establishment or a homeless hostel with shared facilities will surely not find it surprising that 'twice as many people in B & B experience psychological distress than in the general population' (Howard et al., 2001: 115).

Psychological consequences

People who are poor and/or unemployed and/or homeless have significantly worse mental and physical health than the population at large. The causal relationships are complex and not all one-way, but poverty, unemployment and homelessness do impact directly on mental and physical health. The following statements give a flavour of the ways in which poverty is actually experienced. The quotations from Beresford et al. (1999) that I have italicized are comments made by people with personal experience of poverty:

> Children in the bottom social class [in Britain] are five times more likely to die from an accident than those at the top. (Howard et al., 2001: 115)

> *... being poor is just so much work your whole life. You see people going into a shop. They buy what they want and they leave. But you're there, you're having to calculate how much money you've got as you go round, you're having to look at one brand and then another, and meanwhile the store detective is looking over your shoulder ...* (Beresford et al., 1999: 94)

> One in 20 mothers sometimes went without food to meet the needs of their children, with lone mothers on income support 14 times more likely to go without than mothers in two-parent families not on benefit. (Howard et al., 2001: 109, referring to Ashworth and Braithwaite, 1997)

> *It's the boredom of poverty and the boredom is what wears you down and makes you despondent in the end ... It's deadly boring having to penny pinch all the time.* (Beresford et al., 1999: 91)

But the negative impact of social exclusion isn't only about lack of access to material resources. Unemployment, for instance, impacts not only on people's incomes but also on their self-esteem and sense of purpose. For many of us, work is central to our identity. ('What do you do for a living?' is one of the most commonly asked questions on first meeting someone.) Work provides not only money but also 'opportunity for control; skill use; interpersonal contact; external goal and task demands; variety; environmental clarity; ... physical security; and valued social position' (Fryer, 1992: 114).

A Danish author (Christofferson, 2000) suggests that unemployment can impact on the mental health of parents as a result of decreased social status, disruption of family roles and feelings of personal failure as well as of specifically financial problems, and that this in turn is likely to impact on children. Hypothesizing that unemployment is likely to make parents 'less supportive of, or sensitive to their children's needs', and that it might result in increased incidences of child abuse and neglect, Christofferson particularly considered the relationship between abuse incidents and a history of unemployment, and concluded that 'Although it is very seldom that children are hospitalized as a consequence of violence, a disproportionate number of such cases can be observed among the children of the long-term unemployed' (Christofferson, 2000: 431). Aware of the possibility that there could be other factors which caused both unemployment *and* child abuse – and could thus result in a statistical correlation between child abuse and unemployment but no actual causal link between the two – Christofferson tried to tease out the effects of unemployment from those of other social factors, and concluded:

> the analyses revealed that the connection between unemployed parents and abuse of their children was still to be found even after taking account of parents' education and existing risk factors and adverse social circumstances. (Christofferson, 2000: 437)

In Christofferson's view, 'Parental unemployment [and especially *maternal* unemployment] . . . is one of several risk factors which may increase the risk for child abuse even in ordinarily stable families exposed to unemployment' (2000: 436).

Poverty as stressor

As Michael Rutter observes: 'Good parenting requires certain permitting circumstances. There must be the necessary life opportunities and facilities. When these are lacking even the best parents may find it difficult to use their skills' (1974: 20).

I do not think that we should be surprised that researchers find links between the experience of unemployment, poverty and homelessness on the one hand and depression and poor health on the other, along with a whole range of other phenomena such as marital breakdown, crime, drug abuse and suicide. By the same token, I do not think we should be surprised that they are also linked with an increased incidence of child abuse and neglect. It would be a mistake to conclude from this that poverty *causes* abuse and neglect, but I think it reasonable to assume that one of the reasons for the correlation is that poverty and social exclusion are *stress factors* – and, as all parents must surely know from personal experience, cumulative stress is a factor that pushes parents along a continuum that leads towards abusive or neglectful behaviour.

Exercise 12.2

Elsie is a lone parent aged 22, living on state benefits with two children – Ben aged three years and Jack aged nine months – in a fourth-floor council flat. (She has never had paid employment and left school without any qualifications.) Elsie goes shopping for groceries several times a week, a trip which involves a walk of about three-quarters of a mile to a small supermarket in a small shopping precinct. Unless she can arrange for a neighbour to look after them, she takes both children with her in a double buggy.

Elsie is returning from the shops on a hot summer day, pushing the buggy laden with children and groceries. She has spent all her money until her next benefit payment in three days' time. Ben and Jack are hot, tired and bored, as is Elsie, who is rather overweight and has difficulty with the buggy, which has seen better days and now has the annoying habit of pulling constantly to the right. Jack has been crying the whole way home and Ben has been whining and demanding sweets.

In the building where they live, the lift is out of order, as it frequently is. It is impossible to carry buggy, children and groceries up the stairs. Elsie tells Ben to get out of the buggy and walk up the stairs, while she herself carries Jack and one bag of groceries, leaving the buggy and the other groceries for her to come back and collect when the children are installed in the flat. This makes her very anxious because on one occasion she had all her groceries stolen when she left them downstairs like this, so she wants to get back down again as quickly as possible.

Ben is infuriatingly slow on the stairs, complaining all the way up and asking her to carry him too. When they finally reach the landing outside her flat, she puts down her groceries and Jack so as to get out her key. At this point, for some reason, Ben takes it into his head to pull a bottle of cooking oil out of the groceries, which he then drops onto the concrete floor of the landing, where it smashes, right next to where his baby brother is sitting.

Consider Elsie's likely reaction (or your likely reaction if you were in Elsie's shoes).

Now consider the following different scenario: Elizabeth is a university teacher aged 35 who has temporarily given up work to be a full-time mother. She is married to a doctor and lives in a detached house with its own car-parking space right outside the front door. She has just returned from her monthly grocery shop at a large out-of-town supermarket. Coincidentally she also has a Ben aged three and a Jack aged nine months. In the car on the way back Ben has been listening to a story tape and Jack has gone to sleep. Elizabeth helps Ben out of his car seat and then picks up Jack, along with one of the ten bags of groceries. Outside the front door she puts down the groceries to take out her key and Ben, for some reason, takes out a bottle of olive oil, which he promptly drops on the doorstep where it smashes.

What differences do you notice between the two experiences?

Comments on Exercise 12.2

Obviously how Elsie and Elizabeth might react to their respective smashed bottles of cooking oil will depend on their own personalities, what is going on for them at the time, and their own personal histories. It might be that Elsie is the sort of person who can deal calmly with minor crises of this kind while Elizabeth is the sort of person who finds this sort of thing intolerably exasperating.

(Continued)

But other things being equal, I think you will agree that grocery shopping is far more stressful for Elsie than it is for Elizabeth. She has to do it far more often (and has to worry much more about how much she spends), she has to undertake an exhausting journey to do it and, at the end of it, she has the difficulty of getting everything up the stairs. Even the money wasted on the cooking oil is more serious for Elsie than Elizabeth. She has no money left to buy a replacement. Other things being equal, then, you will probably agree that, for the two women, the bottle-smashing incident is much more likely to be the final straw for Elsie than it is for Elizabeth and that – out of the two – Elsie is therefore the one who is more likely to react in an abusive way, perhaps hitting Ben, or screaming at him, or dragging him roughly into the flat.

The example in the exercise related to contrasting experiences of shopping trips, but I would suggest that if you contrast the experiences of middle-class or upper-working-class parents with those of the poorest parents, you would find a whole range of ways in which the experience of the latter is more stressful, and I would suggest that the cumulative impact of these differences must be enormous, although its effects will of course vary from one individual to another.

Intervention and oppression

But how should an awareness of the relationship between poverty and child maltreatment actually change the practice of child protection workers? In many small ways it may be possible to mitigate the effects of poverty in particular situations – assisting with a claim for benefits, arranging for a grant to pay for some day care to allow parent and child a break from one another – and doing so can often be the most effective form of intervention, so it is very important that child protection workers make every possible effort to address these kinds of environmental stresses. But the professionals involved in child protection really are not equipped or mandated to do more than scratch the surface of problems like poverty or homelessness and unemployment. These things have causes at the level of macroeconomics and of national and international politics and economics. They are not amenable to casework. The reality is that the material assistance that child protection professionals can offer *is* extremely limited, and even that limited help comes, from a family's point of view, at a price. By becoming recipients of 'welfare', their status as poor and dependent on others is necessarily underlined and confirmed.

These are very difficult matters which at times make social workers and other professionals question the whole basis on which they work. Child protection workers often have to deal with parents who are failing to cope but would have been able to do so adequately if it were not for the external stressors that they are up against. Of course, children cannot be left to suffer maltreatment just because we are sorry for their parents, and sometimes, even when there are perfectly understandable reasons why parents are struggling, child protection services have to intervene. But frequent interventions by child protection agencies into the lives of poor families can in themselves be a very substantial additional source of stress. I have previously quoted (in Chapter 2) Neil Guterman's warning that, if intervention by child protection agencies 'engenders in parents deeper feelings of powerlessness and adds additional ecological challenges', there is a possibility that it 'may even heighten the risk of child maltreatment – precisely the opposite of the stated purpose of the intervention' (Guterman, 2001: 49). Sadly some interventions do indeed have the effect of making things worse both for the parents *and* the child. For this reason, a 'play it safe', 'belt and braces' approach to child protection doesn't really work. There are risks attached to every course of action and the job of the child protection worker is to strike a balance between them.

And there is another level at which child protection interventions can make things harder for people in poor communities. A pattern of regular interventions can have the effect of making things more difficult not only for families but for *whole neighbourhoods,* by increasing general feelings of powerlessness, threat and alienation. This could in the long run result in more harm being done to children in these neighbourhoods, *even if interventions in any given case were helpful to the children immediately involved.* There are neighbourhoods within which the child protection system must feel at times like something akin to the surveillance system of a totalitarian state (and, in the UK, the increasing levels of surveillance of children and families proposed by *Every Child Matters* and *Working Together* [DfES, 2003, 2006] are likely to exacerbate this problem). Schools talk to social workers about children and their parents, social workers talk to doctors about their patients, schools and social workers hold liaison meetings with the police. A system that is justified on the grounds of protecting children can end up looking awfully like a system to oppress and spy on the poor. And though even an oppressive system may protect some children, there is a danger that, in the long run, this will only be at the expense of others.

Exercise 12.3

In Exercise 12.2, the three-year-old son of Elsie smashed a bottle of cooking oil on the concrete landing outside her flat. For the purposes of this exercise, let us suppose that the bottle incident does indeed feel to Elsie like the final straw and that she slaps Ben hard across the face. He is caught just above the eye by a heavy ring which she is wearing. The result of this is a large bruise and swelling on one cheek and a black eye.

Next day, a neighbour in the flat opposite, Mrs Rowe, sees the injuries and telephones the Local Authority's Children's Social Care service (CSC), reporting that she heard Elsie yelling at Ben on the landing the previous day, following a smashing noise, and heard Ben screaming in distress. She had also heard Jack screaming throughout the incident.

Mrs Rowe says she hears a lot of screaming and shouting coming from the flat, and has sometimes thought she had heard hitting before.

On checking its records, CSC finds that there were several referrals from a different neighbour at a previous address, concerned about Elsie screaming at the children, although on those occasions CSC had decided there was not a basis to take any further action other than talking to the local health visitor and to Elsie's GP, who had both reported that Elsie had a short fuse but that they had never seen evidence of physical injury to the children.

(Continued)

CSC visits Elsie. During the course of this visit Elsie learns for the first time that there have been previous referrals about her to CSC, that CSC has had discussions about her with her GP and her health visitor, and that the agency holds a file on Ben and Jack. Elsie at first attempts to deny that she hit Ben and suggests that he may have fallen and hit his face on a toy car. Taking his cue from his mother, Ben tells the CSC worker that he fell over.

At the insistence of CSC Ben and Jack are taken to a paediatrician, who says the injury has clearly been caused by a blow with the hand across the face. The paediatrician also notes some older bruising on Jack's shoulder, but is unable to suggest a cause for it.

As a result of this investigation, a child protection conference is called and Ben and Jack's names are made subject to a child protection plan. The protection plan is agreed between CSC, the other professionals and (because she feels she has little choice) Elsie. It initially involves:

- Ben and Jack being checked weekly for bruising
- a social worker visiting Elsie weekly for a six-week period to complete a 'core assessment' and work with her on parenting issues
- Elsie being required to attend a family centre with Ben and Jack for a programme on parenting skills.

The social worker assigned to Elsie is Judy, aged 24, single and with no children.

Elsie knows several people who have had dealings with CSC. A friend of Elsie's recently had a child taken into care.

What do you think the effect of this intervention will be on Elsie, and what consequences do you think it will have for Ben and Jack?

Comments on Exercise 12.3

This was a violent assault on a small child and there are some suggestions (though no hard evidence) that it was not an isolated incident. The professional agencies have perfectly legitimate concerns and have put in place a plan which will at least ensure that, if this sort of thing is a regular event, it should be picked up fairly quickly. What is more, the professional agencies might argue, this plan not only provides the safety net of monitoring but also offers some help to Elsie with coping in a different way in the future.

But if we put ourselves in Elsie's shoes – and it is very important to do this, provided that we hold in mind the fact that the point of doing so is to help protect Ben and Jack – it may look rather less helpful.

What has happened is deeply humiliating for Elsie. She has never had a job. She has no qualifications. The most important work she does in life is to parent her children and her ability to do this work is now being called into question by powerful agencies who she knows sometimes take people's children away from them.

Elsie has found out for the first time that her health visitor and GP talked about her 'behind her back' to CSC. (If I was Elsie this would make me feel angry and betrayed, and also make me feel that I was up against a powerful network of professional agencies, who valued each other's opinion more than they valued mine.)

(Continued)

(Continued)

She is being offered a 'core assessment'. This term would probably not mean anything to Elsie. Even if it is explained to her, it seems to me that the idea of an assessment carries an implication that the professionals are better able to understand Elsie's family than she is herself.

Elsie is also being offered 'work' with a social worker 'on parenting issues'. A phrase like 'work on parenting issues', though, is a very social work expression. What would Elsie make of it? And what does it actually mean? In my experience child protection workers often fail to explain these terms, and we are perhaps not always clear about what we mean ourselves. If what is being suggested is some sort of counselling or quasi-therapeutic work, then a clearer understanding with Elsie would be needed, and also her genuine consent. If something much more general and open-ended is being proposed then why not say so? (Perhaps: 'I'd like to visit you for a few weeks just to get to know you a bit better and see if there is any way we can help you to avoid hurting your children when you lose your temper'.)

I mean no disrespect to young or childless social workers, but in my experience, the fact that Judy is not much older than Elsie, and has no experience of parenting, is likely to be a significant issue for Elsie and an additional source of humiliation and resentment if it is not acknowledged in some way.

Parenting skills training at a family centre is a common response in such situations, but again is humiliating – it is like being sent back to school – and perhaps it is beside the point. Is it actually skills that Elsie is lacking? (If I drive badly when I am tired or stressed, it doesn't necessarily mean I am lacking in driving skills.)

In particular, the plan lacks any component aimed at reducing the stress on Elsie. For example, a simple, practical arrangement might be to provide some sponsored daycare to allow Elsie to do shopping without the children once a week. Although it is right and proper that a child protection plan should insist on Elsie taking responsibility for her violent behaviour, this should surely be balanced by some acknowledgement of the difficult task she faces? Otherwise the net effect of the whole approach is to locate the problem entirely inside Elsie, and thereby to amplify any feelings of self-doubt and low self-esteem which she already has.

Incidentally, plans like this often seem to ignore the fact that the children must have a father or fathers. It is rather hard that women in Elsie's position may have to undergo a humiliating scrutiny of their capacities and deficiencies as parents, while absent fathers, who may have abdicated any sort of parental responsibility, do not find themselves at the receiving end of any such scrutiny.

As to the effect on the little boys of this plan, in the short run it does provide a safety net, in that further assaults on Ben or Jack are likely to be quickly picked up. But in the long run a plan like this provides no practical help to Elsie, may well knock her confidence in her parenting, and is likely to embarrass and humiliate her. It is quite possible to imagine that such an intervention could, in the long run, leave Elsie somewhat less well-equipped to manage everyday stresses than she was before. Most parents at times feel trapped by their children, and resentful of the demands made on them. It is possible that the net effect of interventions of this kind might be to increase those feelings of resentment towards the children, so that they would experience a deterioration rather than an improvement in the standard of parenting they received.

How can child protection workers protect the children of poor people without contributing to the stress that may be one of the major causes of child maltreatment in the first place? There is, unfortunately, no simple route out of this dilemma, which sits uncomfortably at the heart of a great deal of child protection work. But the following are a few suggestions that are to do with being sensitive to power differences and avoiding the abuse of power:

- It is important, particularly for professionals who (like myself) come from comfortable, relatively affluent backgrounds, to be aware of the fact that parents in poor neighbourhoods are raising their children in vastly different circumstances, and raising them to cope with vastly different realities to the ones we are familiar with, or perhaps can even imagine. To give an instance of this: middle-class parents in Britain, finding themselves in the 'catchment area' of state schools which have the reputation of being 'rough', typically take evasive action, either by sending their children to private schools, or by lobbying to get their children into other, less 'rough' state schools further away, or even by moving house so as to get into the catchment area of those less 'rough' schools. For poor parents, there may no alternative to letting their children attend the local 'rough' school, and therefore one of the tasks for parents is to equip them to cope in that environment. Some child-rearing practices, which might seem questionable from a middle-class perspective, 'could be adaptive mechanisms within the social context of a low income deprived neighbourhood' (Shor, 2000: 175).
- It is a good practice to check whether your own conduct, and the conduct of your agency, would be acceptable to you should you find yourself on the receiving end. Would you expect your children's school to inform you if they had concerns about your children, prior to contacting other agencies? What would your attitude be if a professional who had never met your children before, told you that she wished to interview them without you being present? As a general rule, poor people are used to a relatively powerless position, are resigned to official scrutiny and are often remarkably compliant with official requests. But when poor people do raise objections or refuse to fall in with the wishes of child protection agencies, they are rather frequently labelled as 'unco-operative', 'difficult' and 'anti-authority'. We should be very wary about this.
- By the same token, it can be salutary to compare your practice with poor families to the way you work with the (relatively few) affluent middle-class families who come to your attention. Are there differences? And if so why?
- All parents and (depending on their level of understanding) all children need to be informed about what is going on, how things have been left, what is being recorded, who is being consulted, and what the possible outcomes are. People who are in a relatively powerless position may not ask questions (or alternatively, may do so in an aggressive rather than an assertive manner), but child protection agencies should treat them the same as they would treat more powerful and assertive people. Jargon ('assessment', 'core group', 'key worker', 'child protection plan') should be carefully explained.
- It is important to avoid making people 'jump through hoops' just for the sake of doing something. For an agency to require parents (or children) to do something simply so as to make the agency feel *it* has done something is an abuse of power. Anything which makes parents feel humiliated and infantilized is unlikely to help them feel confident about being parents, and is therefore unlikely to help their children.
- Clearly there are some practices by parents and carers which are not acceptable, and it is entirely legitimate for a child protection agency, when such lines have been crossed, to insist on parents stopping these practices, and to take other action if parents do not comply. However, child protection workers should be very careful not to engage in 'nagging'. There are many parenting practices which childcare professionals may dislike but which are not illegal and which would not constitute grounds for removing a child. There is no purpose to be served by 'insisting' that parents stop such practices, if in fact, there is nothing that the agency can do if they

carry on. Subjecting people to constant criticism is not a good way of helping them get better at anything, particularly if their self-esteem is already low, and they are already under stress.

- In particular, child protection agencies should not make threats – such as the threat to take a child into care – if they are not in fact going to carry that threat out. It is the awareness that child protection social workers can and do on occasions take children away from their parents that makes them particularly feared in poor communities. Of course, it is sometimes necessary to remove children from their parents to protect them against serious harm and it is entirely appropriate to give parents warning if this action is being seriously contemplated. But the fear should not be exploited.

- In Exercise 12.3, I suggested that practical help would often be more effective than interventions that simply label a parent as failing and require her to prove her ability to change. I believe this to be the case. But it is worth bearing in mind that targeted help of the kind mentioned is still stigmatizing, because a parent must in effect prove that she is failing before she can gain access to it. ('Are you telling me I have to batter my kids before I can get any help?', as more than one parent has observed when trying unsuccessfully to get help from a social work agency.) For resource reasons, agencies often have no choice but to ration services in this way, although it would be much better in many respects if services such as daycare were provided on demand, or perhaps on financial criteria alone, so as to avoid parents having to experience failure before getting help.

Among the various professional groups involved in child protection, social workers in particular are frequently enjoined to work in an 'anti-oppressive' way, but the oppression that results from poverty, unemployment and homelessness are caused by economic and political forces far beyond the reach of individual casework. However, while child protection professionals cannot expect to transform society in their working lives, they are well placed to witness the reality and extent of poverty and social exclusion, something which is largely invisible to the majority of citizens of the affluent 'West' and they do perhaps have a useful contribution to make *outside* the workplace to the wider political debate.

Chapter summary

In this chapter I have discussed poverty, along with the closely related, overlapping issues of social exclusion, unemployment and homelessness, and explored its relationship to child maltreatment. I have considered:

- evidence that links poverty statistically with child maltreatment, making poverty a 'predictor' or 'risk factor' in child maltreatment, and discussed the nature of this connection
- the nature of poverty, including the concepts of relative and absolute poverty and of environmental poverty, the meaning of 'social exclusion', and the links with unemployment and homelessness
- the psychological consequences of poverty and social exclusion

(Continued)

- the idea of poverty as a stressor – a source of stress which can push some parents who might otherwise cope into abuse or neglect
- intervention by social workers and the child protection system and the danger that intervention intended to protect a child may become, in effect, another kind of oppression of the poor. I made some suggestions about ways of avoiding this.

This concludes Part III of this book. Part IV will look at some current issues and dilemmas faced by child protection work as a whole. The next chapter will look further at the ways in which child protection interventions can actually be harmful, and will consider how the child protection system, intended to protect children from abuse, may actually perpetrate abuse in its own right.

Part IV

PROBLEMS AND DILEMMAS

13 | Abusive Systems

- Harm caused by the system
- Abuse in public care
- System abuse
- System abuse by the child protection system
- Multiple placements
- Drift and prevarication

... the practice of child protection can be as abusive as the behaviour of the parents which has brought the situation into the child protection arena in the first place. (Velleman, 2001: 42)

In the previous chapter, I suggested that the actions of child protection agencies can be a source of additional stress to poor families, which means that they may actually at times increase rather than reduce the risk of child maltreatment.

This is the first of two chapters forming the fourth and concluding part of the book looking at problems and dilemmas facing the child protection system. The next and final chapter will look at some real-world constraints that limit our ability to detect and respond to every instance of child abuse. In this chapter I will look further at ways in which the child protection system, and the system of public care for children (called, in England and Wales, the 'looked-after system'), can themselves be harmful to children to the point where they could themselves accurately be described as abusive.

Harm caused by the system

Most of the harm that is done by the child protection and looked-after systems is not deliberate. Although there are dangerous and abusive individuals in social work and in the looked-after system, as there are in every part of society, they are the exception. But systems can be harmful in effect, even when the individuals who operate them are acting with the best of intentions.

Many child protection professionals are motivated by a strong desire to rescue children from situations in which they are suffering and being harmed. On one level this is a very appropriate motive for doing the work. But the danger of being a 'rescuer' is that you can become so taken up with the harm that a child needs protecting from that you can forget to consider the harm that you yourself might do. It is important for child protection professionals to recognize that there is no such thing as absolute safety, and that the likely or possible benefits of any intervention – whether or not this involves removing children from their parents' care – must be weighed against the likely or possible harm that it might do. The children you work with, and their families, will have to live with the *actual* consequences of your actions, not with whatever consequences you might have aspired to. For this reason, decisions about intervention – and decisions at the policy level too – should always be based on what actually one can *realistically expect* to achieve, not on what one would *ideally like* to achieve. Andrew Maynard and I call this general ethical principle 'the duty of realism' (Beckett and Maynard, 2005: 97).

Abuse in public care

All the kinds of abuse and neglect that happen to children in their own homes, can happen too to children who are in public care, including to children who have been removed from their own families *precisely* for the purpose of protecting them against abuse. Indeed, children who have been abused in their own homes may be particularly vulnerable to abuse elsewhere. They may accept abuse as the norm; they may have been taught that it is dangerous to complain about abuse; they may even have learnt to invite abuse as a way of getting attention. Some sexually abused children, for instance, behave in a sexually provocative way and some children who have been physically abused behave in ways that seem to invite violence. Children who have experienced emotional rejection may likewise behave in ways which seem calculated to alienate themselves from their carers (I quoted an example of this on p.98). This may be because it can feel safer to such children to reject others before they have a chance to reject them. Or perhaps it is because when we fear something in the future we sometimes find it easier to 'get it over with', rather than live in anticipation.

The behaviour of looked-after children is, therefore, a stressor which may contribute to the risk of abuse in the public care system. Another is the difficulty on both sides of forming an attachment to people who have their own separate history. As I observed in a previous chapter, placing a child in an adoptive family or a foster-home is a little like grafting a branch from one tree onto another. It can 'take' very successfully, but there is always a risk that it will not. This may help to explain why being an adoptive, foster- or step-child is one of the eight 'characteristics of the child' identified by Cyril Greenland (1987) as risk factors in fatal child abuse, and may be connected too with the finding of Anderson et al. (1993) that step-parents were roughly ten times more likely to sexually abuse than parents.

The latter statistic may also be connected with the fact that paedophiles can be highly predatory and will actively seek opportunities to have contact with children, and this includes establishing relationships with single mothers in order to gain access to their children, like the narrator of the novel *Lolita* (Nabokov, 1992). Getting a job involving children is another obvious tactic, and it is not surprising that predatory paedophiles have been found operating in schools, churches, choirs and cub packs, as well as in residential homes, foster-homes and adoptive families. Whatever checks and safeguards are put in place, it is difficult to see how they can ever be 100 per cent safe. Checking police records, for instance, will not be effective against paedophiles who have so far managed to keep their activities secret.

One of the facts of life that child protection workers have to live with, therefore, is that the system intended to provide a safe haven for children who would be unsafe in their own homes, does in itself contain a small minority of highly dangerous, abusive individuals.

Exercise 13.1

Two sisters are placed with approved adopters Mr and Mrs Brown, after a period in foster-care. It has been decided that they cannot return to their own family. The older sister, Lynne, is 13; the younger, Kate, is eight. Lynne has experienced sexual abuse in her own family. She is restless and anxious, has difficulty concentrating on school work, and has difficulty getting on with her peers. She can be devious and manipulative at times. These problems continue in the placement, but it is hoped that the security of an adoptive home and the regular input of a therapist, who she has started seeing weekly, will help in time. Kate does not have a known history of abuse. She is a much more confident child, and much easier to like.

One month before the adoption is due to go through, Lynne tells her therapist that Mr Brown has been feeling under her clothes and getting her to masturbate him. This happens, she says, on a Saturday morning, when Mrs Brown takes Kate to a ballet class.

The therapist contacts the social services department, as a result of which both children are questioned by a social worker and the police. Lynne repeats her allegation in detail. Kate says nothing has happened to her and that she is very happy with Mr and Mrs Brown. Both girls are moved to a foster-home while investigations continue, though Kate very much resents this.

Mr Brown indignantly denies the allegation, saying that he and his wife have always known that Lynne is a 'lying, spiteful, vicious girl', but that they will fight 'tooth and nail' to get Kate back. Mrs Brown supports him.

You are the social worker responsible for Lynne and Kate, and you placed them with Mr and Mrs Brown. Imagine your reaction if you were to return from your summer holiday to find that all this had unfolded in your absence.

Comments on Exercise 13.1

As the social worker who made this placement you will have got to know both the girls and the Browns and will have a working relationship with all of them. You will probably have found things to like about all of them, and will certainly have decided that both Mr and Mrs Brown have something to offer these girls as parents.

(Continued)

(Continued)

    What has happened would therefore be a severe blow to you, including your confidence in your ability to make judgements about other people. If the allegations are true, as seems probable, then you (and the social worker who assessed the Browns as adopters) have seriously misread Mr Brown. Even if the allegations are not true, the reaction of Mr Brown perhaps reveals a new and worrying side of him that you have not seen before.

    A range of difficult decisions lie ahead, but it is clear that your own involvement up to now will make this especially difficult for you (as a social worker in this position you may be able to glimpse how it might feel to be the non-abusing parent in a family where the other parent is accused by a child of abuse). Although you may have a very important role to play in this case, there is a need for input from another worker who is not encumbered with guilt and baggage from the past.

Abusive foster-parents and adoptive parents

In March 1998, in North Wales, Roger Saint, the former manager of a children's home, and a foster-parent for many years, pleaded guilty to charges of indecent assault against five boys placed with himself and his wife at ages between nine and 14 at time of placement, and subsequently adopted by them. After leaving the Saints, all of them reported having been sexually abused by Roger Saint (Waterhouse, 2000). Saint also pleaded guilty to sexual assaults on a step-son, a foster-son and two pupils at an establishment where he once worked.

    This particular case raised questions about the way that foster- and adoptive parents are assessed and placements are monitored. Saint had a 25-year-old previous conviction for indecent assault on a 12-year-old boy, which, for whatever reason, had not prevented employers from offering him jobs in children's homes, or fostering and adoption agencies from placing children with him: the case led to a tightening of the law. But although in individual cases, we may, in hindsight, see mistakes that were made or procedures that could be tightened up, the fact remains that there will always be an element of risk involved in child placement away from home.

    A US study (Benedict et al., 1994) looked at reports of child abuse and neglect made about 285 foster-carers in the city of Baltimore, comparing them with allegations made against birth families in the same period. They found that, although there were proportionately fewer allegations of neglect against foster-parents than against birth-parents, in the case of physical abuse, the rate of allegations was *seven times higher* than that against birth-parents over the same period, while in the case of sexual abuse the rate was four times higher.

    Caution is necessary with figures like these because foster-parents may be more vulnerable to unfounded allegations than are birth-parents. Bray and Hinty (2001: 56), in a much smaller British study, found that only two out of a sample of 22 allegations against foster-parents were confirmed, and point out that 'it is not unlikely that some birth parents, from motives of either guilt, resentment or parental concern, are very ready to seize upon any sign of failure in the care provided by foster-parents'. This is consistent with the finding of the Benedict et al. study that physical abuse was confirmed in a lower proportion of investigations of foster-parents than was the case in respect of investigations of natural parents. But we should bear in mind too that in the Bray and Hinty study, ten per cent of the allegations against foster-parents *were* found to have been substantiated, while in the Benedict et al. study, when it came to *sexual* abuse, there was actually a *higher* proportion of confirmed allegations against foster-parents than against birth-parents, with 40 per cent of allegations being found to have been substantiated.

In the UK context, one form of fostering that was highlighted following the murder of Victoria Climbié (Laming, 2003), is so-called private fostering. Victoria Climbié died in the care of her great-aunt, Marie Therese Kouao, who was fostering her as a private arrangement with Victoria's parents. There have been many reports (see Philpot, 2001) of children, often of West African origin, being abused or exploited in such private arrangements, often undeclared and illegal ones.

Abuse by residential staff

No one who reads the newspapers in the UK can fail to be aware of the long catalogue of cases where residential care workers have been accused of abusing children in residential establishments. Corby et al. (2001: 77–8) list no fewer than 18 public inquiries held in the UK over the period 1967–2000 into such cases. Among the better-known cases are:

- the Kincora working boys hostel where, in the 1980s, there were allegations not only of sexual abuse of boys by a staff member, but of access being obtained to boys by members of a paedophile ring (Department of Health and Social Security, Northern Ireland, 1985)
- the Pindown inquiry in Staffordshire held in 1991, where there were concerns about cruel and degrading methods of punishment (Staffordshire County Council, 1991)
- a series of allegations about physical and sexual abuse in a number of residential establishments and foster-homes in North Wales, resulting in the Waterhouse inquiry (Waterhouse, 2000).

Such cases are not confined to the UK. Similar concerns have arisen in the USA, Canada, the Irish Republic and elsewhere about abuse of children in public care and also in establishments operated by various religious organizations. In Canada the Episcopal (Anglican) Church was brought to the point of bankruptcy by law suits brought by former pupils of residential schools for native Canadians (Brooke, 2000).

As with allegations of abuse by foster-carers (and indeed any other allegation, including allegations about parents) we should of course be aware that not all allegations are necessarily true. In the case of residential social workers, the methods involved in obtaining evidence for convictions in the UK have, at times, been seriously questionable. They have typically included inviting adult former care residents, many years after the event, to make allegations, and there are instances of demonstrably false allegations being made as well as of allegations that seem pretty clearly to have been motivated by the possibility of substantial financial compensation (see Webster, 1998, 2005). I believe that it is likely that a significant number of imprisoned former residential workers may have been wrongfully convicted (Beckett, 2002).

All the same, there really can be no doubt that abuse by staff has gone on and no doubt continues to go on in residential establishments, as it does in other contexts where adults work with children. Indeed, it would be incredible if paedophiles were *not* found in residential establishments, given what we know about the driven single-minded pursuit of gratification that characterizes paedophilia, in common with other addictive behavioural patterns, and given that paedophiles may be impossible to detect in advance if they do not already have convictions.

Other kinds of abusive personalities too, such as those who like to dominate and control others (in short, bullies) are inevitably to be found among those who work with vulnerable young people. There are also dynamics in residential environments, as in fostering, which may result in some individuals who might not otherwise be abusive, behaving in an abusive way. Children and adolescents in residential care may come from homes where they may have experienced violence, rejection, high levels of family conflict, abuse, neglect, a breakdown of parental authority. They may have had experiences at school and elsewhere that alienated them from authority in general, and which have encouraged them to adopt highly confrontational styles. They may have learnt to get what they want by threats or manipulation. Working in such a context is a difficult, emotionally demanding task and it would not be surprising if some individuals end up behaving in inappropriate ways, as do some parents who are under stress.

Once again, then, it is important that child protection workers do not imagine that residential care necessarily represents a safe haven from abuse.

Abuse by fellow-residents or other foster-children

Abuse by other children or adolescents occurs within and outside of families, but it is a particularly significant risk within residential and foster-care. By their nature residential care and foster-care will tend to bring together children and adolescents who have suffered maltreatment of one kind or another, and a significant minority of these children will have developed abusive behaviour patterns of their own. Indeed a proportion of children and adolescents are brought into public care *because* of their abusive behaviour. Children coming into public care are therefore being brought into an environment where the risk of being exposed to other children who are abusers can often be quite high.

System abuse

I have been discussing abuse that is carried out by abusive individuals in responsible positions. More insidious and difficult to grasp, though, is the idea that child protection and childcare systems may be abusive in effect, *even when the individuals involved may not be abusive and may be acting with the best of intentions.*

In fact, having discussed sexual abuse, physical abuse, emotional abuse and neglect in earlier chapters, I want now to introduce a new category of abuse, *system abuse*, which occurs whenever the operation of legislation, officially sanctioned procedures or operational practices within systems or institutions is avoidably damaging to children and their families. (Williams, 1996: 5)

There are a variety of interacting factors which exist in child protection and childcare work that may lead to the system itself being harmful to children. I will briefly list some of them before looking at some of the ways in which harm can be done.

- Professionals and agencies are interested in their own survival and their own reputation, as well as the well-being of children. Decisions are often to some extent motivated by self-protection. Procedures are to some extent designed to allow agencies to 'cover their backs'.
- Staff shortages and high staff turnover may result in some cases going for long periods without receiving any attention, or in cases being passed on again and again from one temporary member of staff to another. The latter can result in children and parents having to get to know – and explain themselves to – a succession of strangers, each of whom will have her own different ideas. Since any new caseworker has to 'get up to speed' on a complex case, rapid turnover of staff can lead to effective paralysis of decision making.
- Stress and overload experienced by professionals may result in poor decision making and, particularly, in the short term, reactive thinking. The cases of children perceived as not being at immediate risk, for instance, may be ignored, even if there are important decisions to be made about their long-term future. Cases where there is an immediate risk, on the other hand, may be dealt with in a 'firefighting' style, which rushes from one crisis to the next without addressing underlying problems or forming long-term plans.
- Professionals may be reluctant to make painful decisions, such as the decision to remove a child from a parent (or the opposite: a decision to allow a child to remain in a situation where there are some risks), and may be prone to finding reasons for putting off such decisions, even though this has the result of children and parents being left 'in limbo'.
- The resources available in a given area may simply be inadequate for the task. This can be true in relation to material resources (having identified a serious problem and intervened in a family, the child protection system may then be unable to offer more than a metaphorical Band-Aid), but it can also be true in relation to human resources. For example, a child could be removed from her family and placed with a new family intended to be her permanent home. But the new family might find her behaviour impossible to cope with, with the result that she may be subjected to placement breakdown.
- Interventions by professional agencies may be unrealistic and not sufficiently informed by evidence as to what actually works.
- Resource-rationing systems operated by public agencies may mean that it is necessary to have a crisis in order to obtain a service. In order to gain help, a family may have to prove decisively that it is failing. On the other hand, improvement in function can lead to withdrawal of support. To some extent such systems may actually promote 'dysfunctional' family behaviour (because, in terms of obtaining help, such behaviour is actually *functional*).
- It is difficult in some circumstances for child protection agencies to do nothing. This can mean making families 'jump through hoops' for the sake of doing something as much as for the benefit of the children in the family.
- Professional rivalries and boundary disputes between agencies can lead to children and families being passed to and fro or to protracted delays while disagreements are thrashed out.

System abuse by the child protection system

Exercise 13.2

Micky, a boy of six, is reported by his school to the child protection agencies because of a series of suspicious bruises, culminating in a group of clear grip-mark bruises on both his arms. His mother insists that she has done nothing wrong and that he has always bruised easily.

A social worker arranges to take mother and son to a doctor to look at the bruises. The doctor finds that the bruises seem to indicate very excessive force being used not just once but on a number of occasions, but says that it is just possible that the boy might bruise easily as a result of a 'bleeding disorder', and arranges for him to be seen in hospital by a specialist. Social worker, mother and child then find themselves waiting for an hour and a half in a hospital corridor to see the specialist doctor.

The doctor is exhausted after a long shift, and is not good with children in any case. He makes no eye contact with Micky, offers no reassurance, but pushes a large hypodermic needle into the back of his hand to take a blood sample. It is now eight o'clock in the evening.

How might all this be experienced by Micky?

Comments on Exercise 13.2

Waits in hospital corridors are tedious at any age but to a child of six they can feel like an eternity. This eternity of waiting takes place in a very frightening context where his mother is almost certainly agitated and distressed, and where she seems to be powerless against the demands of other more powerful strangers. And hospitals in themselves are frightening places.

Exhaustion and awkwardness are not necessarily interpreted as such by a small child. The specialist doctor, a complete stranger in a frightening environment, may well seem hostile and malign to Micky. Most children are frightened of needles in any case. The syringe used for a blood sample is larger, more alarming and more frightening than those used for injections, and in this context the whole experience probably feels like a violent assault.

This sort of event can become the stuff of a child's nightmares. It is also a good example of system abuse, because none of the participants set out to maltreat Micky. The GP and the social worker doubtless felt that the second medical opinion was in Micky's interests (to help establish whether he was safe at home). The specialist doctor was tired and lacking in social skills, rather than deliberately unkind.

The experience of being on the receiving end of a child protection investigation must be a very frightening experience for a child. As in the example above, children are placed in unfamiliar environments and face unfamiliar demands from people who may be complete strangers. They may be subjected to intrusive physical examination. They may be asked to 'tell tales' about their own parents (and may perhaps fear the possibility that what they say could result in parents going to prison or themselves going into care and/or that they will face retribution from abusive parents). They are placed in the position of witnessing their parents' authority being overruled by strangers.

Of course there are plenty of children who nevertheless welcome child protection investigations because they are being abused and very much want the abuse to stop. But many children who are subject to investigations are not being abused, and many more are not being abused to the extent that they would welcome this kind of outside intervention. Even children who are being *seriously* abused can be so frightened by what they have set in motion that they decide to get some control again by withdrawing the allegation that set the whole thing off, a sequence of events that was described by Roland Summit in the 'Child Sexual Abuse Accommodation Syndrome' (Summit, 1983). A case of this kind was described in Exercise 7.4 (p. 104).

Not only the initial investigation but the protective steps subsequently taken can, in some instances, actually have a harmful impact on a child. Thus, in cases of serious concern about a child's physical safety, removal of a child from a parent's care may be indicated. But this comes at a price, and it can be a very high price indeed. To give an example: if the effect of the removal of a baby from his mother is to disrupt the formation of a mutual attachment between them, it is possible that in the long run this may actually have the effect of *causing* harm, even if the intention was to *prevent* it, and even if, in the short run, prevention of harm was actually achieved.

Any decision to separate a child and parents needs therefore to be carefully weighed in the balance to ensure that the likely benefits exceed the likely harm. Indeed, any plan of action (including decisions to *return* children to parents) should be subjected to a cost–benefit analysis of this kind. And any intervention in family life should be proportionate to the benefits to be gained. (Was it necessary for Micky in Exercise 13.2, for instance, to have a blood test on the same day as the initial investigations, or was the benefit of doing this offset by the distress that it caused?)

These points may perhaps seem obvious, and yet it is very easy for experienced child protection workers, involved in this kind of work on a daily basis, to become inured to the impact that their interventions can have.

Exercise 13.3

Melanie was aware that she might have difficulty in bonding with a baby who was the unplanned child of an abusive, one-off encounter, but had made the decision to have the baby. In particular she was very keen to use breast-feeding as a natural way of establishing a bond.

After the birth of baby Jade, a suspicious injury, seen in the context of her mother's known ambivalence, led the professional agencies to decide to remove her from Melanie and place her with foster-parents pending further investigations. Later, a reasonable non-abusive explanation for the injury was found and Jade was returned, but Melanie had had to abandon breast-feeding and was not able to re-establish it.

What do you think the net effect of the professional intervention might be?

(Continued)

(Continued)

Comments on Exercise 13.3

Of course in such situations it is never possible to know what would have happened if different decisions had been made. Small babies often cope quite well with changes of carers – and bottle-fed babies can be content as well as breast-fed ones – so it may be that the disruption had little direct impact on Jade. But it seems to me that, by disrupting Melanie's own strategy for establishing a bond with her baby, this intervention could well have weakened her own confidence in her ability to do so, and resurrected fears of alienation from her own child. The effect of such things is incalculable, yet they may be the final straw that prevent the growth of a mutually satisfactory attachment. If so, they could have lifelong effects on a child's development.

Clearly when a small baby is injured in suspicious circumstances, child protection agencies must be extremely concerned, because small babies are extremely vulnerable and are more likely than older children to suffer permanent damage or death as a result of physical abuse. If it had emerged that Jade's injury had been deliberately caused by her mother, then the decision to remove her might well have been vindicated. As so often in child protection work, hindsight is needed to know for certain whether or not the decision made was the best one.

But, as the outcome of enquiries could not be known at the start, it would have been better in this case if a way could have been found to monitor Melanie's care of Jade without separating the two of them.

Multiple placements

Children in public care can suffer abuse at the hands of their carers, as I've already discussed, though this is a relatively rare occurrence. But even when a child is looked after by carers who do *not* abuse them, public care can have an effect that amounts to a form of emotional abuse.

One of the experiences that is commonly faced by children in public care is that of repeated placement moves. A British government report (Department of Health, 1998) found that in some local authority areas, as many as a third of all children in public care were going through three or more placements per year. An American study found that children waiting for decisions from the Boston Juvenile Court went through more than two foster-placements on average just during the 18-month average period that their cases were before the court (Bishop et al., 1992). Back in the UK, Bridget McKeigue and I, also looking at children waiting for court decisions, found the following case examples:

[Michael] went through eleven placement changes between the first emergency protection order and adoption. If we disregard short respite breaks, this figure reduces to seven changes involving five sets of carers ...

In the James case, the siblings ... were ... split between two foster homes, with three initially going to one home, one going to another and a new baby, born during the proceedings, joining the three older siblings. While in these foster-homes the children went to other respite foster-homes. The four siblings placed together were subsequently moved to another foster-home. They were then split and moved again to two other foster-homes.

Bill had already been accommodated three times with three different sets of foster-parents at the time that care proceedings were initiated and was with the third set when the interim care order was made. He remained with these carers initially, and was joined by his new-born sibling. They went for respite to another set of foster-carers, but were then moved successively to their mother, to another family member, to a new set of foster-parents, back to the foster-parents Bill was with at the onset of proceedings and on to yet another new set of foster-parents. They were later placed with adopters. (Beckett and McKeigue, 2003: 33. All the names were of course changed)

We commented that, if readers found these accounts of placement moves hard to follow, they might like to reflect on how these moves would have been experienced by the children.

I find it painful to even begin to contemplate the feelings of worthlessness and loneliness that must be experienced by children involved in multiple placement breakdowns. But there are many children who have experienced not just one but a series of rejections within the care system, and have had to face, again and again, first alienation from their carers, then placement breakdown and then a move to one, two or more short-term placements before another long-term placement is found, only for the cycle of alienation and failure to begin again. I would suggest that such children must pick up very powerful messages about being 'worthless or unloved, inadequate, or valued only insofar as they meet the needs of another person', they may well experience themselves as being expected to meet 'developmentally inappropriate expectations', and they almost certainly will feel frequently 'frightened or in danger'. *All of these phrases are direct quotes from the definition of emotional abuse* given in *Working Together* (DfES, 2006: 38) and cited previously in Chapter 5.

Even children who are moved for reasons unconnected with their own behaviour are likely to pick up a lot of these messages. And when, as often occurs now in the UK, changes of placement are paralleled by equally rapid changes of social workers ('Michael', for example, had had three different social workers during the period discussed above) then the experience of being 'in care' must feel like being almost completely alone in the world – a profoundly disturbing and harmful experience for a child.

The problem of multiple placement moves is a good example of system abuse, because it can occur without any of the participants having anything other than good intentions, and yet may do really profound long-term harm. The UK government recognized the seriousness of the problem when it chose as the very first of the sub-objectives of its *Quality Protects* programme: 'To reduce the number of changes of main carer for children looked after' (Department of Health, 1998: 12). But to some extent it is in the nature of public care that such things happen – the examples given above, after all, postdate *Quality Protects* by several years – and professionals should therefore be wary of assuming that the removal of children into public care will necessarily provide children with security or protect them from harm.

A decision to remove children from their own families therefore requires a realistic assessment not only of the shortcomings of their family of origin, but also of the kind of care that is likely to be on offer elsewhere, and the risks that are involved in moving them.

Exercise 13.4

Kelly is taken into care on an emergency protection order at the age of seven, after she was found to have been left on her own in her mother's flat for the better part of a day. This is the fourth reported incident of her being left on her own. Her mother is a heroin user, who insists she is very committed to Kelly, but finds it difficult in practice to prioritize Kelly's needs over her own need to finance and feed her habit.

Kelly is initially placed with Mr and Mrs Brown, the only foster-parents with space available, but the Browns were about to go on holiday so, within a week, she is moved to Mr and Mrs Thompson. The plan at this stage is to return her quickly to her mother, but a decision is then reached that she should remain in foster-care for four months, to allow her mother to go through a programme of rehabilitation and put her life in order prior to Kelly's return. Mr and Mrs Thompson are unable to commit themselves for four months, so Kelly is moved to another set of foster-parents, the Rogers. There are a number of meetings with the Rogers who are very keen to work with Kelly during this difficult period and to provide her with a home until she can return to her mother.

Kelly stays with the Rogers for seven weeks, but during this time there are increasing tensions surrounding Kelly's behaviour with the Rogers' daughter, Emma, aged four, whom the Rogers feel Kelly picks on. This is brought to a head by a particular incident in which Kelly breaks a favourite toy of Emma's. The Rogers demand Kelly's immediate removal. She is placed back with Mr and Mrs Brown while another family is found. She is then informed that she will be moving to a new family, the Youngs. Kelly's social worker tells her that the Youngs are very keen to have her and to help her during the remaining period while her mother gets her life in order (a period which now looks like being longer than originally anticipated).

Comments on Exercise 13.4

Kelly is a child who has been let down more than once before entering public care. I would suggest that to Kelly the assurance that the Youngs really are going to provide her with stability will ring very hollow indeed. Indeed, she would be right to be sceptical on the evidence of her care history already. The Rogers, too, were supposed to be providing her with a stable base.

One cannot blame the Rogers for choosing to put the needs of their own daughter first. Quite possibly Kelly's treatment of Emma was a deliberate attempt to test the Rogers out, aimed at their area of greatest vulnerability. But such testing-out behaviour is commonplace, normal even, among children in Kelly's position. If the care system is unable to stand up to it, then it is pretty inevitable that children such as Kelly will regularly experience placement moves.

Other moves in this scenario were unconnected with Kelly's behaviour, and were to do with the logistics of the system, but this is not a distinction that will make much sense to a seven-year-old. Indeed even an adult would pick up the message from such treatment that her own needs and her own convenience were relatively unimportant compared with the needs of others.

Drift and prevarication

Related to the problem of multiple placements is the form of system abuse – or perhaps we should call it 'system neglect' – that is sometimes known as 'drift'. This problem was brought to light in the 1970s in the UK by Jane Rowe and Lydia Lambert (in *Children who Wait*, 1973) who exposed the plight of children in the public care system who spent long periods of time in supposedly temporary placements, or placements whose duration had not been defined, without any clear plan for their long-term future being made.

This is harmful to children because it deprives them of the security of carers with whom they can safely form an attachment. In such a context, the child must hold something back; the carers, as human beings, almost certainly hold something back too, and the child is, as a result, prevented from being able to meet her very basic need for a home where she can really feel she belongs. The fact that no one seems to be willing to offer this commitment must also for many children be a profound blow to their sense of self-worth – another message (to quote yet again from the *Working Together* definition of emotional abuse) that they are 'worthless or unloved, inadequate, or valued only insofar as they meet the needs of another person' (DfES, 2006: 38). These feelings, and the psychological defences that a child inevitably constructs in order to ward off such feelings, may well do harm to a child's capacity to form relationships in the long as well as the short run.

Although it is 30 years since Rowe and Lambert's book came out, the problem of children spending long periods in supposedly temporary care arrangements (or worse, long periods in a *series* of temporary care arrangements, as discussed earlier) still persists. A British government White Paper on adoption found that 80 per cent of adopted children have spent a year or more in the looked-after system before being adopted (Department of Health, 2000). And, although the 1989 Children Act was the first piece of legislation in England and Wales to require parties to court proceedings about children to avoid delay, the length of care proceedings – and hence of the time that children spend in limbo without knowing what their long-term future is going to be – has grown longer, year on year, since the Act came into effect (McKeigue and Beckett, 2004), doubling in average duration over the period 1993–2002. (The government has attempted to tackle the problem with a new protocol on delay [LCD, 2003] and, in 2004/5, claimed to be making some progress since courts had dealt with 41 per cent of cases in under 40 weeks [DCA, 2005], as against 35 per cent in the previous year However, the remaining 59 per cent of children did of course still wait for over nine months in 2004/5, and some of them, I know from my own ongoing research, for very much longer.)

Once again this is a classic instance of system abuse in that it occurs without any deliberate intention to do harm. Indeed one of the factors that causes delay may well be a determination to be as sure as possible that the final decision is the right one. And yet, the combination of high anxiety situations with the absence of stable attachment figures is uniquely difficult for children because it is *precisely* in those situations that a child needs – and instinctively seeks – the security that comes from the support of an attachment figure. As Paul Steinhauer observed:

> The more continuity is disrupted, be it through multiple moves or through being left too long in limbo while … future plans are being contested, the greater the risk of severe and lasting personality damage. (Steinhauer, 1991: 82)

Drift doesn't only occur in the care system. There are situations too in which natural families are under intense professional scrutiny for long periods of time and where the possibility of children being removed is continuously present. These situations too are surely harmful for the development of secure attachments. It is important to remember – in *all* decision-making processes and not just those that occur in court – that children need decisions to be made in a *reasonable timescale*. Of course it is important, too, to try to get decisions right and to collect as much relevant information and advice as possible to that end. But there can never be absolute certainty in this area of work, and after a certain point the pursuit of certainty becomes simply an excuse to avoid taking the risk that is inevitably entailed in making a decision.

Chapter summary

In this chapter I have looked at the ways that child protection systems, and childcare systems, can in themselves cause harm to children. I have considered:

- abuse perpetrated by abusive individuals in the public care system: foster-parents, adoptive parents, residential workers and other children in care
- the idea of system abuse, and the ways in which the practices and processes of organizational systems can be abusive in effect, even if the individuals within them are not abusive
- ways in which the child protection system itself can be harmful to children
- the problem of multiple placements for children in public care as an instance of system abuse
- the idea of prevarication and 'drift' being a form of system abuse, or neglect, when it delays decisions being made for children.

System abuse occurs because organizational systems are driven and shaped not simply by the needs of children but by a complex set of pressures and constraints. Among the pressures on child protection workers are public expectations, and perhaps their own expectations of themselves. In the next and final chapter I will ask what can reasonably be expected of a child protection system.

14 Facing Reality

- Reaching for the stars
- Information gathering and its limits
- Limited resources
- Having their cake and eating it

In the previous chapter I considered the ways in which systems intended to protect children could themselves end up doing harm. Complex dynamics are at work within the child protection and childcare systems, which mean that many factors other than a purely rational consideration of a child's best interests will play a part in the making of decisions and the formation of policies and procedures. I mentioned the psychological needs of professional workers, the expectations that are placed upon the child protection system by society at large, and the inevitably limited resources that are made available by society at large for the work – resources which are not necessarily well-matched to expectations. ('Paradoxically, while the public continued to demand greater efforts to be made to curb child abuse, it was increasingly unwilling to fund those efforts', wrote Duncan Lindsey, 1994: 97, about the USA.)

In this final chapter, I want to consider the real pressures and constraints that child protection systems operate under. What is, and what is not, possible and what are the dangers of asking for more from a child protection system than it can realistically achieve?

Reaching for the stars

It is commonly said that it is a good thing in life to 'think positive', to 'set your sights high', to 'reach for the stars'. And so it is, in many respects. But to set objectives, or to raise expectations, which cannot possibly be achieved, can be very destructive indeed. This is certainly true in respect of parenting. Good parents encourage and challenge their children, but they do not demand the impossible of their children. In fact it is a recognized form of emotional abuse to impose 'developmentally inappropriate expectations' on children (DfES, 2006: 8). It is true also of work *with* parents that we should not demand the impossible. I have discussed before in this book the dangers of the child protection system demanding unrealistically high standards from parents.

And I suggest that the same principle holds good in respect of the demands made by society of the child protection system. If child protection workers are expected to deliver far more than they can realistically deliver, then the result will not be an improvement in practice but the reverse, bad practice based on defensiveness and fear. This danger was succinctly summarized by a British government minister as follows:

> We must not pretend that actions taken by child protection agencies can ever guarantee that parents will not harm their children. The danger of trying to give such guarantees and of pillorying those agencies when harm does occur is that inappropriate interventions may be made out of fear. (John Bowis, OBE, MP, *Foreword* to Department of Health, 1995)

Mr Bowis might have added that a culture of fear also contributes to staff sickness, poor staff retention and difficulties in staff recruitment, and that striving after unrealistic goals can distort practice in other ways, for example by deflecting resources from areas where they might be more useful into the pursuit of narrow goals and targets.

It is reasonable to expect that a child protection system will identify as many risks to the well-being of children as it can and try to reduce those risks, just as it is reasonable to expect the police to respond to crime and find criminals, or doctors to save lives and cure illnesses. But we do not expect the police to anticipate or solve every crime, we do not expect doctors to abolish death, and we should not expect child protection systems to eradicate child abuse or neglect.

There are a number of reasons why this would be an unrealistic expectation:

- There are limits to the level of surveillance and state intervention that is practicable or desirable. We might detect more child abuse, for instance, if closed circuit television was installed in every home, and we employed large numbers of staff to watch a vast bank of screens, but most people would agree that these benefits would be outweighed by many drawbacks to such an arrangement.
- It is in principle impossible to predict human behaviour with any degree of certainty. This makes it impossible to predict or recognize abuse in every case, and impossible too to predict with certainty the outcome of any intervention. Errors are inevitable and efforts to avoid errors in one direction (failure to protect a child from their parents) will result in new kinds of errors in the other direction (unnecessary break-up of families).
- The ability of child protection professionals are also limited – and always will be limited – by the resources at their disposal, by which I mean material resources (time, money, access to services), personal resources and resources in terms of knowledge and influence.

Information gathering and its limits

In the natural sciences it is accepted that complex natural phenomena, involving a very large number of variables, cannot be predicted except in a probabilistic sense. The following discussion, for instance, describes the difficulties involved in accurately predicting the weather:

> ... suppose the earth could be covered with sensors spaced one foot apart, rising at one foot intervals all the way to the top of the atmosphere. Suppose every sensor gives perfectly accurate readings of temperature, pressure, humidity, and any other quantity a meteorologist could want. Precisely at noon an infinitely powerful computer takes all the data and calculates what will happen at each point at 12.01, then 12.02, then 12.03.
>
> The computer will still be unable to predict whether Princeton, New Jersey, will have sun or rain on a day one month away. At noon the spaces between the sensors will hide fluctuations that the computer will not know about ... By 12.01, those fluctuations will already have created small errors one foot away. Soon the errors will have multiplied to the ten-foot scale and so on up to the size of the globe. (Gleick, 1988: 21)

In practice, of course, meteorologists attempt to predict the weather with *far* less detailed data than this (using sensors separated by many miles), and we all know that the predictions they make, even a single day in advance, are quite often wrong. This does not reflect incompetence on the part of the meteorologists, or even lack of knowledge about the workings of the weather. The fact is that it simply is not practical to know precisely what is going on in every single bit of the atmosphere. And even if it *were* practical, and meteorologists could know the precise state of every molecule in the atmosphere at a given moment, it is inconceivable that a human system would ever be capable of processing such a vast quantity of information.

This might seem a far cry from child protection, but in fact child protection professionals are also in the business of making judgements on the basis of limited information, and with a limited capacity for processing information at their disposal. Doctors have to decide whether or not bruises are symptomatic of physical abuse, and have to do so quickly because there are a lot of other patients waiting to be seen. Teachers have to decide whether or not they ought to be worried that an unhappy child may be being abused at home, and have to do so quickly because there are 34 other children in the class and a pile of homework to mark. Social work agencies have to decide which cases to prioritize, and they have to do so quickly because they are already working with many families and new referrals keep coming in.

The fact that these judgements have to be based on limited information has led British child protection policy makers in recent times to try to rectify this by placing an enormous emphasis on information gathering and information sharing. But this may create as many problems as it solves.

Assessment uses up resources

The more time is spent on information gathering and information sharing, the less time is available for actually doing anything else. In the UK, the agencies involved in child protection work are already seriously limited in the degree to which they can offer a service. Eileen Munro points out the fallacy of believing that more detailed information will necessarily result in a better service:

> For most parents the suggestion that children are not currently receiving help for low level problems because professionals are not sharing information is ludicrous. The experience for parents is of asking for help and being turned away because limited resources mean that there is a high threshold for access. (Munro, 2004: 5)

Writing from an American perspective, Neil Guterman makes the similar point that a narrow preoccupation with 'screening, decision making and monitoring activities' can drive out 'any remaining capacity to provide direct services' (Guterman, 2001: 44).

Of course information is important – and in the various Exercises in this book I have repeatedly emphasized the importance of gathering information before coming to a decision – but we need to recognize that there is a trade-off between information gathering and acting. Most important decisions in life have to be made on limited information because if we waited to be completely certain we would never act at all.

Surveillance undermines trust

The more that professional agencies are co-opted into the child protection information-gathering system, the less they will be trusted and confided in by their service users. In Chapter 9 I gave the example of mothers with post-natal depression keeping this secret for fear of having children taken from them. In Chapter 7, I quoted David Finkelhor's comments on the 'enormous, unexpected, and devastating increase in powerlessness' that children feel in the aftermath of abuse, 'when they find themselves unable to control the decisions of the adult world' (Finkelhor, 1988: 72). Eileen Munro notes that, if an advocate is not allowed to offer confidentiality to a child, 'this is likely to increase the number of children who will conceal their problems' (Munro, 2004: 5).

There is another trade-off here. We have to strike a balance between gathering and sharing information and allowing a degree of privacy to parents and children, which will allow them to feel able to talk. This balance is in danger of being lost if we proceed on the basis that more and more information sharing is necessarily a good thing.

Too much information is overwhelming

A large quantity of information is only of use if you have the capacity and the tools to interpret it, otherwise it can be worse than nothing. I can illustrate this by returning to my weather example. Suppose that a meteorologist were presented with a computer print-out giving the precise location and state of every one of the many billions of molecules in the atmosphere. This would certainly be a much more complete set of data than the meteorologist normally has to work with, but of course there would be far too much data there for the meteorologist to even know where to start.

In relation to moves towards a national database on children in the UK which would allow professionals to log their concerns, Eileen Munro observes:

If literally any cause for concern is logged, then professionals will spend a considerable amount of time entering data or responding to the entries, most of the alerts being false alarms. The sheer amount of data will make the system grind to a halt. Also information about serious cases of abuse will be hidden amongst the plethora of minor concerns, increasing the risk that children like Victoria Climbié will go unprotected. (Munro, 2004: 5–6)

False negatives and false positives

When it comes to extremely rare events, such as the killing of a child, our ability to pin-point when that event will occur is limited by the nature of the task itself. Most of us are quite muddled in our thinking about this because it involves thinking about uncertainty and probability, which most of us (myself included) find very difficult (Gigerenzer, 2002, in a useful layman's guide to the subject, suggests that it is in the nature of the human brain to overestimate certainty, just as it is in the nature of the brain to be predictably misled by certain optical illusions). I will make the following analogy with football because I believe it may help, but without in any way wishing to trivialize a very serious subject.

At the time of writing, the 2006 World Cup has recently been completed, with Italy as the winner. Prior to the tournament, no one could have predicted for certain that Italy would win, but Italy was certainly one of a relatively small number of teams, along with teams such as Brazil and Germany, that experts agreed were likely to make it into the knockout stages of the tournament. Likewise, there were other countries, such as Angola or the USA, that experts were generally agreed were likely not to get that far. Now let us suppose that, at the beginning of the tournament, we attempted to divide teams up into two categories: High Performers, who were likely to get through into the knockout stage, and Low Performers, who were unlikely to do so. Experts in possession of detailed information about the teams, their players, managers, recent history and so on, would have been able to assign teams much more accurately to these categories than the rest of us, but even so they would have classified some teams as High Performers who did not make it through to the knockout stage and other teams as Low Performers who did in fact make it through. And, regardless of the amount of information available, *none* of them could have predicted for certain who the actual winner would be. Indeed none of them would even *claim* to be able to know for certain.

In the same way, competent child protection professionals looking at the risk of (for example) serious physical injury to a child are able to separate out high-risk cases from low-risk ones. But sometimes, even if competent and in possession of a reasonable amount of information, they will incorrectly assign to the low-risk category a case where an injury does in fact occur. This is analogous to my football experts assigning a team to the Low Performer category who do in fact get through to the knockout stage (Ukraine, for example) and it is known in the literature as a false negative (see, for example, Gigerenzer, 2002). Equally, they will sometimes assign to a high-risk category a family where in fact, even if the family was left to its own devices, no serious injury would occur. This is known as a false positive and is equivalent to my football experts assigning a team to the High Performer category which does not in fact get past the preliminary group round (for example, the Czech Republic). Even competent experts cannot with certainty predict serious injury accurately in every case, though they can certainly tell the families in which this is more likely to occur.

When it comes to picking out which exactly of the high-risk families will actually end up with a child being killed if no action is taken, the task is much more difficult and the error rate much higher, just as the error rate of football experts would go up enormously if asked to predict precisely which country would win the Cup. (If asked to list the teams that would make it through to the knockout stage, most of them might well be, say, 80–90 per cent right. If asked to pick the winner, most of them would be 100 per cent wrong though of course a few would be 100 per cent right.)

When members of the general public get to hear that the child protection system has failed to recognize that a family was dangerous, they hear the details of the family circumstances, which sound *so* much more troubled than their own, and they wonder how the professionals could possibly fail to see that this was a high-risk situation. But in fact professionals often *have* correctly identified the family as high risk. The problem lies not in distinguishing high-risk cases from those which are very low risk, but in deciding which out of a number of high-risk cases is the one that most urgently needs attention. In other words, child protection professionals trying to identify children in extreme danger are not (as the outsider might imagine) like a football expert trying to decide whether Brazil or Togo is more likely to win the World Cup, for that would be easy (even I know the answer and I know next to nothing about football) but rather they are like experts looking at the High Performing teams, such as Brazil, Italy, Germany, Argentina and France, and trying to decide which one of them will win.

To take the football analogy one step further. Information about the teams would help to make the decision, but you can see that no amount of information would result in certainty. Information would also only be as useful as our capacity to interpret it. And it would only be useful if we had *time* to interpret it.

Exercise 14.1

Look at the cases below referring to an imaginary social work team. For the sake of this exercise please imagine that, due to staff shortages in the team, it is only possible to follow up on one of these referrals immediately. The others will only be able to be followed up when more staff time becomes available.

Decide which of these referrals should be the one that is followed up and the order in which you would follow up the others. Assume that the information below is all that is available to make this decision. After all, getting more information itself requires staff time.

Case (a)

Children: James (five) and Matthew (four)
Mother: Mandy Baker (25)

Neighbours have been very worried about the environment in which the boys are living. Mandy keeps open house to local teenagers who come and go at all hours. There are loud noises – shouting, music and quite often fights – until the early hours.

(Continued)

The house is described as dirty and bare. The garden fence has been broken up for firewood. The front door was kicked in during a fight and never properly mended. Several windows have likewise also been broken. On one occasion, neighbours report, a young man who visited the house brought a horse right into the living room, which was the subject of a lot of excitement in the house.

The boys' school are also worried about them. They are absent about one day in five and late on most days. When in they always seem very tired (quiet, withdrawn, with rings under their eyes) and sometimes hungry. Their clothes are often not changed for a week.

Mandy often seems to teachers to be under the influence of drugs or alcohol and frequently does not come to collect them from school, several different friends of hers (some very young) coming in her place. Mandy has recently been asked to collect them herself or to let the school know who will be collecting them – and she agreed to do so.

But today a young friend of Mandy's, a girl of about 16, arrived to collect the boys from school, saying that Mandy was unwell. Teachers have seen her before with Mandy but the boys did not seem to know her very well. Teachers wonder if they made the right decision in letting them go with her and want the social work team to check the boys are alright.

Mandy is known to have suffered abuse as a child and to have grown up in care. The boys' father has never had contact with them.

Case (b)
Child: Hazel Maddox (13)
Mother: Tammy Maddox (34)
Father: Bill Maddox (32) (parents separated)

Hazel was admitted to hospital as a result of a paracetamol overdose. This is thought to have been a para-suicide rather than a real attempt on her own life. Hazel had been living with her mother but her mother now refuses to have her home, saying that she is fed up with her daughter's aggressive and difficult behaviour.

Hazel has a history of unexplained absences from school. Her health record includes enuresis to age ten a hearing impairment for which no organic cause has ever been found and numerous urinary tract infections. When at school she is said to be rather isolated, and to find it difficult to make friends.

She is now medically ready for discharge.

Her father, Bill, who lives on his own, is willing to have her to stay with him, but Hazel is adamant that she does not want to go to him. The only reason she is able to give for this, however, is that he nags her a lot. Her contact with him has been somewhat erratic. She had little contact as a small child, but quite a lot in recent years until about six months ago, and since then has consistently refused to go.

Case (c)
Child: Annette Foster (four)
Mother: Judy Young (26)
Step-father: Mike Young (28) (father has no contact)

(Continued)

(Continued)

A referral has come from a Debbie Johnson, who is Judy's sister (Annette's aunt). Annette has a learning disability and attends a special school where she has a male one-to-one helper who is also her regular babysitter. Debbie is concerned that Annette has (according to Judy) recently been displaying a lot of behaviour that is overtly sexual and seems inappropriate for her age. For example, getting dolls to enact sex, masturbating with objects.

Debbie says that Mike was very angry with Judy when he heard that Judy had talked about this with her, and has since tried to prevent the two sisters from having contact.

Debbie and her husband have themselves noticed some of this sexual behaviour for themselves. When Debbie visited with her husband, Annette climbed onto her husband's lap and rubbed up against his groin.

Mike and Judy married six months ago after quite a brief previous relationship.

Comments on Exercise 14.1

I don't believe there is a 'right' answer to this. There are long-term risks to children and immediate dangers in all of the cases, but the dangers are different in each one and difficult to weigh up against one another.

In case (a) there are reasons to believe that the boys are being neglected, but no definite immediate danger, although James' and Matthew's teachers are understandably worried that they are being picked up from school by someone they seem to hardly know.

In case (b) I can see a distinct possibility of sexual abuse, though there is no firm evidence of this. The immediate issue is that Hazel has one parent who refuses to have her home and another parent who she refuses to go to. The immediate danger is that a clearly very unhappy 13-year-old, who has already taken one overdose, running the risk of permanent liver damage if not death, may do so again.

In case (c) there is clearly a possibility of sexual abuse, with some suspicion being attached to the step-father, though the male helper is also in a position to abuse Annette. There is no new danger today, but if Annette is being abused, then she will probably have to endure more abuse the longer the case is left.

There are also features of these cases which might, with the benefit of hindsight, become significant, but which, in advance, it is impossible to accurately weigh. For example, you quite probably did not choose case (a) as your highest priority. However, suppose you were to discover, after the event, that Mandy had not collected the boys because she was too drunk to stand, that there were a group of about a dozen teenagers at home with her, also drunk, and that later the same evening the two little boys were made to simulate sexual acts with each other for the amusement of the whole gathering. You might then look back again at the information you had received and notice, for instance, how it suggested a complete absence of boundaries in this household: the horse, the burnt fence, the noise, the constant coming and going.

The hindsight fallacy

Certainty is not achievable in child protection work. Even a competent, functional child protection system will, some of the time, make decisions that turn out not to have been in the best interests of the child.

> If a decision involves risk, then even when one can demonstrate that one has chosen the unarguably optimal course of action, some proportion of the time the outcome will be suboptimal. It follows that a bad outcome in and of itself does not constitute evidence that the decision was mistaken. The hindsight fallacy is to assume that it does. (Macdonald and Macdonald, 1999: 22)

To illustrate this point, imagine that I throw four dice and ask you to tell me how likely it is that they will all come up as sixes. You tell me that it is very unlikely. I then throw the dice and four sixes come up. Does this mean you were wrong in saying that it was unlikely? Of course not. In fact the chance of this happening is only one in 1296, which is very unlikely indeed. But this doesn't mean it will never happen. It means that on average one out of 1296 throws will come up as four sixes.

After a child known to the child protection system has died, it is easy to see that more attention should have been paid to that child, and less to other children, in the same way that after four sixes have been thrown we see that it would have been to our advantage to place a bet on four sixes and not on something else. But this does not mean that we could have known this in advance, when this combination of numbers (in the dice example), or a bad outcome for this particular child (in the real-ife situation), was only one of a number of different possibilities that we were faced with.

> The [Climbié] inquiry comments on several things that [the social worker] failed to do but tells us nothing about what she was doing instead. Presumably, they seemed more important to the worker at the time and, without further detail, how can we judge whether she was wrong or not? (Munro, 2005: 537)

The trouble with the hindsight fallacy is that it can lead to an anxious and fruitless endeavour to ensure that 'mistakes' are never made. British child protection policy is shaped to a very large degree by enquiries into very rare events like the death of Victoria Climbié. This does not really seem to prevent such tragedies from occurring, but it does mean that the system is actually less useful than it might be in dealing with the problems that are referred to it every day. It may result, for instance, in:

- A culture of fear, as described in the quote from John Bowis MP above, in which agencies act to 'cover their backs' rather than in the best interests of children.
- High levels of state intervention in family life and high levels of removal of children from their own families. This may help to explain the rapidly increasing number of children being taken into public care annually in England and Wales (McKeigue and Beckett, 2004).
- As discussed above, a disproportionate investment of limited time and resources into information gathering, at the expense of actual services for children and families.

- A paralysis of decision making resulting from an anxious quest for a level of certainty which can never actually be achieved. This can and does result in all kinds of 'drift' and prevarication such as I discussed in the last chapter, including the increasing levels of prevarication that occur in court proceedings about children.

If the only acceptable definition of a successful child protection system is that it succeeds in ensuring that no child is ever seriously harmed, then we will never have a successful child protection system, just as we would never have a successful health service if success were to be defined as never failing to save a patient's life. We need another, more realistic, criterion of success.

Limited resources

The task in Exercise 14.1 is, in essence, a task that I myself used to carry out on a regular basis as the manager of a children and families team during the 1990s. Duty social workers would take new referrals and collect together information about cases, and, on the basis of that information, I would then decide which of these cases could be allocated to social workers within the team, which ones could be dealt with by 'no further action' and so on. Although in real life the constraints are seldom quite so cut and dried as in the exercise, essentially the same difficulties arose.

I could not realistically allocate all new referrals – not even all new referrals where I could see there were significant risks – because the team's social workers were already busy and the more cases they took on, the less they would be able to do on each case. The arithmetic is simple. If a social worker has 20 cases, she has less than two hours per week per case to spend on all the visits, telephone calls, recording, travelling, completing forms, going to court and attending meetings that the case requires.

One local authority that I know of recently conducted a survey on how children and family social work staff spent their time. As I understand it, the survey found out that, because of paperwork, meetings and other competing demands on their time, social workers only spent 12 per cent of their week – less than five hours – in actual direct contact with children and families. For a social worker with 20 cases, that would translate into an average of *15 minutes* a week – an hour per month – direct contact with the members of each family. Even for a social worker with just ten cases, the amount of direct contact time would be just two hours a month.

When you consider that social workers may be trying to work to bring about change in the way that a family has been functioning for years and maybe generations, this an extraordinarily – perhaps even absurdly – small amount of time. Any rational person can surely see that, if those social workers are going to be able to achieve anything useful at all, their workload needs to be strenuously protected from yet more demands.

Another option open to me as team manager was to hold less urgent cases for allocation later. This was useful at times when members of the team were busy or absent for temporary reasons, but in the long run it is not sensible to place cases on the 'awaiting allocation' list at a faster rate than they are coming off it, because otherwise the list gets longer and longer, and children and families end up waiting longer and longer for a service. The end result of this is situations such as a case described by Sarah Banks and Robin Williams (2005: 1012–13) in which an embarrassed social worker began an assessment *two years* after a baby's name had been placed on the child protection register. The absurd double message they were being given was, of course, not lost on the family: 'we've never seen anybody for two years and now you turn up and you're asking all these questions' is the social worker's recollection of the family's reaction (ibid.: 1013).

Another option open to me was to refer cases on to other agencies. In the UK, a huge amount of store is currently put on inter-agency collaboration as a means of resolving these resource problems, and this was a large part of the thrust of the Green Paper, *Every Child Matters* (DfES, 2003). But while good working relationships are highly desirable for many reasons, and some time is certainly saved if energies are not dissipated in inter-agency wrangling, the fact remains that other agencies were just as busy as my own, and were themselves carrying out the same kind of juggling exercise as I was. Teachers, for example, are busy teaching, marking and preparing lessons, not to mention dealing with the voluminous paperwork that they too are expected to complete for monitoring purposes, and therefore have limited time left for more pastoral work.

One more option open to me was to defer a decision by asking a social worker to obtain more information. But this carries its own costs, since (as already discussed) information gathering itself takes time, and therefore takes time away from other tasks.

I appreciate that the system within which I operated was a relatively unsophisticated one, and that nowadays the various operations that I have just described are commonly undertaken in the UK by different teams or units, rather than within the confines of a single team, but essentially the same constraints still apply. For example, if a social work agency has separate 'assessment teams' undertaking assessments and 'continuing care' teams working with families identified as needing a service, the managers of that agency still have to determine how to divide their resources between assessment and service provision. It is just that this decision will be made not so much on a case-by-case basis, as I described it, but more as a policy decision about the respective sizes of the two teams, and about the point at which cases are passed from one to the other.

Whatever the organizational structure, it remains the case that resource constraints set limits on the level of assessment that is possible, and involve agencies in trying to balance the need for assessment with the need to actually provide some kind of service.

Having their cake and eating it

This concept of a trade-off between competing objectives does not, I am sorry to say, seem to feature heavily in current policy-making in the UK, which of course is the product of a political process rather than of an entirely rational examination of the facts. Eileen Munro and Martin Calder comment on the British government's stance as follows:

> They want to shift practitioners' focus *towards* preventative services; this has the logical implication of shifting the focus *away from* its current emphasis on child protection. The consequences of this have not been explicitly addressed, leaving it to agencies and individual practitioners to grapple with the inconsistency of being told to focus on family support without taking attention

away from child protection. What is the priority? Family support or child protection? What happens if another Victoria [Climbié] dies? Will government do a knee-jerk reaction and blame the professionals, or will it accept some responsibility for introducing a range of changes that have not only failed to tackle the problems in child protection but also have distracted front line staff from this vulnerable group of children as they meet the new demands being made on them? (Munro and Calder, 2005: 444)

In fact policy-making that takes no account of the difficulties and trade-offs involved in practice, is not really policy-making at all but merely 'wishlisting' (Beckett, 2006: 175). Listing laudable objectives is quite easy. We can all agree that we would like every child to be happy and healthy and safe. But in policy-making, as in child protection practice itself, the hard part lies in balancing competing and often incompatible objectives. In child protection policy, as Munro and Calder indicate, we need to strike a balance between a service that is supportive and helpful to struggling families, and one that leaves no stone unturned in trying to detect maltreatment. But wherever we strike that balance there will be children who lose out. More abuse will go undetected if we adopt an approach which prioritizes providing helpful services. More families will be broken up if we adopt an approach which uses up most of its resources on surveillance. This is hard to bear, but we will not move forward unless we face the reality and confront the hard choices that are to be made.

It may seem rather negative to have ended this book with a chapter in which I insist that there are severe limits to the ability of child protection agencies to prevent child maltreatment, and in which I question the assumptions on which reform of the system is currently based. In fact I believe that every day social workers and other professionals, help many children to escape from intolerable abuse and neglect, and many families to steer themselves onto happier, less self-destructive paths. I believe that this is important work, essential in any civilized society, and I hope that this book will have offered a few useful insights to those who are embarking on it, or are already engaged in it.

The purpose of this chapter, therefore, has not been to cast doubt on the value of child protection work itself, but to suggest that child protection work would be able to help more children and more families if we were more honest about its limitations. If perfection is what the child protection system has to achieve in order to be seen as successful, then it is doomed forever to be seen as a failure. This is not an environment that is conducive to strong, imaginative, constructive child protection work.

Chapter summary

In this chapter I considered the practical and theoretical constraints under which the child protection system operates. In it I have:

- warned about the negative consequences of imposing unrealistic expectations on the child protection system

(Continued)

- discussed the limits to what can be achieved by gathering more and more information
- considered the difficult, and inevitably risky, choices that are imposed on child protection agencies by resource constraints
- criticized current UK government policy for failing to confront the dilemmas inherent in child protection work.

In conclusion I argued that child protection work, in spite of these problems, has been helpful to many children and families, and suggested that its helpfulness would increase if it could be allowed to be more positive and less preoccupied by the fear of failure.

References

Abel, G., Mittleman, M., Becker, J. (1985) 'Sexual offenders: results of assessment and recommendations for treatment', in H. Ben-Aron, S. Hucker and C. Webster (eds), *Clinical Criminology*. Toronto: MMGraphics.

AIMS [Association for Improvements in Mental Health Services] (2004) Press release: Health visitors are now the health police – and the government's campaign to stop aggression against NHS staff is backfiring, says maternity pressure group', 1 Oct., www.aims.org.uk (accessed July 2006).

Anderson, J.C., Martin, J.L., Mullen, P.E., Romans, S.E. and Herbison, P. (1993) 'The prevalence of childhood sexual abuse experiences in a community sample of women', *Journal of the American Academy of Child and Adolescent Psychiatry*, 32: 911–19.

Ashworth, K. and Braithwaite, I. (1997) *Small Fortunes: Spending on Children, Childhood Poverty and Parental Sacrifice*. London: Joseph Rowntree Foundation.

Bagley, C. and Thurston, W. (1995) *Understanding and Preventing Child Sexual Abuse – Critical Summaries of 500 Key Studies, Vol. 2*. Aldershot: Arena.

Banks, S. and Williams, R. (2005) 'Accounting for ethical difficulties in social welfare work', *British Journal of Social Work*, 35 (7): 1005–22.

Barnard, M. and McKegany, N. (2004) 'The impact of parental problem drug abuse on children: what is the problem and what can be done to help?', *Addiction*, 99 (5): 552–9.

Batchelor, J. (1999) *Failure to Thrive in Young Children: Research and Practice Revisited*. London: The Children's Society.

BBC News (2005) 'Angola witchcraft's child victims', 13 July, http://news.bbc.co.uk/1/hi/world/africa/4677969.stm (accessed May 2006).

Beckett, C. (2002) 'The witch-hunt metaphor: and residential workers accused of abuse', *British Journal of Social Work*, 32 (5): 621–8.

Beckett, C. (2006) *Essential Theory for Social Work Practice*. London: Sage.

Beckett, C. and Maynard, A. (2005) *Values and Ethics in Social Work: an Introduction*. London: Sage.

Beckett, C. and McKeigue, B. (2003) 'Children in limbo: case where care proceedings have taken two years or more,' *Adoption and Fostering*, 27 (3): 31–40.

Beckett, C., McKeigue, B. and Taylor, H. (2007) 'Coming to conclusions: social workers' perceptions of the decision-making process in care proceedings', *Child and Family Social Work*, 12 (1): 54–63.

Beitchman, J.H., Zucker, K.J., Hood, J.E., da Costa, G.A., Akman, D. and Cassavia, E. (1992) 'A review of the long-term effects of child sexual abuse', *Child Abuse and Neglect,* 16: 101–18.

Benedict, M.I., Zuravin, S., Brandt, D. and Abbey, H. (1994) 'Types and frequency of child maltreatment by family foster care providers in an urban population', *Child Abuse and Neglect,* 18 (7): 577–85.

Bentovim, A. (2002) 'Working with abused families', in K. Wilson and A. James (eds), *The Child Protection Handbook, 2nd edn.* London: Baillière Tindall, pp. 456–80.

Beresford, P., Green, D., Lister, R. and Woodard, K. (1999) *Poverty First Hand: Poor People Speak for Themselves.* London: CPAG.

Bishop, S., Murphy, M., Jellinek, M., Quinn, Sister D. and Poitrast, Judge F. (1992) 'Protecting seriously mistreated children: time delays in a court sample', *Journal of Child Abuse and Neglect,* 16: 465–74.

Black, D. (1995) 'Parents who have killed their partner', in P. Reder and C. Lucey (eds), *Assessment of Parenting: Psychiatric and Psychological Contributions.* London: Routledge, pp. 219–34.

Blackburn, C. (1991) *Poverty and Health: Working with Families.* Buckingham: Open University Press.

Booth, T. and Booth, W. (1993a) 'Parenting with learning difficulties: lessons for practitioners', *British Journal of Social Work,* 23: 459–80.

Booth, T. and Booth, W. (1993b) 'Parental adequacy, parenting failure and parents with learning difficulties', *Health and Social Care,* 2: 161–72.

Booth, T. and Booth, W. (1994) *Parenting under Pressure: Mothers and Fathers with Learning Difficulties.* Buckingham: Open University Press.

Booth, T. and Booth, W. (1996) 'Parental competence and parents with learning difficulties', *Child and Family Social Work,* 1: 81–6.

Booth, T., Booth, W. and McConnell, D. (2005) 'The prevalence and outcomes of care proceedings involving parents with learning difficulties in the family courts', *Journal of Applied Research in Intellectual Disabilities,* 18 (1): 7–17.

Bowker, L.H., Arbitel, M. and McFerron, J.R. (1988) 'On the relationship between wife beating and child abuse', in K. Yllo and M. Bograd (eds), *Feminist Perspectives on Wife Abuse.* Newbury Park, CA: Sage.

Bowlby, J. (1980) *Attachment* (Vol. 1 of *Attachment and Loss*). London: Pimlico.

Bray, S. and Hinty, B. (2001) 'Allegations against foster carers and the implications for local authority training and support', *Adoption and Fostering,* 25 (1): 55–66.

Brooke, J. (2000) 'Indian lawsuits on school abuse may bankrupt Canada churches', *New York Times,* 2 Nov.

Browne, A. (1987) *When Battered Women Kill.* New York: Free Press.

Burck, C. and Speed, B. (1995) 'Introduction', in C. Burck and B. Speed, *Gender, Power and Relationships.* London: Routledge.

Bureau of Labor Statistics (2006) at www.stats.bls.gov (accessed May 2006).

Burke, P. and Cigno, K. (2000) *Learning Disabilities in Children.* Oxford: Blackwell Science.

Burton, S. (1997) *Where there's a Will there's a Way. Refocussing Childcare Practice: a Guide for Team Managers.* London: National Children's Bureau.

Butler-Sloss, Lord Justice E. (1987) *Report of the Inquiry into Child Abuse in Cleveland*. London: HMSO.

Calder, M. (2004) *Children Living with Domestic Violence: Towards a Framework for Assessment and Intervention*. Lyme Regis: Russell House Publishing.

Calder, M., with Hanks, H., Epps, K., Print, B., Morrison, T. and Henniker, J. (1997) *Juveniles and Children who Sexually Abuse: Frameworks for Assessment*. Lyme Regis: Russell House Publishing.

Carr, A. (1989) 'Counter-transference to families where child abuse has occurred', *Journal of Family Therapy*, 11: 87–97.

Carter, B. and McGoldrick, M. (1989) 'Overview: the changing family life cycle: a framework for family therapy', in B. Carter and M. McGoldrick (eds), *The Changing Family Life Cycle – a Framework for Family Therapy*, 2nd edn. Boston/London: Allyn & Bacon, pp. 3–28.

Chaffin, M., Kelleher, K. and Hollenberg, J. (1996) 'Onset of physical abuse and neglect: psychiatric, substance abuse, and social risk factors from prospective community data', *Child Abuse and Neglect*, 20 (3): 191–203.

Christofferson, M.N. (2000) 'Growing up with unemployment: a study of parental unemployment and children's risk of abuse and neglect based on national longitudinal 1973 birth cohorts in Denmark', *Childhood*, 7 (4): 421–38.

Cleaver, H., Unell, I. and Aldgate, J. (1999) *Children's Needs – Parenting Capacity: the Impact of Parental Mental Illness, Problem Alcohol and Drug Use, and Domestic Violence on Children's Development*. London: The Stationery Office.

Clyde, Lord (1992) *Report of the Inquiry into the Removal of Children from Orkney in February 1991*. Edinburgh: HMSO.

Cohen, F. and Densen-Gerber, J. (1982) 'A study of the relationship between child abuse and drug addiction in 178 parents: preliminary results', *Child Abuse and Neglect*, 6: 383–7.

Coleman, R. and Cassell, D. (1995) 'Parents who misuse drugs and alcohol', in P. Reder and C. Lucey (eds), *Assessment of Parenting: Psychiatric and Psychological Contributions*. London: Routledge, pp. 182–93.

Community Care (2002) 'Crucial moments in a tragic case', reporters L. Revans, S. Gillen and R. Downey, 21–27 Feb., pp. 18–21.

Cooper, A., Hetherington, R., Baistow, K., Pitts, J. and Spriggs, A. (1995) *Positive Child Protection: a View from Abroad*. Lyme Regis: Russell House Publishing.

Corby, B., Doig, A. and Roberts, V. (2001) *Public Inquiries into Abuse of Children in Residential Care*. London: Jessica Kingsley.

Corner, R. (1997) *Pre-Birth Risk Assessment in Child Protection*. Norwich: Social Work Monographs.

Daily Mail (2005) 'Scandal of the stolen children', 14 May, at http://www.dailymail.co.uk/pages/live/articles/news/newscomment.html?in_article_id=348650&in_page_id=1787 (accessed July 2006).

Davies, J. (1997) *The Myth of Addiction*, 2nd edn. Amsterdam: Harwood.

DCA [Department for Constitutional Affairs] (2005) *Court Service Annual Reports and Accounts 2004/5*. London: The Stationery Office (accessed via www.hmcourts-service.gov.uk, April 2006).

Delaney, R. (1998) *Fostering Changes: Treating Attachment-Disordered Children*, 2nd edn. Oklahoma City: Wood & Barnes.

Department of Health (1989) *Introduction to the Children Act.* London: HMSO.

Department of Health (1991) *Working Together under the Children Act 1989: a Guide for Inter-agency Co-operation for the Protection of Children from Abuse.* London: HMSO.

Department of Health (1995) *Child Protection: Messages from Research.* London: The Stationery Office.

Department of Health (1998) *The Quality Protects Programme: Transforming Children's Services*, Local Authority Circular (98) 28. London: The Stationery Office.

Department of Health (1999) *Working Together to Safeguard Children.* London: The Stationery Office.

Department of Health (2000) *Framework for the Assessment of Children in Need and their Families.* London: The Stationery Office.

Department of Health and Social Security, Northern Ireland (1985) *Report of the Committee of Inquiry into Children's Homes and Hostels.* Belfast: HMSO.

DfES [Department for Education and Skills] (2003) *Every Child Matters* [Green Paper]. London: The Stationery Office.

DfES [Department for Education and Skills] (2006) *Working Together to Safeguard Children: a Guide to Interagency Working to Safeguard and Promote the Welfare of Children.* London: The Stationery Office.

Dowdney, I. and Skuse, D. (1993) 'Parenting provided by adults with mental retardation', *Journal of Child Psychology and Psychiatry,* 34 (1): 25–37.

Doyle, C. (2006) *Working with Abused Children*, 3rd edn. Basingstoke: Palgrave.

Duncan, S. and Reder, P. (2003) 'How do mental health problems affect parenting?', in P. Reder, S. Duncan and C. Lucey (eds), *Studies in the Assessment of Parenting.* Hove: Brunner-Routledge, pp. 195–210.

Erooga, M. and Masson, H. (eds) (1999) *Children and Young People who Sexually Abuse Others.* London: Routledge.

Falkov, A. (1996) *Study of Working Together 'Part 8' Reports.* London: Department of Health.

Family Policy Studies Centre (2000) *Family Poverty and Social Exclusion (Family Briefing Paper 15).* London: Family Policy Studies Centre.

Farmer, E. and Owen, M. (1995) *Child Protection Practice: Private Risks and Public Remedies.* London: The Stationery Office.

Featherstone, B. (1996) 'Victims or villains? Women who physically abuse their children', in B. Fawcett, B. Featherstone, J. Hearn and C. Toft (eds), *Violence and Gender Relations: Theories and Interventions.* London: Sage, pp. 178–90.

Featherstone, B. and Trinder, L. (1997) 'Familiar subjects? Domestic violence and child abuse', *Child and Family Social Work,* 2 (3): 147–59.

Feerick, M. and Snow, K. (2005) 'The relationships between childhood sexual abuse, social anxiety, and symptoms of posttraumatic stress disorder in women', *Journal of Family Violence,* 20 (6): 409–19.

Feldman, M. and Case, L. (1999) 'Teaching child-care and safety skills to parents with intellectual disabilities through self-learning', *Journal of Intellectual and Developmental Disability,* 24 (1): 27–44.

Feldman, M., Varghese, J., Ramsay, J. and Rajska, D. (2002) 'Relationships between social support, stress and mother–child interactions in mothers with intellectual disabilities', *Journal of Applied Research in Intellectual Disabilities*, 15 (4): 314–23.

Fergusson, D.M. and Mullen, P.E. (1999) *Childhood Sexual Abuse: an Evidence Based Perspective*. London: Sage.

Finkelhor, D. (1988) 'The trauma of child sexual abuse: two models', in G. Wyatt and G. Powell (eds), *Lasting Effects of Child Sexual Abuse*. Newbury Park, CA: Sage, pp. 61–82.

Finkelhor, D. and Browne, A. (1986) 'The traumatic impact of child sexual abuse: an update', *American Journal of Orthopsychiatry*, 55: 530–41.

Fisher, D. (1994) 'Adult sex offenders: who are they? Why and how do they do it?', in T. Morrison, M. Erooga and R.C. Beckett (eds), *Sexual Offending Against Children: Assessment and Treatment of Male Abusers*. London: Routledge, pp. 1–24.

Flores, P. (2004) *Addiction as an Attachment Disorder*. Lanham, MD: Jason Aronson.

Foreman, D. (2006) 'Detecting fabricated or induced illness in children', *British Medical Journal*, 331: 978–9.

Forrester, D. (2000) 'Parental substance abuse and child protection in a British sample', *Child Abuse Review*, 9: 235–46.

Fryer, D. (1992) 'Psychological or material deprivation: why does unemployment have mental health consequences?', in E. McLaughlin (ed.), *Understanding Unemployment: New Perspectives on Active Labour Market Policies*. London: Routledge, pp. 103–25.

Gath, A. (1977) 'The impact of an abnormal child upon the parents', *British Journal of Psychiatry*, 130: 405–10.

Gaudin, J.M. (1999) 'Child neglect: short-term and long-term outcomes', in H. Dubowitz, *Neglected Children: Research, Practice and Policy*. Thousand Oaks, CA: Sage, pp. 89–108.

Gibbons, J., Gallagher, B., Bell, C. and Gordon, D. (1995) *Development after Physical Abuse in Early Childhood*. London: HMSO.

Gigerenzer, G. (2002) *Reckoning with Risk*. London: Penguin.

Gilman, M. (2000) 'Social exclusion and drug using parents', in F. Harbin and M. Murphy, *Substance Misuse and Child Care*. Lyme Regis: Russell House Publishing, pp. 21–6.

Glaun, D. and Brown, P. (1999) 'Motherhood, intellectual disability and child protection: characteristics of a court sample', *Journal of Intellectual and Developmental Disability*, 24 (1): 95–105.

Gleick, J. (1988) *Chaos: Making a New Science*. New York: Viking Penguin.

Greenland, C. (1987) *Preventing CAN Deaths: an International Study of Deaths due to Child Abuse and Neglect*. London: Tavistock.

Gregory, J. (2004) *Sickened: the Memoir of a Münchhausen by Proxy Childhood*. London: Century.

Guardian Society (2001) '"Ineffective", authorities failed to protect Lauren', http://society.guardian.co.uk, 1 Oct.

Guterman, N. (2001) *Stopping Child Maltreatment before it Starts: Emerging Horizons in Early Home Visitation*. Thousand Oaks, CA: Sage.

Harlow, H. (1963) in Foss, B.M. (ed.), *Determinants of Human Behaviour*. London: Methuen.

Harold, G. and Howarth, E. (2004) 'How marital conflict and violence affects children: theory, research, and future directions', in M. Calder (ed.), *Children Living with Domestic Violence: Towards a Framework for Assessment and Intervention.* Lyme Regis: Russell House Publishing, pp. 56–73.

Headey, B., Scott, D. and de Vaus, D. (1999) 'Domestic violence in Australia: are women and men equally violent?', *Australian Social Worker*, 2: 57–62.

Henning, K., Leitenberg, H., Coffey, P., Turner, T. and Bennett, R.T. (1996) 'Long term psychological and social impact of witnessing physical conflict between adults', *Journal of Interpersonal Violence*, 11: 35–51.

Hester, M. and Radford, L. (1996) *Domestic Violence and Child Contact Arrangements in England and Denmark.* Bristol: Policy Press.

Hester, M., Pearson, C. and Harwin, N. (2000) *Making an Impact: Children and Domestic Violence, a Reader.* London: Jessica Kingsley.

Hodapp, R.M. (1996) 'Down syndrome: developmental, psychiatric and management issues', *Child and Adolescent Psychiatric Clinics of North America*, 5: 881–94.

Hodapp, R. (1998) *Development and Disabilities: Intellectual, Sensory and Motor.* Cambridge: Cambridge University Press.

Hodapp, R.M. and Krasner, D.V. (1995) 'Families of children with disabilities: findings for a national sample of eighth-grade students', *Exceptionality*, 5: 71–81.

Howard, M., Garnham, A., Fimister, G. and Veit-Wilson, J. (2001) *Poverty: the Facts*, 4th edn. London: CPAG.

Howe, D. (2005) *Child Abuse and Neglect: Attachment, Development and Intervention.* Basingstoke: Palgrave.

Humphreys, C. (1999) 'Avoidance and confrontation: social work practice in relation to domestic violence and child abuse', *Child and Family Social Work*, 4 (1): 77–87.

Humphreys, C. and Stanley, N. (2006) 'Introduction' to C. Humphreys and N. Stanley (eds), *Domestic Violence and Child Protection.* London: Jessica Kingsley, pp. 9–16.

Janis, I. (1982) *Groupthink: Psychological Studies of Policy Decisions and Fiascos.* Boston, MA: Houghton Mifflin.

Johnston, J. and Campbell, L. (1993) 'A clinical typology of interparental violence in disputed-custody divorces', *American Journal of Orthopsychiatry*, 63 (2): 190–9.

Kanel, K. (2003) *A Guide to Crisis Intervention.* Pacific Grove, CA: Brooks/Cole.

Kearney, P., Levin, E. and Rosen, G. (2003) *Alcohol, Drug and Mental Health Problems: Working with Families.* London: SCIE.

Kelly, L. (1994) 'The interconnectedness of domestic violence and child abuse: challenges for research, policy and practice', in A. Mullender and R. Morley (eds), *Children Living with Domestic Violence, Putting Men's Abuse of Women on the Child Care Agenda.* London: Whiting & Birch.

Kennedy, M. (2002) 'Disability and child abuse', in K. Wilson and A. James (eds), *The Child Protection Handbook*, 2nd edn. London: Baillière Tindall, pp. 147–71.

Klee, H., Wright, S. and Rothwell, J. (1998) *Drug Using Parents and their Children: Risk and Protective Factors. Report to the Department of Health.* Manchester: Centre for Social Research on Health and Substance Use, Manchester Metropolitan University.

Knight, J. and Brent, M. (1998) *Access Denied: Disabled People's Experience of Social Exclusion*. London: Leonard Cheshire.

Kroll, B. and Taylor, A. (2003) *Parental Substance Abuse and Child Welfare*. London: Jessica Kingsley.

Kurz, D. (1993) 'Physical assaults by husbands: a major social problem', in R. Gelles and D. Loseke (eds), *Current Controversies in Family Violence*. London: Sage, pp. 88–103.

La Fontaine, J. (1998) *Speak of the Devil: Tales of Satanic Abuse in Contemporary England*. Cambridge: Cambridge University Press.

Laming, Lord H. (2003) *The Victoria Climbié Inquiry*. London: The Stationery Office.

Lancaster, S. (1999) 'Being there: how parental illness can affect children', in V. Cowling (ed.), *Children of Parents with Mental Illness*. Melbourne: ACER Press, pp. 14–34.

Lantz, P., Sinal, S., Stanton, C. and Weaver, R. Jr (2004) 'Perimacular retinal folds from childhood head trauma', *British Medical Journal*, 328 (7451): 754–6.

LCD [Lord Chancellor's Department] (2003) *Protocol for Judicial Case Management in Public Law Children Act Cases*. London: Lord Chancellor's Department.

Leopold, B. and Steffan, E. (1997) *Special Needs of Children of Drug Misusers: Final Report, 1997*. Brussels: European Union.

Lindsey, D. (1994) *The Welfare of Children*. New York: Oxford University Press.

London Borough of Brent (1985) *A Child in Trust: Report of the Panel of Enquiry Investigating the Circumstances Surrounding the Death of Jasmine Beckford*. London: Borough of Brent.

MacDonald, G. (2001) *Effective Interventions for Child Abuse and Neglect: An Evidence-based Approach to Planning and Evaluating Interventions*. Chichester: Wiley.

Macdonald, K. and Macdonald, G. (1999) 'Perceptions of risk', in P. Parsloe (ed.), *Risk Assessment in Social Work and Social Care*. London: Jessica Kingsley, pp. 17–52.

Mamen, M. (2006) *The Pampered Child Syndrome*. London: Jessica Kingsley.

Marsh, P. and Crow, G. (1998) *Family Group Conferences in Child Welfare*. Oxford: Blackwell Science.

Marsh, P. and Doel, M. (2005) *The Task-centred Book*. London: Routledge.

McConnell, D., Llewellyn, G., Mayes, R., Russo, D. and Honey, A. (2003) 'Developmental profiles of children born to mothers with intellectual disability', *Journal of Intellectual and Developmental Disability*, 28 (2): 122–34.

McGaw, S. (1996) 'Services for parents with learning disabilities', *Tizard Learning Disability Review*, 1 (1): 21–8.

McGaw, S. and Sturmey, P. (1993) 'Identifying the needs of parents with learning disabilities: a review', *Child Abuse Review*, 2: 101–17.

McGaw, S. and Sturmey, P. (1994) 'Assessing parents with learning disabilities: The Parental Skills Model', *Child Abuse Review*, 3: 36–51.

McKeigue, B. and Beckett, C. (2004) 'Care proceedings under the 1989 Children Act: rhetoric and reality', *British Journal of Social Work*, 34 (6): 831–49.

Menzies Lyth, I. (1988) 'The functions of social systems as a defence against anxiety: a report on a study of the nursing service of a general hospital', in I. Menzies Lyth (ed.), *Containing Anxiety in Institutions: Selected Essays, Vol. 1*. London: Free Association Books, pp. 43–88.

Middleton, L. (1992) *Children First: Working with Children and Disability*. Birmingham: Venture Press.

Middleton, L. (1999) *Disabled Children: Challenging Social Exclusion*. Oxford: Blackwell Science.

Milner, J. and O'Byrne, P. (2002) *Assessment in Social Work*, 2nd edn. Basingstoke: Palgrave.

MIND (2006) 'How common is mental illness?', at http://www.mind.org.uk/Information/ Factsheets (accessed July 2006).

Minnes, P. (1988) 'Family stress associated with a developmentally handicapped child', *International Review of Research on Mental Retardation*, 15: 195–226.

Morris, J. (1999) 'Disabled children, child protection systems and the Children Act 1989', *Child Abuse Review*, 8: 91–108.

Munro, E. (2002) *Effective Child Protection*. London: Sage.

Munro, E. (2004) 'Tracking children: a road to danger in the Children Bill?', at http://tracking-children.lse.ac.uk/report.pdf (accessed May 2006).

Munro, E. (2005) 'A systems approach to investigating child abuse deaths', *British Journal of Social Work*, 35 (4): 531–46.

Munro, E. and Calder, M. (2005) 'Where has child protection gone?', *The Political Quarterly*, 76 (3): 439–45.

Murphy, J.M., Jellinek, M., Quinn, D., Smith, G., Poitrast, F. and Goshko, M. (1991) 'Substance abuse and serious child mistreatment: prevalence, risk and outcome in a court sample', *Child Abuse and Neglect*, 15: 197–211.

Murphy, M. and Harbin, F. (2000) 'Background and current context of substance misuse and child care', in F. Harbin and M. Murphy (eds), *Substance Misuse and Child Care*. Lyme Regis: Russell House Publishing, pp. 1–8.

Nabokov, V. (1992) *Lolita*. London: Everyman's.

National Research Council (1993) *Understanding Child Abuse and Neglect*. Washington, DC: National Academy Press.

National Statistics (2006) at www.statistics.gov.uk (accessed May 2006).

NCCANI [National Clearing House on Child Abuse and Neglect Information] (2004) 'Child abuse and neglect fatalities: statistics and interventions', at http://nccanch.acf.hhs. gov/pubs/factsheets/fatality.pdf (accessed June 2006).

NPI [New Policy Institute] (2006) 'Key facts', at www.poverty.org.uk/summary/ key_facts.htm (accessed May 2006).

ODPM [Office of the Deputy Prime Minister] (2006) *Statistical Release: Statutory Homelessness: 4th Quarter 2005, England*, at www.odpm.gov.uk (accessed March 2006).

O'Hagan, K. (1993) *Emotional and Psychological Abuse of Children*. Buckingham: Open University Press.

Palmer, G., Carr, J. and Kenway, P. (2005) *Monitoring Poverty and Social Exclusion 2005*. York: Joseph Rowntree Foundation.

Pantazis, C. and Gordon, D. (1997) 'Poverty and crime', in D. Gordon and C. Pantazis (eds), *Breadline Britain in the 1990s*. Aldershot: Ashgate, pp. 115–33.

Park, J., Solomon, P. and Mandell, D. (2006) 'Involvement in the child welfare system among mothers with serious mental illness', *Psychiatric Services*, 57 (4): 493–7.

Parton, N. (1991) *Governing the Family: Child Care, Child Protection and the State.* Basingstoke: Macmillan.

Perry, R. and Cree, V. (2003) 'The changing gender profile of applicants to qualifying social work training in the UK', *Social Work Education*, 22 (4): 375–83.

Philpot, T. (2001) *A Very Private Practice: a Report into Private Fostering.* London: BAAF.

PIU [Performance and Innovation Unit] (2000) *Prime Minister's Review on Adoption.* London: Cabinet Office.

Quas, J., Goodman, G. and Jones, D. (2003) 'Predictors of attributions of self-blame and internalizing behavior problems in sexually abused children', *Journal of Child Psychology and Psychiatry*, 44 (5): 723–36.

Robinson, B. and Rhoden, J. (1998) *Working with Children of Alcoholics*, 2nd edn. London: Sage.

Rooney, R. (1992) *Strategies for Work with Involuntary Clients.* New York: Columbia Press.

Rowe, J. and Lambert, L. (1973) *Children who Wait: a Study of Children Needing Substitute Families.* London: Association of British Adoption and Fostering Agencies.

Russell, D. (1986) *The Secret Trauma: Incest in the Lives of Women and Girls.* New York: Basic Books.

Rutter, M. (1974) in DHSS, *The Family in Society: Dimensions of Parenthood.* London: HMSO.

Rutter, M. and Rutter, M. (1993) *Developing Minds: Challenge and Continuity across the Lifespan.* London: Penguin.

Rutter, M. and the English and Romanian Adoptees Study Team (1998) 'Developmental catch-up, and deficit, following adoption after severe global early privation,' *Journal of Child Psychology and Psychiatry*, 39: 465–76.

Saradjian, J. with Hanks, H. (1996) *Women who Sexually Abuse Children: from Research to Clinical Practice.* Chichester: Wiley.

Schofield, G. (1996) 'Parental competence and the welfare of the child: issues for those who work with parents with learning difficulties and their children. A response to Booth and Booth', *Child and Family Social Work*, 1: 87–92.

Schwartz, D. (1997) *Who Cares? Rediscovering Community.* Boulder, CO: Westview Press.

SCODA [Standing Conference on Drug Abuse] (1997) *Drug Using Parents: Policy Guidelines for Inter-agency Working.* London: Local Government Association.

Sherr, V. (2005) 'Munchausen's syndrome by proxy and Lyme disease: medical misogyny or diagnostic mystery?', *Medical Hypotheses*, 65: 440–7.

Shor, R. (2000) 'Child maltreatment: differences in perceptions between parents in low income and middle income neighbourhoods', *British Journal of Social Work*, 30: 165–78.

Silbert, M. and Pines, A. (1981) 'Sexual child abuse as an antecedent to prostitution', *Child Abuse and Neglect*, 5: 407–11.

Silvern, L., Karyl, J., Waelde, L., Hodges, W.F., Starek, J., Heidt, E. and Min, K. (1995) 'Retrospective reports of parental partner abuse: relationships to depression, trauma symptoms and self-esteem among college students', *Journal of Family Violence*, 10: 177–202.

Smith, M. (2005) *Surviving Fears in Health and Social Care: the Terrors of Night and the Arrows of Day.* London: Jessica Kingsley.

Solnit, A. and Stark, M. (1961) 'Mourning and the birth of a defective child', *Psychoanalytic Study of the Child*, 16: 523–37.

Somander, L. and Rammer, L. (1991) 'Intra- and extrafamilial child homicide in Sweden, 1971–1980', *Child Abuse and Neglect*, 15 (1): 45–55.

Sperlinger, A. (1997) 'Introduction' to J. O'Hara and A. Sperlinger, *Adults with Learning Disabilities: a Practical Approach for Health Professionals*. Chichester: Wiley.

Staffordshire County Council (1991) *The Pindown Experience and the Protection of Children: the Report of the Staffordshire Child Care Inquiry 1990*. Stafford: Staffordshire County Council.

Stanley, J. and Goddard, C. (2002) *In the Firing Line: Violence and Power in Child Protection Work*. Chichester: Wiley.

Steel, J., Sanna, L., Hammond, B., Whipple, J. and Cross, H. (2004) 'Psychological sequelae of childhood sexual abuse: abuse-related characteristics, coping strategies, and attributional style', *Child Abuse and Neglect*, 28 (7): 785–801.

Steinhauer, P. (1991) *The Least Detrimental Alternative: a Systematic Guide to Case Planning and Decision-making for Children in Care*. Toronto: University of Toronto Press.

Stovall-McClough, K. and Cloitre, M. (2006) 'Unresolved attachment, PTSD, and dissociation in women with childhood abuse histories', *Journal of Consulting and Clinical Psychology*, 74 (2): 219–28.

Straus, M. (1992) 'Children as witnesses to family violence: a risk factor for life-long problems among a nationally representative sample of American men and women', in *Children and Violence: a Report of the Twenty-third Ross Roundtable on Initial Approaches to Common Paediatric Problems*. Columbus, OH: Ross Laboratories.

Straus, M. (1993) 'Physical assaults by wives: a major social problem', in R. Gelles and D. Loseke (eds), *Current Controversies in Family Violence*. London: Sage, pp. 67–87.

Styles, C. and Knight, M. (1999) '"Kids with confidence": a peer support group for children', in V. Cowling (ed.), *Children of Parents with Mental Illness*, Melbourne: ACER Press, pp. 150–8.

Sullivan, P. and Knutson, J. (2000) 'Maltreatment and disabilities: a population-based epidemiological study', *Child Abuse and Neglect*, 24 (10): 1257–73.

Summit, R. (1983) 'The child sexual abuse accommodation syndrome', *Child Abuse and Neglect*, 7: 177–93.

Tarleton, B., Ward, L. and Howarth, J. (2006) *Finding the Right Support: a Review of Issues and Positive Practice in Supporting Parents with Learning Difficulties and their Children*. London: Baring Foundation (www.baringfoundation.org.uk).

Townsend, P. (1979) *Poverty in the United Kingdom*. London: Penguin.

Trotter, C. (1999) *Working with Involuntary Clients: a Practice Guide*. London: Sage.

Trotter, C. (2004) *Helping Abused Children and Their Families*. London: Sage.

Tucker, M. and Johnson, O. (1989) 'Competence promoting vs. competence inhibiting social support for mentally retarded mothers', *Human Organisation*, 48 (2): 95–107.

Tymchuk, A. (1992) 'Predicting adequacy of parenting by people with mental retardation', *Child Abuse and Neglect*, 16: 154–78.

Tymchuk, A. and Andron, L. (1994) 'Rationale, approaches, results and resource implications of programmes to enhance parenting skills of people with learning disabilities', in A. Craft (ed.), *Practice Issues in Sexuality and Learning Disabilities*. London: Routledge.

US Conference of Mayors (2005) *Hunger and Homelessness Survey: a Status Report on Hunger and Homelessness in America's Cities*, at www.usmayors.org/uscm/hungersurvey/2005/HH2005FINAL.pdf (accessed May 2006).

Velleman, R. (2001) 'Working with substance misusing parents as part of court proceedings', *Representing Children,* 14 (1): 36–48.

Vostanis, P. (2002) 'Mental health of homeless children and their families', *Advances in Psychiatric Treatment,* 8 (6): 463–9.

Waterhouse, Sir Ronald & the Tribunal of Inquiry into the abuse of children in care in the former county council areas of Gwynnedd and Clwyd since 1974 (2000) *Lost in Care.* London: The Stationery Office.

Watson, G. (1989) 'The abuse of disabled children and young people', in W.S. Rogers, D. Hevey and E. Ash (eds), *Child Abuse and Neglect.* Buckingham: Open University Press.

Watts, P. (2000) 'Solution focussed brief therapy used in a substance misuse setting', in F. Harbin and M. Murphy (eds), *Substance Misuse and Child Care.* Lyme Regis: Russell House Publishing, pp. 95–110.

Webster, R. (1998) *The Great Children's Home Panic.* Oxford: Orwell Press.

Webster, R. (2005) *The Secret of Bryn Estyn.* Oxford: Orwell Press.

Weir, A. (1999) 'An introduction to the issues: a new holistic approach outlined', in A. Weir (ed.), *Child Protection and Adult Mental Health.* Oxford: Butterworth-Heinemann, pp. 1–9.

Westcott, H. and Cross, M. (1996) *Thus Far and No Further: Towards Ending the Abuse of Disabled Children.* Birmingham: Venture Press.

Williams (Lord Williams of Mostyn, Chair) (1996) *Report of the National Commission of Inquiry into the Prevention of Child Abuse, Vol. 1, the Report.* London: The Stationery Office.

Wolf, S.C. (1984) 'A multifactor model of deviant sexuality', paper presented at Third International Conference on Victimology, Lisbon.

Yusuf Ali, A. (1989) *The Holy Qur'an* (English translation). Brentwood, MD: Amana Corporation.

Index

Abel, G., 121
'absence of love', 113, 115
abuse by children *see* children as abusers
actuarial approach, 111, 112
addiction, 97, 114, 115
ADHD *see* Attention Deficit Hyperactivity
    Disorder
adoptive families, 189
adult authority (importance of), 76
Africa, 171
AIMS (pressure group), 138
alcohol, linked to violence, 124
alcoholic parents, 127 *see also* drug and
    alcohol problems
Ali, Yusuf, 159
allocation of cases, 210
ambivalence, 79, 89, 195
American Sign Language, 85
Anderson, J., 188
Andron, L., 144
Angola, 75
Ashworth, K., 174
attachment, 95, 115, 125, 127, 133, 188,
    195, 196, 199, 200
    and parental drug and alcohol abuse, 126–127
    and parental mental health problems, 133
Attention Deficit Hyperactivity Disorder, 76
autism, 88

baby-farming, 8
Bagley, C., 94, 101
Banks, Sarah, 211
Barnard, M., 125
Batchelor, J., 94
battered baby syndrome, 9, 12
battering, ongoing or episodic male
    (of women), 160
BBC News, 76

Beckett, Chris, 9, 17, 26, 27, 139, 153, 169,
    188, 191, 197, 199, 209, 212
Beckford, Jasmine *see* Jasmine Beckford
bed and breakfast, 173, 174
Benedict, M., 190, 191
Bentovim, Arnon, 42
bereavement, 52, 79, 97
Beresford, P., 174
betrayal, 103
Bible, The, 8
Bishop, S., 196
Black, Dora, 156, 158
Blackburn, C., 173
blame, fear of, 49
blaming victims (of domestic violence), 163–164
boarding school, 85
Booth, Tim and Wendy, 144, 145, 147,
    148, 151, 153
Boston Juvenile Court, 196
'boundary setting', 41
Bowis, John (MP), 202, 209
Bowlby, John, 95, 96
Braithwaite, I., 174
Bray, S., 190
Brent, London Borough of, 49, 110
British Sign Language, 85
Brooke, J., 191
Brown, P., 145
Browne, A., 113, 159
Burck, C., 167
Bureau of Labor Statistics, 173
bureaucracy, 57–58
Burke, P., 84
Burton, S., 32
Butler-Sloss, Dame Elizabeth, 55

Calder, Martin, 8, 67, 121, 156, 157, 211, 212
Campbell, Linda, 160, 161

Canada, 191
Care Order, 9, 18
    numbers of, 9
Carr, Alan, 53, 54
Carter, Betty, 116
Case, Laurie, 144, 148
Cassell, D., 127, 130
causality, 112
certainty, unattainability of, 203–210
Chaffin, M., 125
change, promotion of, 32–45
Child Protection Conference
    Initial, 23
    Review, 27
Child Protection Plan, 24, 25, 27, 28, 32, 34, 35, 36,
        37, 38, 39, 40, 41, 43, 55, 58, 119, 180
Child Protection Register, 24
Child Protection Review Conference, 27
child protection system
    confidentiality and trust, 35
    in England and Wales, 16–28
    history of, 8–9
    international comparisons, 10
    'child rescue' (versus 'family support'), 10,
        53–55, 57
Child Sexual Abuse Accommodation Syndrome, 195
Child Welfare Officers, 9
child, focussing on, 55–56
child-directed work, 38–40
Children Act 1948, 9
Children Act 1989, 8, 9, 16, 17–18, 21, 31, 35,
        69, 145, 152, 199
    general principles of, 17–18
    Section 1, 17
    Section 17, 18
    Section 37, 17
    Section 44, 17
    Section 47, 17, 18
    welfare checklist, 17
Children Act 2004, 8, 9, 16, 18–19, 25, 64
children as abusers, 121, 192
'children in need', 18
'children in need of protection', 18
Children who Wait, 199
children with disabilities *see* disabled children
Children's Commissioner, 18
Children's Social Care, 9, 16, 21, 23, 24, 27,
        28, 29, 52, 68, 72
Christofferson, M., 175
Cigno, K., 84
circumcision, 11
class *see* social class
Cleaver, Hedy, 124

Cleveland, 9, 12, 55, 67
Climbié, Victoria *see* Victoria Climbié
clitoridectomy, 11
Cloitre, M., 98
Clyde, Lord, 31
Cohen, E., 125
Coleman, R., 127, 130
collaboration between agencies
        see inter-agency/multi-disciplinary work
collaborative problem-solving (in work with
        involuntary clients), 34
Colwell, Maria *see* Maria Colwell
communicating
communicating with children, 39–40, 85–86
    with disabled children, 85–86
Community Care (Journal), 12
competence-related abuse and neglect, 113, 120
confidence (parental lack of), 121
confidentiality, 6, 25, 30, 34, 35, 204
conflict (between agencies/professions), 29, 30
consequences of abuse and neglect *see* harm
control, lack of, 25
Corby, Bryan, 191
Core Assessment, 20, 23, 25, 28, 179, 180
Core Group, 20, 24, 25, 27, 28, 30, 58, 181
Corner, Ruth, 46
Côte d'Ivoire, 75
counter-transference reaction, 53–54
court delay *see* delay (in court proceedings)
court proceedings, 28, 152, 199
creative tension, 29, 146
Cree, V., 157
critical periods, 95
Cross, M., 84
Crow, Gill, 44
CTR *see* counter-transference reaction
cultural differences, 10, 22, 23, 86, 90
culture, 21

Daily Mail, The, 141, 142, 144, 153
database, national, 7, 18, 204
Davies, J., 124
deaf children (language needs of), 85
defence mechanisms (psychological)
    bureaucracy as, 57
        see also 'defensive exclusion', denial, repression
'defensive exclusion', 96
Delaney, Robert, 98
delay (in court proceedings), 152, 199
delusional ideas, 133, 134
demonizing men/perpetrators, 167
denial, 96
Densen-Gerber, J., 125

denying agency (to victim of domestic violence), 166
Department for Education and Skills *see* DfES
Department of Health, 20, 21, 23, 35, 135, 191, 196, 197, 199, 202
depersonalizing, 57, 58
depression, 20, 72, 76, 88, 94, 99, 100, 103, 104, 126, 132, 133, 134, 136, 138, 156, 175, 204
de-skilling, 121
DfES, 8, 14, 16, 18, 19, 20, 21, 25, 63, 66, 67, 69, 73, 79, 178, 197, 202, 211
dice, 209
Directors of Children's Services, 18
disabilities, children with *see* disabled children
disabled children, 63, 78–90
    communicating with, 85
    different professional systems dealing with, 84
    families of 79–83
    social context of, 83
    vulnerability of, 78–79
distorted thinking, 102, 114, 128, 161
distress
    fear of causing, 51
    of children, 52
    of parent as factor in child abuse, 119
doctors, 5, 12, 23, 29, 66, 80, 126, 152, 178, 202
Doel, Mark, 43
domestic violence, 76, 155–168
    as form of emotional abuse of children, 156
    children's exposure to, 76
    different patterns of, 160
    effects on children of, 156
    euphemisms for, 162
    feminist view of, 159
    impact on parenting capacity, 156
    male and female perpetrators *see* gender: and violence in families
    meaning of, 159
    minimization of, 161–162
    pitfalls for child protection workers dealing with, 161
    systemic view of, 159
Dowdney, I., 143, 144, 146
Down's Syndrome, 79, 81, 86, 88
Doyle, Celia, 51
drift, 198–200
drug and alcohol problems, 121, 123–131
    direct effect of parental substance abuse on children, 125
    direct effects of parental substance abuse on parenting, 126
    family assessment issues 130
    involvement of whole family in, 128

drug and alcohol problems, *cont.*
    more likely following maltreatment as child, 125
    problems with definition of, 123
    social effects of, 128
Duncan, Sylvia, 132, 134, 136

Emergency Protection Order, 17, 164
emotional abuse, 63, 68–72, 73, 75, 76, 80, 91, 92, 94, 99, 101, 102, 113, 116, 128, 156, 196, 197, 202
    definition of, 69
    domestic violence as, 156
    over-protection as, 73
    recognizing, 69–72
    system abuse as, 197–199
emotional pressure, 71
EPO *see* Emergency Protection Order
Erooga, M., 113, 121
ethnicity, 21, 22, 173
Every Child Matters, 8, 9, 16, 18, 25, 178, 211
executive role (of social workers), 27
expertise (professional), 29
extended family, 6, 10, 20, 38, 44, 54, 138
external resources (of families with children with disabilities), 89

fabricated or induced illness, 66
Factory Act 1833, 8
Failure to Thrive (FTT), 94
Falkov, Adrian, 134, 135
false negatives, 205
false positives, 205
Family Group Conferences, 44
Family Policy Studies Centre, 173
family relationships,
    of disabled children, 79–83
    respecting, 56–57
'family support' (versus 'child rescue') 53–55
family systems, 123, 128
family's perception (of child with disabilities), 89
Farmer, E., 164
fatal abuse, 56, 110
    and parental mental health problems, 134–135
fear (as factor in child protection work), 49–52
Featherstone, Brid, 158, 159, 160, 162
feedback loops, 98
Feerick, M., 98
Feldman, Maurice, 142, 144, 148
female initiated violence, 161
Fergusson, D., 111, 112, 113
Finkelhor, David, 102, 103, 104, 113, 204
Fisher, Dawn, 114

Flores, Philip, 97, 125
Foetal Alcohol Syndrome, 125
Foreman, David, 66
Forrester, D., 125
foster parents, 98, 150, 189, 191, 196, 197
    abuse by, 190–191
    private, 8, 191
Fryer, D., 175

Gath, A., 81
Gaudin, J., 101
gender
    and focus of child protection intervention, 164
    and physical abuse, 158
    and violence in families, 157–161
    of child protection professionals, 157
    of sex abusers, 157
Gibbons, Jane, 99, 170
Gigerenzer, G., 205
Gilman, M., 125
Glaun, D., 145
Gleick, J., 203
Goddard, Chris, 50, 51, 167
Gordon, D., 172
GPs, 36
Greenland, Cyril, 110, 111, 116, 117, 170, 188
Gregory, Julie, 66
'groupthink', 30–31, 32, 49, 75
Guardian, The, 12, 158
Guterman, Neil, 10, 18, 33, 127, 170, 177, 178, 204

Harbin, Fiona, 130–131
Harlow, H., 97
harm, 91–106
    caused by emotional abuse and neglect, 101
        see also domestic violence; system abuse
    caused by physical abuse, 99–101
    caused by sexual abuse, 101–104
    physical, 93–94
    psychological, 94–99
    significant *see* significant harm
Harold, G., 156
Headey, B., 158
health visitors, 29, 43
'help', 32–33
Henning, K., 156
heroin, 41, 42, 43, 111, 125, 126, 129, 130
Hester, M., 160
'hindsight fallacy', 209–210
Hinty, B., 190
Hodapp, Robert, 81, 88, 89
homelessness, 171, 173–174
    links to child neglect and domestic violence, 174

horizontal stressor, 116
horror videos, 71
hostage theory, 50, 167
hostility, 50
Howard, M., 171, 174
Howarth, E., 156
Howe, David, 96, 115, 125, 127, 132, 133, 134
humiliation, 71
Humphreys, Catherine, 161, 162, 164

ICS (IT system), 24
immediate protection, 17, 37
Infant Life Protection Act 1872, 8
information
    information-sharing, 7, 24, 25, 30, 33, 120, 203,
        204 *see also* confidentiality
    limits to usefulness of, 203–210
instrumental assistance, 152
interactive violence, male-controlled, 161
inter-agency/multi-disciplinary work, 28–31, 211
internal resources (of families with disabled
    children), 89
internalized working models
        see working models (internalized)
interpreter, use of, 21, 22
intervention *see* change, promotion of
    as discussed in *Working Together* guidelines, 26
investigate, duty to, 17
involuntary clients, 33, 34
invulnerability, illusion of, 30
IQ, 142, 144, 147, 149
    and parenting ability, 144
Irish Republic, 191
Islam, 11

Janis, Irving, 30
Jasmine Beckford, 49, 110
Johnson, O., 121
Johnston, Janet, 160, 161
judgement, 34

Kanel, Kristi, 97
Kelly, L., 156
Kempe, Henry, 12
Kennedy, Margaret, 83, 84, 86
Key Worker, 20, 24, 25, 26, 28, 181
Kincora working boys hostel, 191
Knight, Melissa, 138
Knutson, John, 78
Kouao, Marie Therese, 191
Krasner, D., 81
Kroll, B., 124, 126, 127
Kurz, Demie, 159

labelling, 147
Lambert, Lydia, 199
Laming, Lord, 18, 75, 191
Lancaster, S., 133, 134
language, 12, 13, 22, 23, 26, 34, 58,
    69, 80, 85, 86, 143
Lantz, P., 94
Lauren Wright, 12, 158
learning difficulties/disabilities
    children with, 88
    definition of, 142
    history of institutional care, 141
    parents with, 121, 141–154
    social exclusioin resulting from, 146
    two professional systems, 145
legal profession, 14
limbo, 26, 199
Lindsey, Duncan, 201
Local Authority children's social care
        see Children's Social Care
Local Safeguarding Children's Boards, 18, 19
Lolita, 189
lone parenthood, 171
    incidence of linked to male unemployment, 171
looked-after system (UK terminology)
        see public care
LSCB *see* Local Safeguarding Children's Boards

Macdonald, Geraldine, 209
MacDonald, Geraldine, 76, 101
Macdonald, Kenneth, 209
Makaton, 85
Mamen, Maggie, 76
mandated clients, 33 *see also* involuntary clients
Maria Colwell, 9
marital violence *see* domestic violence
Marsh, Peter, 43, 44
Masson, H., 113, 121
Maynard, Andrew, 188
McConnell, D., 143
McDonald, Geraldine, 42
McGaw, S., 142
McGaw, Susan, 148, 151, 152
McGoldrick, Monica, 116
McKegany, N., 125
McKeigue, Bridget, 9, 17, 26, 139, 153,
    196, 197, 199, 209
medical approaches to child protection, 12
mental health problems
    assessment of parents with, 135–137
    implicated in fatal child abuse, 134–135
    of parents, 123, 132–139
    problems with definition of, 132

mental health problems *cont.*
    support to children of parents with, 138
    support to familes where parents have, 137–139
mental retardation *see* learning difficulties/disabilities
Menzies Lyth, Isabel, 58
messages
    emotional abuse as negative message, 70–72
    given to parents, 36, 52, 83, 121
    negative, given to children, 70–72, 103,
        119, 121, 135, 197
micro and macro planning, 37
Middleton, Laura, 78, 83
Milner, Judith, 34, 166
MIND, 132
'mindguards', 31
Minnes, Patricia, 88
Morris, Jenny, 79, 80, 85
MSBP (Münchhausen's Syndrome by Proxy) *see*
        fabricated or induced illness
Mullen, P., 111, 112, 113
multi-agency work *see* inter-agency/
        multi-disciplinary work
multiple placements, 196–198
    as emotional abuse, 197
Münchhausen's Syndrome by Proxy *see* fabricated or
        induced illness
Munro, Eileen, 7, 8, 25, 30, 204, 205, 209, 211, 212
murder, of mother by father, 156
Murphy, Michael, 130, 131

Nabokov, Vladimir, 113, 189
National Research Council, 170
National Society for the Prevention of Cruelty to
        Children *see* NSPCC
National Statistics, 173
NCCANI (National Clearing House on Child Abuse
        and Neglect Information), 93
neglect, 40, 42, 51, 68–75, 84, 93, 94, 96, 98, 100, 101,
        117, 124, 125, 128, 129, 136, 144, 148, 151, 174,
        190, 198
    definition of, 69
    developmental harm caused by, 101
    emotional abuse and, 68–75
    fatal, 93
    long-term physical injury caused by, 93
    parental drug abuse and, 124, 125, 128, 129
    parental mental illness and, 136
    parents with learning disabilities and,
        144, 148, 151
    signs and symptons of, 72–75
    system abuse could be seen as, 198
    versus over-protectiveness, 73, 84
Neonatal Abstinence Syndrome, 126

New Zealand, 44
nicotine, 123
nonvoluntary clients, 33 *see also* involuntary clients
'no order principle', 17
North Wales, 191
NPI (New Policy Institute), 171, 172
NSPCC, 9, 17, 18, 19, 24, 25, 27
nursing, 58

observation, 23, 112, 121
O'Byrne, Patrick, 34, 166
ODPM (Office of the Deputy Prime Minister), 173
offending cycle, 114
O'Hagan, Kieran, 76
ongoing or episodic male battering, 160, 161
Orkney islands, 31
over-protectiveness, 73, 84
Owen, M., 164

paedophiles, 42, 128, 188, 189, 192
Pantazis, C., 172
paperwork, 210
parent-directed work, 40–43
parenting skills, 41, 42–43, 120, 148, 149, 151, 179
parents
    who abuse drugs or alcohol *see* drug and alcohol
        problems
    with learning difficulties *see* learning difficulties/
        disabilities: parents with
    with mental health problems *see* mental health
        problems
Park, J., 135
Part 8 Reviews, 135
Parton, Nigel, 9, 67
patterns of maltreatment, 112
permanent family placement, 44
Perry, R., 157
personal feelings (of child protection professionals),
    46–59
Philpot, T., 191
physical abuse, 9, 49, 56, 63, 64, 66, 70, 75, 82, 85,
    91, 92, 99, 101, 102, 111, 112, 116, 117, 125,
    158, 164, 170, 190, 191, 203
    definition, 63, 66
    fabricated or induced illness as form of, 66
    signs and symptoms of, 64–66
'Pindown', 191
Pines, A., 102
PIU (Performance Indicators Unit), 44, 116
placement breakdown, 44, 116
placement in substitute families, 188 *see also*
    foster parents

playing it safe, 35
poisoning, 63
police, 5, 6, 8, 12, 14, 18, 21, 24, 27, 35, 50, 56, 104,
    117, 128, 164, 178, 202
political dimension, 7, 8, 13, 145, 169, 182, 211
pornography, 71, 115
Post-Traumatic Stress Disorder, 97, 102
Post-Traumatic Stress Disorder (PTSD), 97–98, 102
poverty, 7, 13, 117, 118, 125, 146, 169–183
    absolute, 171
    as factor in drug and alcohol problems, 125
    as risk factor, 170
    crime and, 172
    disability and, 173
    environmental, 172
    psychological consequences of, 174
    relative, 171
power differences (between adults and children),
    40, 67
powerlessness, 103–105
prediction
    constraints on, 203
    football comparison (World Cup), 205–206
    in the physical sciences, 203
    weather comparison, 203
pregnancy, effect of drug or alcohol use during, 125
premeditated abuse, 112–113
prevarication *see* drift
Prevention of Cruelty to Children Act 1889, 8
primary client (differences as to), 29
private fostering, 8, 191
procedures (excessive focus on), 32
pro-social modelling, 34
prostitution, 102
protective networks, 43
psychological abuse, 76
psychological perspectives, 13
psychosis, 126, 133, 161
PTSD *see* Post-Traumatic Stress Disorder
public care
    abuse by children in, 192
    abuse in, 188–192
    multiple placements in *see* multiple placements
punishment, 101

Quality Protects, 197
Qur'an, The, 159

race, 21
Radford, L., 160
Rammer, L., 134
rape, 66, 79, 102, 160

realism, 188, 201–213
recording, 24
recovery (from maltreatment), 39
Reder, Peter, 132, 134, 136
religious organizations, abuse allegations against, 191
repression, 96
'rescuing the child', 53
'rescuing the parents', 53
residential care, abuse in, 191–192
residential establishments, 85
resources, 35, 193, 202, 203
   limits imposed by, 210–211
respite care, 138
revictimization, 102, 104
Rhoden, J., 125, 127, 128
right to parenthood, 145
rights of children, 152
risk factors, 81, 109–112, 116, 117, 132, 135,
     170, 174, 175, 188
   in fatal child abuse, 110
   poverty as, 170
   sexual abuse, 111
ritual abuse, 75
Robinson, Bryan, 125, 127, 128
Rochdale, 31
role reversal, 127, 134
Romania, 94, 95
Rooney, Ronald, 33
Rowe, Jane, 199
Russell, D., 102
Rutter, Michael, 94, 95, 175

'safeguarding children', 5, 14
Saint, Roger, 190
Saradjian, J., 157
Schofield, Gillian, 146
Schwartz, David, 7
SCODA (Standing Conference on Drug Abuse), 126
screaming child as stressor, 116
self-protection, 38
separation and post-divorce violence, 161
sexual abuse, 12, 23, 37, 48, 55, 63, 66–68, 70, 71, 75,
     80, 83, 91, 98, 101, 102, 103, 104, 111, 112, 113,
     114, 120, 121, 124, 157, 164, 189, 190, 191, 208
   by women and girls, 157
   definition of, 66
   signs and symptoms of, 67–68
sexual abusers
   characteristics of, 111–112
   link to own childhood abuse, 103
sexual performance problems, 103
Shaken Baby Syndrome, 94

shaking, 93–94
Sherr, Virginia, 66
Shor, Ron, 11, 181
significant harm, 17, 18, 21, 24, 27, 28, 44, 69, 71, 91,
     142, 146, 170
Silbert, M., 102
Silvern, L., 156
Skuse, D., 143, 144, 146
smacking, 63, 64, 153
Smith, Martin, 49
Snow, K., 98
social class, 11, 73, 174
   and likelihood of accidents, 174
social construction of child abuse, 13
social exclusion, 7, 13, 169, 173, 174, 175, 182
    see also poverty
Social Services departments, 9
social work role, 27–28
sociological perspectives, 13
Solnit, A., 79
Somander, L., 134
special needs (of children), 39
Speed, B., 167
Sperlinger, A., 143
'spoiling' children, 76
Stanley, Janet, 50, 51, 161, 167
Stark, M., 79
statistical associations, 112
status differences (profesessional), 29
Steel, J., 103
Steinhauer, Paul, 199
step-parents, 111, 112, 116, 188
stereotypes, 29, 30
stigmatization, 103
Stockholm syndrome, 50, 51, 167
Stovall-McClough, K., 98
Strategy Discussion, 21
Straus, Murray, 156, 158
strengths (of families), 36
stressors, 81, 88, 116, 117, 118, 120,
     131, 147, 175, 188
   horizontal and vertical, 116, 118
   professional intervention as, 120
stress-related abuse and neglect, 43, 113, 116–120
structural factors in child maltreatment, 169
Sturmey, Peter, 142, 148
Styles, Cathy, 138
substance abuse *see* drug and alcohol problems
substitute care, 44
suicide, 103, 110, 134, 175, 207
   combined with child homicide, 134
Sullivan, Patricia, 78

Summit, Roland, 195
support, 139
  need for long-term, 151
surveillance, 204
system abuse, 76, 187–200
  by the child protection system, 194–196
  causes of, 193
  definition of, 192–193
  in public care system, 196–200
system levels, 116, 117

taboos, 46
Tarleton, B., 141, 146
task-centred casework, 43
Taylor, A., 124, 126
Taylor, Hilary, 139
teachers, 23, 27, 29, 36, 39, 43, 52, 82, 136, 207, 208
therapy, 12, 26, 39, 42, 86, 120
Thurston, W., 94, 101
Times, The, 9
timescales, 26, 28, 152, 200
Townsend, Peter, 173
trade-offs, 212
'traumagenic dynamics' (Finkelhor), 102–105
traumatic sexualization, 102
Trinder, Liz, 159, 160, 162
Trotter, Chris, 34, 35, 36, 41
trust, 35, 204
Tucker, M., 121
Tymchuk, A., 144

unanimity, illusion of, 30
unemployment, 171, 173, 175
  as risk factor in child maltreatment, 175
  link to heroin use, 125
urinary tract infections, 67
US Conference of Mayors, 173

values, 34, 46
Velleman, R., 124, 187
vertical stressors, 116
vicious circles, 98, 125, 127
victim-blaming *see* blaming victims (of domestic violence)
Victoria Climbié, 12, 18, 75, 191, 205, 209
violence
  against women *see* domestic violence
  and gender *see* gender: and violence in families
  underestimation of, 51, 161, 162
Vostanis, Panos, 174

Waterhouse, Sir R., 190, 191
Watson, G., 84
Watts, P., 130
Webster, R., 191
Weir, Amy, 132, 133, 134, 135, 136, 138
Welsh Assembly, 18
Westcott, H., 84
Williams, Lord, 193
Williams, Robin, 211
'wishlisting', 212
Wolf, S., 114
Women's Aid, 155
working models (internalized), 39, 95–99, 102
Working Together
  1991 version: *Working Together under the Children Act 1989*, 135
  1999 version: *Working Together to Safeguard Children*, 20
  2006 version: *Working Together to Safeguard Children*, 16, 20–28, 63, 69, 178, 197
workload, 210
World Cup, 205
Wright, Lauren *see* Lauren Wright